D1237835

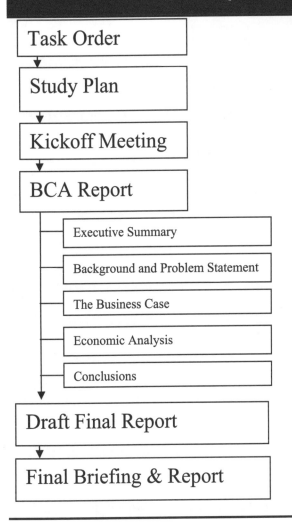

Business Case Analysis
Basic Steps

Task Order

Study Plan

Kickoff Meeting

BCA Report

- Executive Summary
- Background and Problem Statement
- The Business Case
- Economic Analysis
- Conclusions

Draft Final Report

Final Briefing & Report

Knowledge is of two kinds: we know a subject ourselves, or we know where we can find information upon it.
Samuel Johnson (circa 1764)

The wise man is he who knows the relative value of things.
William Ralph Inge (circa 1944)

> ### *BCA: Business Case Analysis*
> **The practical guide for business and economic decisions**

§ BCA §

BUSINESS
CASE
ANALYSIS

**Examples, Concepts
& Techniques**

Featuring the 8-Day BCA

James W. Brannock

STS Publications
www.STSpublications.com

BCA: Business Case Analysis
Examples, Concepts & Techniques
by James W. Brannock

Published by:
STS Publications
Post Office Box 3732
Plant City, FL 33563-0013 U.S.A.
Orders
Orders@STSpublications.com
Information
http://www.STSpublications.com

Copyright © 2004 by James W. Brannock. All rights reserved.
Printed in the United States of America. No part of this book may
be reproduced or transmitted in any form or by any means electronic or mechanical, including photocopying, recording or by
any information storage and retrieval system, without written
permission from the author, except for the inclusion of brief quo-
tations in critical articles or reviews. For information, write to
STS Publications, P.O Box 3732, Plant City, FL 33453-0013.

Printed in the United States of America

Publisher's Cataloging-in-Publication
(Provided by Quality Books, Inc.)

Brannock, James W.
     BCA : business case analysis : examples, concepts &
techniques : featuring the '8 day BCA' / James W.
Brannock – 1st ed.
  p. cm.
  Includes bibliographical references and index.
  LCCN 2004090290
  ISBN 0-9747813-9-8
  ISBN 0-9747813-8-X (hardbound)
    1.   Industrial management.   I. Title

HD31.B7264 2004   658.4'01
                        QBI04-200040

Contents

About the Author

Jim Brannock is a principal and partner in a prestigious management consulting firm based in the Northern Virginia–Washington D.C. area. He has over thirty years experience with business management situations, including business case analysis, strategic planning, and sociotechnical systems analysis. He holds a double bachelor degree in economics and history, an MBA, and a PhD with a concentration in business management. He has authored and coauthored numerous management studies, journal articles and professional business analysis presentations.

Dr. Brannock was prompted to write this book after observing, repeatedly, that otherwise professional business managers had little background in the basics for even the most simple business case analysis procedures and techniques. Time and again, clients were either already committed to, or about to make expensive business decisions without even reviewing the rudimentary facts and economic comparisons of alternatives.

As you will see in this book, business case analysis is not that big a deal—it's not 'rocket surgery.' Jim takes the reader through a very simple 8-Day BCA that demonstrates most of the basics. He then reveals, in detailed examples, many of the 'secrets' that expensive consultants use for all sorts of business analysis situations. Following these basic approaches and techniques will help you learn how to conduct your own business case analysis and to evaluate potential opportunities and risks of important business decisions.

Preface

This is the book that I looked everywhere for on my first real job as a new second lieutenant in the U.S. Air Force, many years ago. My assignments continually involved situations where last minute end-of-year funds were available for many of the needed programs, but where justification for budget support never seemed strong enough. At first, when unable to make the winning case, I wrote most instances off, assuming 'somebody up there' really knows better.

In the years that followed, while serving in nearly all echelons of management in some very larger organizations, I became involved in increasingly more complex situations. As my decision responsibilities grew in importance, I realized that needed decision support was often even more obscure 'up the organization.' Eventually I realized that the 'somebody up there' (who should really know better) was *me,* and that I often did not have a clue of what was really needed.

I dug in. I began to build on my academic knowledge about business and economic analysis. I continually took notes about 'real world' situations, from local operations to strategic planning. Eventually, many of the concepts, tools and techniques became clear. The culmination of this knowledge quest is presented in this book—under the general title of Business Case Analysis.

This book is the general how-to reference that I have needed so many times, and in so many business decision situations. These decision support tools include both human (social) and technical (mathematical) applications, both needed for good decisions. I hope concepts and techniques will be as fun for you to use as they were for me to learn.

JWB

Warning—Disclaimer

This book is designed to provide information on concepts and techniques that can help managers make informed decisions for evaluation of business situations. It is sold with the understanding that it is a general reference, and not the definitive source in rendering legal, accounting or other professional business services. If legal or other expert assistance is required, the services of competent professionals should be sought.

The purpose of this manual is to provide a simplified, general reference for business case analysis. Every effort has been made to compose this manual as completely and as accurately as possible. However, there may be mistakes, both typographical and in content. Also, this book contains information that is current only up to the printing date. The author and STS Publications shall have neither liability nor responsibility to any person or entity with respect to any loss or damage caused, or alleged to have caused, directly or indirectly, by the information contained in this book.

It is not the purpose of this manual to reprint all the information that is otherwise available, but rather to complement, amplify, and supplement more comprehensive sources. You are urged to read all other available material relevant to a specific business situation, learn as much as possible about business analysis, and tailor the information to your business case needs. Comprehensive references are provided at the end of this book for the sources used herein.

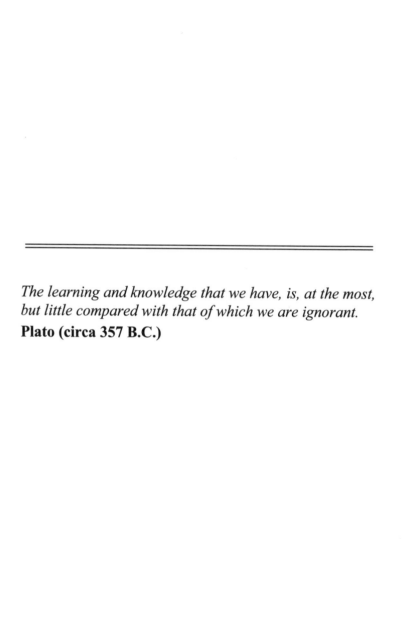

The learning and knowledge that we have, is, at the most, but little compared with that of which we are ignorant.
Plato (circa 357 B.C.)

I

A SIMPLE BUSINESS CASE ANALYSIS EXAMPLE

Day 1—The Assignment
Day 2—The Study Approach
Day 3—The Problem and Alternatives
Day 4—The Costs
Day 5—The Benefits
Day 6—The Benefit-Cost Comparisons
Day 7—The Summary, Conclusions
and Recommendations
Day 8—The Final Report and Presentation

Learning teaches how to carry things in suspense, without prejudice, till you resolve.
Francis Bacon (circa 1610)

CHAPTER ONE

The 8-Day BCA

We always have enough time, if we will but use it right.
Goethe (circa 1800)

Day 1—The Assignment

Jim was browsing his e-mails over coffee Wednesday morning when he noticed a message from his supervisor, Maria, who requested he meet with her at 9:00 concerning a special project.

At the nine o'clock meeting Maria indicated that a headquarters memo suggested that some end-of-year budget funds might be available. Office chiefs had been asked to submit budget requests for remaining office projects that still required funding. Additionally, headquarters requested a *Business Case Analysis* (BCA) accompany any project requests expected to cost more that $10,000.

Maria continued, "The office computer PC workstations are approaching five years of age. We have continual computer freeze-ups, and the quarterly repair and maintenance price tag for technician service calls is 'eating our lunch.'"

She then indicated that competition for the possible 'fallout' money would be stiff, and asked Jim to prepare a convincing Business Case Analysis to support purchase of new computer workstations for the office. "One more thing," Maria said, as the meeting was about to come to a close, "we need the BCA by close of business Friday, eight days from now, to allow me time to go over it before the budget meeting on the following Monday."

Back in his cubicle, Jim pondered what to do next. Eight days was not a long time.

Jim's first question: "Fine, why me?"

His second question: "Just what is a Business Case Analysis (BCA), and how is one developed?"

Jim decided to spend the rest of the day finding out what is required to do a Business Case Analysis. He first searched the office files for previous BCAs and for instructions on how to perform them. When he found no old BCAs in his office area, he asked around if anyone had either performed or had copies of past BCAs. He also contacted technicians in the information technology office.

The information technology office assistant showed Jim two completed Business Case Analyses, one done fairly recently. Upon their review he found that they were very comprehensive, and had been done by professional consultants. They dealt with major strategic enterprise level information modernization issues, and unfortunately were too broad to serve as a template for Jim's relatively simple task of justifying new computer workstations for the 18 workers in his office.

He was able, however, to pick up one reference that might be helpful, and was able to locate it on the Internet:

OMB Circular A-94[i]
Guidelines and Discount Rates for
Benefit-Cost Analysis in Federal Programs

Browsing the OMB A-94 Circular, Jim noticed topics such as *present value*, identifying *benefits* and *costs*, and *cost effectiveness analysis*.

Reading further (the document is only 14 pages), he discovered many of the principles he had seen demonstrated in the comprehensive BCAs from the information technology office. He read further.

While the OMB Circular is written on a high level and applies to the overall evaluation of projects in the federal government, Jim was able to determine, in combination with formats from the two previous BCAs, several key elements that would be useful for his own study effort. These included:

1) Clearly state what the problem is; the reason for the study.
2) Develop explicit assumptions about *what the problem is*, and about *alternatives* that might solve it.
3) Evaluate the alternatives; select the best.
4) Develop a plan for implementation and feedback methods to monitor how well the selected alternative works as it is implemented.

Jim also found, searching the Internet for "Business Case Analysis," numerous references. Some offered case studies and testimonials of clients—including large corporations, nonprofit organizations, educational institutions, government and military organizations.

---

[i] Office of Management and Budget (OMB) Circular A-94, *Guidelines and Discount Rates for Benefit-Cost Analysis of Federal Programs:* http://www.whitehouse.gov/omb/circulars/a094/a094.html.

He also noticed that most of the referenced studies generally used some form of payback indicator, such as benefits-to-cost, savings-to-investment or breakeven analysis comparisons. Examples included benefits due to improved work processes, better resource planning, automated distribution and inventory management.

Jim began to formulate an idea that might useful for his BCA—new PCs would more likely be less prone to downtime, thus reducing the number of technician service calls, and therefore costs causing the budget problem Maria had mentioned. Additionally, reduced service calls meant that there would be fewer lost worker hours awaiting computer repairs, leading to improved productivity. So, there were at least two sources of benefits, reduced service call costs and reduced productive lost time from office workers.

Day 2—The Study Approach

Intuitively, Jim realized that he needed the help of his coworkers to help explain the severity of the problem. The first thing the next morning Jim sent an e-mail to all 18 employees, explaining that he had a 'short fuse' task to develop a BCA to compete for possible end-of-year budget fallout funds. He requested a short (by end-of-day) reply to answer the following questions:

In your opinion:

1) Are new PCs required, and why?
2) Roughly, how many times over the past year have you had computer downtime and required computer technicians for repair?
3) Approximately how long, as an average, have such repairs taken between work order call in and 'up and running' status?
4) Roughly, what percentage of work time do you spend using the PC? 10%? 50%? 70%? Other? Please state %.

5) What features would you add to enhance your PC capability?

He then revisited the information technology office where he interviewed several computer service technicians in a group. He asked for their advice concerning how he might go about selecting up-to-date PCs as candidates for replacements of the existing desktops in his office. They recommended that he could review media advertisements and call or visit PC vendors such as Dell, Gateway, Office Depot, or Best Value. He might also find the Internet useful.

Jim's visit yielded another benefit. He discovered that the *information technology office* kept a log service calls. Recorded in the log were the number of service calls per month and the start and completion times of the work orders. Jim was allowed to make a copy of the past year's service calls to his office area.

By lunchtime on Thursday, Jim had browsed several additional case studies on the Internet. He also had visited the nearby public library, and browsed several business management texts. He checked out one with a section on how to perform financial case studies. Later, he contacted the organization's *operations research office* and was given some helpful suggestions concerning the analysis process.

Jim knew he was no expert—but he only had a few days, so he decided to begin organizing notes from his brief search into needed steps for the BCA. Sketching together best ideas from the OMB Circular, example BCAs, the business management textbooks, and conversations with the operations research office, he developed the outline of study approach, as shown in *Exhibit 1-1*:

Exhibit 1-1

BCA Study Approach

- Formally State the Problem
- Develop the Business Case Alternatives
- Compare Benefits-Costs of Alternatives
- Summary and Conclusions

Produce Final Report and Briefing

At the end of the day, Jim browsed responses from coworkers to his early morning e-mail concerning their opinions of the need for new PCs. Eleven had responded. He went over the responses and jotted down a list of PC options the office workers desired. It was late, so he decided to catch up on his other e-mails, and then get a fresh start on the study the next morning.

DAY 3—The Problem and Alternatives

Statement of the Problem

Early Friday, Jim felt he had absorbed most of the information about what the BCA should cover, and had a good start on what the office workers needed from PCs to do their job better. Now he began the phase of developing potential alternatives to the current situation. He began by formally stating the problem of the current situation. His narrative follows:

The Problem Statement

A need exists to replace desktop PC computers in the contracts management office. Existing PCs were originally installed nearly five years ago, and lack required storage and speed to support the new and evolving software used in daily work. The PCs are frequently 'down' due to maintenance and operations problems.

Further, the problems are increasing. Files are becoming too large for storage, requiring time-consuming manual searches among paper hard copy files and reports. 'Lock-ups' and 'screen freezes' occur often, especially for documents with larger graphics files. Finally, the workload for service call repairs has become very costly, as has the cost of lost productive time by office workers.

Specific problems include excessive delays of loss of files and e-mails with attachments. This affects efficiency of normal operations, as well as worker morale and potentially, customer satisfaction. Also, due to limited PC capacities, installation of updated software for word processing, databases, scanners, spreadsheets, and for preparing briefing presentations is often delayed or not possible. These problems are expected to become more acute with time.

Having completed the problem statement, Jim reviewed the list of suggested PC improvements and requirements from his coworker e-mails. He gathered a list of desired features—including upgraded scanner-copier-fax 'all-in-one' printers, voice activated software, better PC virus protection, faster uploads and software response times, and more hard drive storage capacity.

Next, Jim went online to search for information about PCs. He reviewed promotional materials from large vendors specializing in PCs, including Dell, Compaq and Gateway. He also found several firms that specialize in office information systems, including PCs. He annotated useful information, including prices, features, technical comparisons of software-hardware packages, and so forth. From this he worked up a list of desired workstation PC features, careful to include those his fellow office workers had mentioned. He then verified that the list was essentially complete with the information technology office. The following is the list of desired workstation PC features:

- Industry Standard GHz Processor
- Industry Standard GB Memory
- Industry Standard GB Hard Drive
- Plasma Screen Monitor
- All-in-One Color Printer, Scanner, Copier, Fax
- DVD and CD RW Drives
- Industry Standard Operating System
- Modem
- Industry Standard Internet Wideband
- Wireless Networking Card
- Industry Standard Graphics
- Industry Standard Office Suite
- 6 USB Ports

Jim was also able to locate several large, reputable vendors on the Internet and in the telephone yellow pages who offered state-of-the-art workstations. The most economical of the packages that included all of these features was from a reputable vendor. The desired 18 PCs could be assembled, delivered and installed at the unit price of $1,500 per assembly. Further, this vendor offered two alternatives: *buy* (i.e., paid in full upon delivery), or *lease-to-own* (i.e., pay one-third down, with additional payments of one-third due at the beginnings of year two and three, respectively). Ownership would then transfer to the buyer. This was essentially an installment purchase loan with a zero interest rate.

Statement of the Alternatives

Jim now considered possible alternatives to solve the problem. Armed with the information about potential costs and required technical features of new PCs, he laid out the following alternatives in his BCA narrative:

> **Alternative 1**: Status Quo (delay purchase of new workstations).
>
> **Alternative 2**: Upgrade components of existing workstations.
>
> **Alternative 3**: Buy new workstations.
>
> **Alternative 4**: Lease new workstations.

Jim then began to outline the expected advantages and disadvantages of each alternative.

Evaluation of Alternatives

Alternative 1: Status Quo

Pros: Existing workstations are paid for. Keeping existing workstations avoids the need to obligate a substantial cash investment. The office personnel are well trained and acclimated to existing workstations.

Cons: The existing workstations have excessive costs due to technician service calls and lost personnel work hours. There are unnecessary productivity disruptions due to repeated manual recovery actions for system freeze-ups.

Quality of work outputs is also affected by the retrieval of (often out-of-date) information from manual hard copy sources when electronic files have been lost. Existing PCs will progressively become more inadequate with the new advances in the technology.

Morale and customer response management are being impacted adversely with continually increasing dysfunctions of the PCs.

Alternative 2: Upgrade Existing PCs

Initial consultations with the information technology office indicated that required upgrades would potentially cost more than new PCs, and pose unacceptable risks due to incompatibilities between new and old internal PC components. Also, preliminary review of rebuilt systems offered on the Internet indicated that upgraded systems would still contain an older hardware infrastructure.

Upgraded or refurbished PCs would not solve many of the coming performance issues for new software requirements.

This alternative was considered infeasible.

Alternative 3: Purchase New PCs

Pros: New PCs can potentially reduce service call maintenance costs significantly. In addition, excessive loss of productive work hours can be prevented due to reduction of PC downtime.

Employee morale and customer response management will likely be improved as a result of timely, accurate information.

Cons: The new workstations require budget outlays for acquisition and installation. These are estimated at $1,500 per workstation PC, or $27,000 for the required 18 PC computer systems. Also, there is an acquisition procurement expense to purchase the new PCs.

Additional training will be required to adapt office workers to the new workstation capabilities.

Alternative 4: Lease-to-Own New PCs

Pros: Lease-to-own has identical technical benefits as the buy alternative. These include reduction of lost production time, fewer required repair service calls, and potentially improved morale and customer response management.

In addition, the leasing option spreads the budget burden from a single total payment of $27,000 to three payments of $9,000. The first payment would be due at delivery, with the remaining two at the beginning of each successive year. Additionally, since there is no interest for the time-delayed payments, the there would be potential savings due to the 'time value of money.' Present value of deferred payments can be calculated using the discount rates published in OMB Circular A-94.

Cons: The lease-to-own alternative requires budgeting for a multi-year period, which may have policy or additional administrative cost elements.

Similar to the buy alternative, additional training will be required to adapt office workers to the new hardware/software operations and capabilities.

Selection of Alternatives

Alternative 1, maintaining the status quo, is feasible for the near future but has significant costs associated with lost productive time and payments for maintenance and repair service calls. It should be retained only if the benefit/cost ratio of new replacement PCs is not positive.

Alternative 2, upgrade or remanufacture of the older workstations, was determined to be unfeasible. It was eliminated from further economic analysis.

Alternative 3, *buy* new PCs, was considered technically feasible and selected for further economic analysis comparisons with the remaining alternatives.

Alternative 4, *lease-to-own,* was also considered technically feasible, and selected for further comparisons.

In conclusion, the following alternatives were chosen for evaluation of benefits and costs:

Alternative 1: *status quo*
Alternative 3: *buy new PCs*
Alternative 4: *lease-to-own new PCs*

Jim decided to e-mail a draft copy of the problem statement and proposed alternatives to his supervisor and fellow office workers. He included the proviso that no comments were required, but that any constructive statements would be appreciated. This would keep all concerned 'in the loop.'

"This was a good day's work," Jim thought to himself. He decided to 'fold up his tent' and go home for the weekend. He would begin gathering the costs and benefits for comparing alternatives with a fresh outlook the following Monday morning.

DAY 4—The Costs

Early Monday morning Jim began to evaluate the dollar value of potential costs of the alternatives. He decided, following OMB Circular A-94 guidelines, that the most feasible approach would be a *cost-effectiveness analysis*. Under this approach, the benefits are assumed to derive primarily from net cost reductions or cost avoidance. Also, to classify costs, Jim decided to use the concept of *total cost of ownership*, which was referenced in the literature review. Total costs are comprised of three subcategories:

1) Costs of Acquisition
2) Purchase Price
3) Costs of Ownership

He realized that the *costs of acquisition* (i.e., administrative procurement) and the *purchase price* would put the new PC options under a considerable disadvantage unless their *costs of ownership* could produce sufficient cost reductions. But, since the status quo alternative offered 'zero' dollar benefits and substantial operations costs, new PC alternatives would be preferred if they could show any savings at all. In fact, Jim would only need to show that potential cost savings resulting from new PCs surpass the combined acquisition and purchase costs for them to be preferred. If this could be shown, then the relative merits of the two acquisition alternatives could be evaluated to choose the best between them.

Cost of Acquisition

The *cost of acquisition* is normally comprised of several elements. These can include the costs of personnel to identify needed product attributes, select qualifying vendors, and develop purchase orders with correct product specifications. Jim phoned the organization's financial management office and was able to obtain a cost factor used for acquisition of new items that had been developed from historical costs for budget preparation purposes. That factor was 7.6% of the unit cost of the deliverable item.

However, after review, Jim learned that the cost factor did not include distribution and receipt costs. In one of the references Jim had found a study based on American merchandisers that indicated delivery costs to be estimated at 11.1% of the item cost.[1] However, since the selected PC vendor was local and would deliver and set up the new workstations at no additional charge, Jim reduced the 11.1% estimate to 2.5% by eliminating transportation costs (7.4%), and packaging costs (1.2%). The remaining cost of 2.5% was used as an estimate for receiving, order closeout, and administration.

The final combined acquisition and receipt cost estimate was now 10.1%. This factor was comprised of 7.6% (acquisition) and 2.5% (receipt and handling). He developed the following draft section for the BCA:

Economic Evaluation of Alternatives

Total Costs of Ownership

The alternatives were compared using the expected total costs of ownership. The costs consist of:

1) Cost of Acquisition
2) Unit Purchase Price
3) Cost of Use

Cost of Acquisition

A cost factor of 10.1% of the purchase price was determined to account for order and receiving costs if new workstations are acquired. This is comprised of 7.6% of total acquisition costs for ordering administrative costs, and 2.5% cost of receiving and processing the order. The former percentage was derived from company records, the latter from a published study distribution of costs from American merchandising companies.

Purchase Price

For purchase price, Jim had already narrowed down his purchase alternatives to the vendor who offered the state-of-the-art PCs at the most competitive price of $1,500 per unit. Jim continued his narrative, describing the two purchase alternatives, *buy* or *lease-to-own*:

Unit Purchase Price

An extensive review of vendors offering state-of-the-art PCs at market prices was conducted reviewing Internet prices from reputable vendors, including Gateway, Compaq, Dell, Office Depot, Best Value, and other major suppliers.

Similar prices were offered for the specified workstation PCs, with the most competitive at $1,500 per PC system. However, one vendor also offered special financing at this price, allowing a lease-to-own option. This vendor was tentatively selected as the PC supplier, should an acquisition alternative be chosen. This vendor's offer was considered the most competitive since it both quoted the best purchase price and allowed for time payments over two years, helping offset initial capital outlays.

The *buy* offer consists of purchase of the 18 workstation PCs, delivered and installed, acquisition at $1,500 per unit, for a total purchase price of $27,000, due on delivery and setup of PCs. The *lease-to-own* offer consists of acquisition at $1,500 per unit, but the cash outflow is different. One-third of the total is due upon delivery of the workstations (i.e., $500 per unit), with two successive payments of $500 per unit the beginning of the second and third year of the lease, respectively. The vendor requires no (zero interest) financing charge.

The *buy* and *lease-to-own* alternatives are similar in nearly every aspect except the timing of cash outlays. Jim decides, from his review of OMB Circular A-94 guidelines, to determine the effects of discounting, should the acquisition alternatives survive to face-off. Using the section on the *Net Present Value* from the Circular, he learns more about discounting and calculation of net present value.

Net Present Value

OMB Circular A-94 states: "The standard criterion...for justification of a program...is *net present value*...discounting future benefits and costs...to a common unit of measurement.... This discounting reflects the *time value of money*...benefits and costs are worth more if experienced sooner...."

Jim ponders this. Then he gets it! If, for example, he chooses the lease alternative, then two of the three payments are delayed until the out years and paid in cheaper 'then year' dollars relative to today's dollars. The theory seemed simple enough. A dollar paid today is worth more than one paid next year.

The logic is as follows. If the entire purchase is paid for today, the present value of the investment is obviously 100%. But, under the lease alternative, only one-third of the amount is payable up front. The second payment is due in one year; the third in two years. If we hang on to that money, say, in an interest paying market fund or bank savings account, we will be able to make the second and third payments with the original dollars, and pocket the interest. The net effect is a 'cheaper' cost, since we end up keeping the interest (thus offsetting the total costs). Also, under the lease-to-own alternative, since there are no additional finance or loan interest charges to the vendor, the potential cost savings are not offset by any other costs.

Using these principles, Jim then calculated the present value of dollar outlays for the lease-to-own alternative. He used the discount rate of 4.1%, published in the OMB Circular A94, Appendix C.[ii] Applying this rate to the current lease alternative, the present value cost of each computer would actually be less than if paid for all at once. Jim extended this logic to compare the expected difference in *present value* of paying for the all of PC workstations now, versus stretching payments over the three-year period offered by the vendor. Jim's computations are shown in *Exhibit 1-2.*

[ii] 4.1% was the rate as of this writing. The OMB Circular A94 publishes 'real' and 'nominal' interest rates. The 'real' rates assume 'no inflation' (i.e., represent true growth in productivity), and are normally used in low inflation periods. Appendix C rates are updated annually.

Exhibit 1-2

Present Value (PV)
Costs of One PC

Formula: $PV = 1/(1+i)^t$

Where: PV=Present Value; i = discount rate (interest rate); t = number of years (time)

Totally Paid for at Purchase

$$\$1500 \div 1/(1.041)^0 = \underline{\$1500}$$

Paid for over Three Payments

At purchase:	$\$500 \div 1/(1.041)^0 = \$500$
2nd Payment:	$\$500 \div 1/(1.041)^1 = \$480$
3rd Payment:	$\$500 \div 1/(1.041)^2 = \underline{\$461}$

PV of Total Payments	$\underline{\$1441}$

Jim's BCA narrative continues:

Present Value Comparison of *Buy* and *Lease-to-Own* Alternatives

Workstation PCs are offered at the same purchase price of $1,500 per unit under the *buy* and *lease-to-own* alternatives. The only difference is that under the *buy* alternative, the entire purchase price is paid on the date of delivery; under *lease-to-own* outlays are one-third down, with equal one-third payments due the beginning of the second and third year, respectively.

The vendor offers the lease agreement with no interest charge (rate of 0%) for the delayed installment payments, with transfer of ownership of the PCs upon making the third payment. Administrative cost of acquisition has been estimated at 10.1%. Present value of purchase prices are calculated using a 4.1% the discount rate from OMB Circular A94, Appendix C, as follows.

Exhibit 1-3(a) shows the calculation of the present value of total purchase price for the *buy* alternative of $27,000. This is, of course, the same as the purchase price, since there are no delayed payments.

Exhibit 1-3 (a)

					Total Purchase Price (x 18 Workstations)
	Year 1	Year 2	Year 3	Unit Totals	
$PV = 1/(1+i)^t$					
Buy $1,500				$1,500	$27,000.00
				Acquisition Cost (10.1% of Purchase Price)	+$2,727.00
					$29,727.00

The acquisition cost of $2,727 (i.e., 10.1% of the purchase price) is factored into the total. *Exhibit 1-3(b)* shows the calculation for the *lease-to-own* alternative. Because of the delayed cash outlays, the *present value* of total payments is discounted to $28,677.

Exhibit 1-3 (b)

Present Value Cost of Lease-to-Own Alternative				
$PV = 1/(1+i)^t$ Year 1	Year 2	Year 3	Unit Totals	Total Purchase Cost (x 18 Worksta-tions)
Lease $500				
	PV = 500 x $1/(1+.041)^1$ = $480.30			
		PV = 500 x $1/(1+.041)^2$ = $461.39		
Lease Totals $500.00	$480.30	461.39	$1,441.69	$25,950.42
			Acquisition Cost (10.1% of Purchase Price)	+ $2,727.00
				$28,677.42

Net Difference=Savings	
Per Unit ($1,500 – $1,441.69) =	$58.31
For 18 Units ($29,727 – $28,667.42) =	$1,049.58

From the calculations, the total present value of the purchase cost is reduced by $58.31 per workstation PC. This totals to $1,049.58 savings for 18 workstations.

At this point, the total acquisition costs for the *lease-to-own* alternative offers a slight economic advantage over the *buy* alternative. Jim now had two of the *total cost of ownership* elements: *acquisition costs* and *purchase price*. He next prepared to calculate the third, the *cost of use* category.

Jim recognized that the key data source for *costs of use* could be derived from the service call log data. First, there were the actual costs for the service calls. These could be determined by the reimbursable rates for service call technician hours expended during service calls. The service call log also served as an indicator for *lost productive hours* by workers as they awaited repairs. There were no data sources for *cost of use* for new PCs (since there was no history), so Jim assumed he would need to estimate their costs of use as a percentage of the status quo costs.

Cost of Use

Jim continues his narrative:

Cost of Use

Cost of Use, the third cost category under total *costs of ownership*, was defined by two cost elements, the costs of *service calls* for equipment repairs, and cost of *lost productive hours* of office workers when workstations are down.

The *status quo* hours spent on these two cost areas were derived from historical records obtained from the service call log kept by the information technology office. These hours form the basis for computing the costs of existing workstation PC downtime.

He arrayed the computer log numbers in a spreadsheet, as illustrated in *Exhibit 1-4: Workstation Service Calls*, below. Looking over the spreadsheet, Jim calculated that each PC averaged about five service calls per year for one problem or another. Each service call averaged a little more that three hours from open-to-close. The standard reimbursable rate for technicians was $44.00 per hour, according to the information technology office. Just over 285 service call hours were charged to Jim's office for the previous 12 months. This calculated to an annual cost for service calls of $12,553 (i.e., $44 x 285.3 hours).

Exhibit 1-4

Workstation Service Calls		
Month	**# Events**	**Total Hours:** **Open-to-Close of Work Orders**
1	*7*	*22.0*
2	*5*	*12.5*
3	*10*	*22.1*
4	*8*	*31.0*
5	*9*	*33.7*
6	*6*	*27.0*
7	*5*	*21.0*
8	*9*	*25.0*
9	*7*	*22.0*
10	*8*	*21.0*
11	*6*	*15.0*
12	*10*	*33.0*
Totals	*90*	*285.3*
Annual cost of Service Calls		*$12,553* ($44 x 285.3 hours)
Visits per Worker per Year	*5* [iii]	
Hours per Service Call		*3.2* [iv]
Yearly Average Downtime per Workstation	*5 x 3.2*	*= 16 Hours (per PC per Year)*

[iii] 90 service calls ÷ 12 months = 5 visits per worker per year.
[iv] 285.3 hours ÷ (5 service calls x 18 workstations) = 3.2 hours per service call.

Jim's BCA narrative continues:

Cost of Use (continued)

Cost of Service Calls

Service calls have averaged a little more than three hours from open-to-close of work orders. The standard reimbursable rate for technicians is $44.00 per hour, according to the information technology office. Just over 285 service call hours were charged to Jim's office for the previous 12 months. This calculated to an annual cost for service calls of $12,553 (i.e., $44 x 285.3 hours).

It was obvious that at least part of the *cost of use* was the $12,553 Jim's office had reimbursed for maintenance and repairs during the one-year period. What was not so obvious, however, was how to convert workstation downtime into *lost productive hours* for office workers as they awaited repairs. Jim intuitively felt that not all computer workstation downtime could be attributed to lost productive time. For example, workers do not spend all of their productive working hours on the computer. Only that proportion of working time spent using the PC would be affected by workstation downtime.

Jim called the company's operations research office and asked for advice on how to make this calculation. The operations research analyst was quite helpful. She suggested that Jim review another government document, OMB Circular A-76.[v] In particular, the guidelines in *Part II, The Revised Supplemental Handbook*, might provide useful approximations of expected useful workers' productive time during normal business hours.

---

[v] Office of Management and Budget (OMB) Circular A-76, *Performance of Commercial Activities:*
http://www.whitehouse.gov/omb/circulars/a076/a076.html .

Jim was given a 'heads up,' however, that Circular A-76 gives relative percentages of the base pay level. It was suggested that Jim use actual pay grades if known. But since people are sensitive about such information, he was also advised that the operations research office often uses a rule of thumb to approximate office worker salaries—the pay rate of a US Federal Employee at the career grade level of GS-11, Step 9. General Schedule (GS) rates are often considered comparable to commercial rates for office type jobs.[vi] These rates can provide a convenient proxy for average salaries of office workers in large companies and organizations, and can usually be verified as appropriate or not by the local human resources office. Current GS rates are available on the Internet.[vii]

Also, Jim was advised to get an estimate of *what percentage of time is normally spent using the computer* by office workers during their normal daily work routines. This information would not be available in company records, and Jim needed to re-query the 18 office workers to develop the average estimate.

Reviewing OMB Circular A-76, *Part II, The Revised Supplemental Handbook*, Jim noted that the Handbook provides a way to calculate two key adjustments to worker costs: relative productive rates, fringe benefits.

Relative Productivity

The notion of *relative productivity* assumes that workers will have legitimate nonproductive periods during normal working hours, including time taken for leave, sick days,

---

[vi] Also, for factory, skilled labor and trades, the U.S. federal government publishes Wage Grade (WG) rates related to a particular local.
[vii] GS Pay Schedules can be found on the Internet at http://www.opm.gov/oca.

training, administrative activities, and so on. Jim was able to estimate the productivity rate to be approximately 85% of paid working hours.[viii]

Using this factor, Jim could now estimate the percentage of lost productive hours directly attributable to PC downtime. This lowered the estimate of lost worker time, but was a necessary adjustment for accurate assessment of potential savings.

Fringe Benefits

Jim also reviewed a section relating to *fringe benefits*. Fringe benefits represent real costs the organization and have the effect of increasing value of lost productive hours. This is often a hidden cost of labor to the employee that comes from employer contributions for retirement plans, health care insurance, Medicare, and miscellaneous.

Using the OMB Circular A76 guidelines, these costs are estimated to add 32.45% to the basic cost of salaries. Jim calculated the total 'loaded' hourly cost of lost productive hours by multiplying the base pay by the *fringe benefits factor* of 1.3245, as shown in *Exhibit 1-5*.

For every hour of productive labor reduced by an alternative solution, Jim could now estimate the monetary benefits by multiplying the hourly salary by this factor.

[viii] OMB Circular A-76 indicates that actual available hours per Full Time Equivalent (FTE) employee can be calculated as 1,776 available hours per year. Assuming a 40-hour week, 2,080 hours are expected for a full-time employee, $1,776_{\text{ available productive hours}} \div 2080_{\text{ total paid hours}} \approx .85$, or 85%.

Exhibit 1-5

Total 'Loaded' Cost of Pay (Base Pay + Fringe Benefits)	
Base Pay	100%
Retirement	+ 27.00%
Health Benefits	+ 5.60%
Medicare	+ 1.45%
Miscellaneous	+ 1.70%
Total Cost	= 132.45%
Fringe Benefit Factor	*1.3245*

Lost Productive Hours

Now Jim nearly had enough information to calculate the value of *lost productive hours*. He needed only to develop and estimate of how many of their total hours were dependent upon PCs, then multiply this value by the appropriate pay factors.

Jim took his copy of the spreadsheet of logged workstation service calls and visited each cubicle in his office area. He found 15 of the 18 workers were available for interview. He showed each respondent the log sheet (see *Exhibit 1-4*) and asked, "Does the average number of service calls of about 5 per year seem reasonable?" Is a service call visit about every 2½ months about right?"[ix] The consensus of these workers was that these averages seemed fairly accurate. They also verified that the average downtime per service call of about 3 hours seemed reasonably

---

[ix] Five visits per worker per year (from *Exhibit 1-4*), or about one visit per workstation every 2½ months.

accurate; corresponding with average 3.2 hours calculated using the log.

The general agreement about the frequency and duration of service calls with actual log records gave Jim confidence about answers to a final question, "What percentage of total working time do you estimate is spent actually using your PC?" This estimate provided the final link for calculating the cost of lost hours due to workstation downtime. The consensus from the 15 office workers who were interviewed was that about 70% of their available working hours was spent using the workstation PCs.

Using this information, Jim's BCA narrative continues:

Cost of Use (continued)

Cost of Lost Productive Hours

Calculation of the projected amount of *lost productive hours* began with analysis of the log of service calls made to each organizational office area, kept by the information technology office. The log indicates the office area visited, and the date and time work orders were opened and completed. Records were available for the past 12 months.

The total length of time in hours between opening and closing of service call work orders provided an initial measure of lost productive time at the work site. This enabled calculation of a lost productivity cost, given the assumption that workstations are required for a certain percentage of productive output.

Two factors were calculated to determine the proportion of lost productive output that is attributable to workstation PC downtime. First, using OMB Circular A-76 guidelines for determining productive work hours expected from civilian employees, 85% of scheduled work time is estimated to be productive, reducing productive hours by 15%. Calculations for this factor are footnoted.[x]

The second factor concerns an estimate of the total workstation PC downtime that is used for productive work. Interviews with 15 of the 18 office workers who were available at interview time produced an average response that about 70% of the normal working time is spent using the workstation, reducing usable lost productive hours by 30%.

Finally, the combined effect of the two factors was used to estimate costs subject savings: reduced reduction of *productive work hours* (i.e., 85% of total hours) and of usable lost productive time (i.e., 70% of working time). This computes to approximately 60% of total work hours subject to savings with improved PC reliability.[xi]

Lost Productivity Cost Calculations

Lost productivity costs required calculation of an estimated salary basis to use in the lost productivity calculations. A base pay salary of $54,440 per year (using U.S. Office of Personnel Management wages for a mid-level office employee) was used as an estimate of the average salary for the 18 office workers.[xii] This salary was multiplied by a factor of 1.3245, derived from OMB Circular A-76, to account for fringe benefits. This brought the estimated average annual salary to $72,106 (i.e. $54,440 x 1.3245). This fully loaded salary cost was then divided by

---

[x] From: OMB Circular No. A-76, *Part II, Revised Supplemental Handbook,* Chapter 1 (1966). In-house productive work hours are established as 1776 hours per year for a full-time employee. Assuming employees work 2080 hours per year (i.e., 52 weeks x 40 hours), the ratio of 1776/2020 = 85%.

[xi] That is, .85 x .70 = .595, or 60% rounded off.

[xii] The base pay rate is for a US Civilian GS-11, Step 9, which was published under US Office of Personnel Management tables on the Internet at http://www.opm.gov/oca. This rate was indicated as an appropriate estimate by the corporate Operations Research Office Subject Matter Expert, and verified by a telephone call to a corporate Human Relations Office as representative of rates in the office area for this study.

2080 hours (i.e., 52 weeks x 40 hours per week) to yield $34.67 as the cost per labor hour.

Calculation of the cost of *lost productive hours* can now be computed. First, the expected loss of productive hours due to PC downtime is calculated. This was estimated at 60% of total PC downtime hours, and was computed to be 171.2 hours, as shown in *Exhibit 1-6*.

Exhibit 1-6

Lost Productive Hours			
Month	**# Events**	**Total PC Downtime**	**Productive Hours Lost** (60% of Downtime)
1	*7*	*22.0*	*13.2*
2	*5*	*12.5*	*7.5*
3	*10*	*22.1*	*13.3*
4	*8*	*31.0*	*18.6*
5	*9*	*33.7*	*20.2*
6	*6*	*27.0*	*16.2*
7	*5*	*21.0*	*12.6*
8	*9*	*25.0*	*15.0*
9	*7*	*22.0*	*13.2*
10	*8*	*21.0*	*12.6*
11	*6*	*15.0*	*9.0*
12	*10*	*33.0*	*19.8*
Totals		**285.3**	**171.2**
Cost of Lost Productive Hours		**171.2 x 34.67 = $5,935**	

Total cost was then calculated by multiplication of estimated productive hours lost by the fully loaded pay rate of $34.67 per hour. This tallies to a total cost of $5,935 (i.e., 171.2 hours x $34.67) for the twelve-month historical period.

Total Cost of Use

The total costs of use of PC downtime can now be calculated, as shown *Exhibit 1-7*.

Exhibit 1-7

Costs of Use
Value of Status Quo PC Downtime

Month	Total Hours Machine Downtime	Cost of Service Calls (# Hours x $44)	Productive Hours Lost (60% of Downtime)	Cost of Lost Production (# Hours x $34.67)	Combined Costs (Service Calls + Lost Productive Hours)
1	22	$968	13.2	$458	$1,426
2	12.5	$550	7.5	$260	$810
3	22.1	$972	13.3	$461	$1,434
4	31	$1,364	18.6	$645	$2,009
5	33.7	$1,483	20.2	$700	$2,183
6	27	$1,188	16.2	$562	$1,750
7	21	$924	12.6	$437	$1,361
8	25	$1,100	15	$520	$1,620
9	22	$968	13.2	$457	$1,426
10	21	$924	12.6	$437	$1,361
11	15	$660	9	$312	$972
12	33	$1,452	19.8	$686	$2,138
Totals		$12,553	+	$5,935 =	$18,488

It combines the cost of service calls and of lost productive hours. Service call reimbursable fees were $12,533 (i.e., 285.3 x $44). Added to the cost of lost worker productive hours, the total tallies to $18,488 (i.e., $12,553 + $5,935).

Jim now had calculations to compare costs of the three alternatives. The total procurement costs (i.e., *costs of acquisition* and *purchase price* of new PCs) provided the added 'get in' costs, if new PCs were to be procured. The *costs of use* for the status quo alternative provided the basis from which *expected reduced costs* could be calculated, given that new PCs were expected to have less downtime. All Jim needed now was an estimate of how much the reliability might be expected to improve with new PCs.

Preliminary Total Costs of Ownership Comparisons

To get an estimate of how much more reliable new PCs were likely to be, Jim again contacted the information systems office. The service call supervisor indicated that previous offices had reduced service calls an *average of 75%*. Further, in her experience, new state-of-the-art PCs would probably maintain the better reliability for *about three years*. This estimate of 75% improvement in reliability provided Jim with the needed factor to compute potential savings from new PCs. Jim's BCA narrative continues:

Exhibit 1-8 displays a chart of preliminary estimates of *total ownership costs* of the alternatives for three years.

Exhibit 1-8

Total Ownership Costs *Preliminary Estimates*			
	Alternative 1: **Status Quo**	**Alternative 3:** **Buy New PCs**	**Alternative 4:** **Lease-to-Own**
Cost of:		(estimated 75% reduction in service calls)	
Year 1			
Acquisition	$0	$2,727	$2,727
Price	$0	$27,000	$9,000
Use	$18,488	$4,622	$4,622
Year 2			
Acquisition	$0	$0	$0
Price	$0	$0	$8,645 (i.e., $480.30 x 18)
Use	$18,488	$4,622	$4,622

Total Ownership Costs Preliminary Estimates (continued)			
	Alternative 1: Status Quo	Alternative 3: Buy New PCs	Alternative 4: Lease-to-Own
Year 3			
Acquisition	$0	$0	$0
Price	$0	$0	$8,305 (i.e., $461.39 x 18)
Use	$18,488	$4,622	$4,622
Three-Year Cumulative Costs			
Acquisition	$0	$2,727	$2,727
Price	$0	$27,000	$25,950
Use	$55,464	$13,866	$13,866
TOTALS	$55,464	$43,593	$42,543

The information technology office subject matter expert (SME) estimated that the expected economic life for these savings is three years. It became apparent that initial acquisition and purchase price investments would reach breakeven for both the buy and lease alternatives within the three-year period. Reduced costs from new PCs offset acquisition expenses at a rate of $13,866 per year (i.e., $18,488 - $4,622 = $13,866). The *cost of use* for new machines is estimated to be 25% of status quo costs, based on an interview with the SME.

These cumulative costs are considered preliminary, however, since they do not account for potential worsening of service call frequencies. They are merely a 'first estimate,' based on service calls during the past year. It is reasonable to assume that the unfavorable PC downtime trends will continue to increase if status quo workstations are not replaced. Forecasted estimates of these worsening trends, calculated next, were necessary to calculate potential future costs and benefits from underlying trends in the historical data.

However, the first estimate of a breakeven within three years was encouraging, given the information technology expert's estimate that the improved reliability of PCs would likely 'hold' for only about three years. By then, the replacement PCs would be expected to begin losing efficiency.

Jim felt he had 'nailed' the essentials of costs for the alternatives. Next step would be to develop estimates of the trend of increasing service calls, and from that the expected benefits from forecasted values. However, it had been a long day with much reading and thinking, and it was getting late, so Jim took time to catch up on his e-mails and other postponed projects. He'd take the evening to consider what to do next, and start fresh in the morning.

Day 5 – The Benefits

Early Tuesday morning Jim was eager to get started projecting potential benefits. Looking over the previous study development, he pondered, "What are the benefits?" "How can they be calculated?" Rereading the section about benefits and costs in OMB Circular A-94, Jim noted the distinction made between *benefit-cost analysis* and *cost-effectiveness analysis*.

> *Benefit-cost analysis* is recommended … (but) *Cost-effectiveness analysis* … a less comprehensive technique … can be appropriate when benefits from competing alternatives are the same … or … have the same effects, but dollar amounts cannot be assigned to the benefits.

The difference for the distinction was not intuitively obvious, so Jim gave a call to the operations research analyst and asked for help. The O.R. analyst explained that *benefits* and *savings* are the two basic payback measurements used in traditional economic analysis—but that benefits are often difficult to quantify. *Benefits* generally apply to increased effectiveness (i.e., doing the right things), and *savings* to increased efficiency (i.e., doing things right). Said a different way, benefits can be defined as producing relatively greater outputs with the same resources; savings as producing relatively the same outputs using reduced resources.

The operations research analyst then recommended a cost-effectiveness approach for Jim's study. He also suggested that Jim use *savings-to-investment ratio (SIR)* as the primary indicator for selection of alternatives.

The analyst also gave Jim some pointers on modern forecasting techniques to help project potential savings. Since the service call history represented only one year, forecasting capabilities to quantify other factors such as seasonality and cycles were probably limited for this study. Of great help, however, would be the ability to use the monthly historical variation of service calls to compute estimates of risk. By convention, the operations research analyst recommended estimating required savings that would provide a 95% confidence of having enough savings for breakeven.

Armed with this tutorial, Jim accepted the recommendations, and proceeded to develop a *cost effectiveness analysis.* He began by operationally defining benefits as savings due to higher reliability of new PCs versus status quo. His narrative continues:

Analysis of Benefits

Tangible *benefits for this study were defined as potential cost savings* due to acquisition of more reliable PCs. These savings were calculated from two sources: reduced costs of service calls and lost productive hours of office workers. To be feasible, each alternative's savings must equal or exceed acquisition costs, as measured by the savings-to-investment (SIR) ratio. The alternative with the highest SIR was defined as the most cost efficient.

As previously noted (see *Exhibit 1-8*), the information systems subject matter expert estimated that service calls would probably be reduced by 75% with new PCs. This estimate was considered valid over an expected economic life of three years for new PCs.

Preliminary estimates of savings showed potential breakeven of investment costs for new PCs would occur within the three-year period of useful economic life. This was based on the historical *PC service call rates* from the service call log. However, examination of the data indicated a *trend* of increasing service calls over past the twelve months. Forecasting techniques were used to mathematically determine likely effects of this trend over future periods, should the status quo alternative be selected. Savings estimates were then calculated as 75% of the forecasted service calls.

Forecasting Expected Workstation Downtimes

At this point, Jim realized that he needed more information about forecasting. The basic data available were provided by the service call records in *Exhibit 1-4*, and are partially repeated in *Exhibit 1-9* for easy reference.

Exhibit 1-9

Workstation Service Calls		
Month	# Events	Total Hours: Service Calls
1	7	22.0
2	5	12.5
3	10	22.1
4	8	31.0
5	9	33.7
6	6	27.0
7	5	21.0
8	9	25.0
9	7	22.0
10	8	21.0
11	6	15.0
12	10	33.0

Again Jim called the operations research analyst, who offered an overview of potential ways to forecast future events, using the historical numbers. He suggested that review of a textbook on business statistical forecasting methods would be helpful. He informed Jim that his existing office spreadsheet software had analytical and graphics capabilities that could perform many of the simple forecasting routines.

Hoowaa!! This was a little more than Jim could grasp without better references. Off to the library again, this time to review the forecasting texts that the operations research analyst had suggested. Jim spent the rest of the morning taking notes. Finally, he checked out a forecasting textbook for further reference, and then was off to lunch.

After lunch, Jim began to reexamine the service call data in *Exhibit 1-9*. Combining what he had learned about forecasting techniques and using historical data, Jim's narrative continues:

Forecasting Service Call Hours

Recorded data from the information technology office service call log were examined to determine observable patterns that could be useful for forecasting future expected service call hours (i.e., level, trends, etc.). Since only one year of data was available, seasonal patterns could not be examined.

Exhibit 1-10 presents a graphical representation of the values from the workstation downtime table. Using spreadsheet analytical tools, a *least squares trend line* was calculated using time series regression. Also shown is the scatter plot of the actual service call values around the trend line, indicating the amount of *variability* on the number of service calls from month to month.

From the spreadsheet calculations, it was observed that a slight upward trend in service call hours existed over the 12-month period. The 'fitted trend' increased from a value of 22.6 to a value of 24.8, representing a trend of increasing service calls of nearly 10% over the twelve months.

Exhibit 1-10

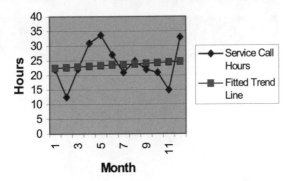

Historical Data (jagged line) and Fitted (Least Squares) Trend Line

A second type measure that is useful for forecasting is shown in *Exhibit 1-11*[xiii] (see next page). There, the accuracy of the forecasting equation was tested for *bias* and degree of *uncertainty*. The flat 'zero error' line represents the 'perfect fit' if the forecasting equation was able to predict actual events with 100% accuracy. That is, the errors for all forecasts would actually be zero, and the array of error points would all fall exactly on the flat line.

This is, of course, highly unlikely, due to the averaging nature of the regression equation. However, if forecasts are systematically correct, the errors (computed by subtracting the computed values from observed values) will vary randomly around the flat

[xiii] These charts were generated automatically using Microsoft Excel spreadsheet software (i.e., select Tools, Data Analysis, and Regression). However, for relatively simple data such as these, one could fairly accurately 'eyeball' the trend and manually draw the trend lines.

'zero error' line. If the number of errors is about equal above and below, and the forecast is said to be 'unbiased.' And, of course, if amplitude of errors above and below the zero error line is generally large, there will be relatively more uncertainty in predictions.

Exhibit 1-11

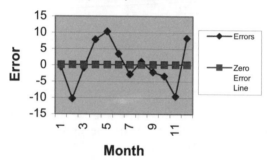

The objective was to develop as accurate and unbiased a forecasting equation as possible, given the historical data. This 'best' equation was then used to forecast future values, assuming that they would follow similar trend/variation patterns to historical observations.

For the service calls, the *errors* appeared to vary in an up-down serpentine pattern. This indicated the possibility of some underlying cause, such as cyclic or seasonal activity. However, there were not enough data points to calculate such possible effects.

There were approximately an equal number of 'misses' above and below the line, which indicates that the trend line is relatively unbiased (i.e., forecasts using this basis will probably not be systematically too high or too low).

The conclusion for the analysis of errors (*Exhibit 1-11*) was to accept the trend line (*Exhibit 1-10*) as representative of the basic underlying average process of events. This allowed use of the trend line equation to forecast future expected service call hours. The spreadsheet software calculated this equation. The general equation for time series linear regression forecasting is illustrated in *Exhibit 1-12*:

Exhibit 1-12

Simple Linear Regression Forecasting Equation

$$F = a + bx$$

where: *F = the forecasted value*
    a = the Y intercept value (if b = 0)
    b = month
    x = the calculated trend factor

The calculated values for a and b, using computer spreadsheet software, were:

$$a = 22.4$$
$$b = .2$$

Using these values, the actual regression equation becomes:

$$F = 22.4 + .2X$$

From this, the 'fitted' values of the *past history* were calculated as shown in *Exhibit 1-13*. These are the values that were actually plotted along the fitted trend line in *Exhibit 1-10*.

Exhibit 1-13

Historical Trend Line

$$M_{onth\ 1} = 22.4 + .2 \times 1 = 22.6$$
$$M_{onth\ 2} = 22.4 + .2 \times 2 = 22.8$$
$$M_{onth\ 3} = 22.4 + .2 \times 3 = 23.0$$

. . .

. . .

$$M_{onth\ 12} = 22.4 + .2 \times 12 = 24.8$$

Forecasts of *future events* extended the historical trend line, beginning with the next month beyond the historical 12-month data period, at month 13. Forecasted future months were calculated using the same regression equation, as follows in *Exhibit 1-14*:

Exhibit 1-14

Forecasted Trend Line

$$M_{onth\ 13} = 22.4 + .2 \times 13 = 25.0$$
$$M_{onth\ 14} = 22.4 + .2 \times 14 = 25.2$$
$$M_{onth\ 15} = 22.4 + .2 \times 15 = 25.4$$

. . .

. . .

$$M_{onth\ 24} = 22.4 + .2 \times 24 = 27.2$$

. . .

. . .

$$M_{onth\ 48} = 22.4 + .2 \times 48 = 32.0$$

For forecasts three years (36 months) out.

Exhibit 1-15 shows a graph of the forecasted service call trend line through the 36-month forecast horizon.

Exhibit 1-15

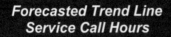

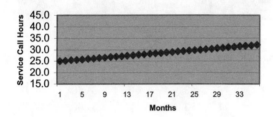

Forecasted Cost of Use

The total costs of PC downtime were attributed to two causes: reimbursable *service call hours* and *lost productive hours* by office workers. Service call hours were available and extracted from the log provided by the information systems office. These data were analyzed, and a linear regression equation was developed to forecast their expected values.

Forecasted hours were then multiplied by the billing rate for computer service call technicians of $44 per hour to estimate future costs. Values of the combined expected *cost of use* values under the status quo (no change) scenario are shown in *Exhibit 1-16*. (Note that the time scale has expanded to quarterly to facilitate presentation of the data).

Similar calculations were made for *lost productive hours*. As previously developed in this study, these hours are simply 60% of the total service call hours, and their value was $34.67 per hour.

Exhibit 1-16

	Status Quo Forecasted Cost of Use				
	Service Call Costs		Lost Productive Hours		
Quarter	Hours	X $44	60% of Hours	x $34.67	Combined Costs
1	76	$3,344	46	$1,581	$4,925
2	77	$3,388	46	$1,602	$4,990
3	79	$3,476	47	$1,643	$5,119
4	81	$3,564	49	$1,685	$5,249
5	83	$3,652	50	$1,727	$5,379
6	85	$3,740	51	$1,768	$5,508
7	86	$3,784	52	$1,789	$5,573
8	88	$3,872	53	$1,831	$5,703
9	90	$3,960	54	$1,872	$5,832
10	92	$4,048	55	$1,914	$5,962
11	94	$4,136	56	$1,955	$6,091
12	95	$4,180	57	$1,976	$6,156

Forecasted Savings

Savings are calculated from difference between status quo and new PC service call costs. The 75% reduction factor from status quo costs is estimated, as shown in *Exhibit 1-17*.

"At last," thought Jim, "I have some tangible evidence to support the acquisition alternatives over the status quo. I'll take some time to think just how to best show this relationship." He then took a well-deserved break, checked his e-mails for the day, and departed for the evening. He felt elated that the study was finally coming together.

Exhibit 1-17

Quarter	Combined Status Quo Costs	Benefits due to Cost Avoidance (75% savings)	Costs of Use with New PCs
Forecasted Costs of Use			
1	$4,925	$3,694	$1,231
2	$4,990	$3,742	$1,248
3	$5,119	$3,839	$1,280
4	$5,249	$3,937	$1,312
Year 1 Subtotal	20,283	$15212	$5,071
5	$5,379	$4,034	$1,345
6	$5,508	$4,131	$1,377
7	$5,573	$4,180	$1,393
8	$5,703	$4,277	$1,426
Year 2 Subtotal	22,163	$16,622	$5,541
9	$5,832	$4,374	$1,458
10	$5,962	$4,472	$1,490
11	$6,091	$4,568	$1,523
12	$6,156	$4,617	$1,539
Year 3 Subtotal	24,041	$18,031	$6,010
Three-Year Totals	$66,487	$49,865	$16,622

Jim now had good evidence for his BCA alternative comparisons, and was sure he would be able to finish the report in the short time Maria had given him.

Day 6—The Benefit-Cost Comparisons

Bright-eyed and bushy tailed, Jim now set out to compare the alternatives. He began with the comparison of the status quo to the two acquisition alternatives. His narrative continues:

Comparison of Total Cost of Ownership

With forecasted values for likely future PC downtime, more accurate *cost of ownership* values could then be calculated. *Exhibit 1-18* shows these calculations.

Exhibit 1-18

Total Ownership Costs *From Forecasted Trend Values*			
Cost of:	**Alternative 1:** **Status Quo**	**Alternative 3:** **Buy New PCs** (estimated 75% reduction in service calls)	**Alternative 4:** **Lease-to-Own**
Year 1			
Acquisition	$0	$2,727	$2,727
Price	$0	$27,000	$9,000
Use	$20,293	$5,071	$5,071
Year 2			
Acquisition	$0	$0	$0
Price	$0	$0	$8,645 (i.e., $480.30 x 18)
Use	$22,163	$5,541	$5,541
Year 3			
Acquisition	$0	$0	$0
Price	$0	$0	$8,305 (i.e., $461.39 x 18)
Use	$24,041	$6,010	$6,010
Cumulative Costs			
Acquisition	$0	$2,727	$2,727
Price	$0	$27,000	$25,950
Use	$66,487	$16,622	$16,622
TOTALS	**$66,487**	**$46,349**	**$45,299**

Recall that previously, under the costs section, preliminary *costs of ownership* were based on historical values, rather than forecasted trends. By taking advantage of the forecasted data, more accurate estimates of future cost savings became possible. The forecast enabled explicit calculations of expected increased service calls under the status quo alternative.

It is clear from the table that both the *buy* and *lease-to-own* acquisition alternatives are more cost efficient than status quo, and were improved relative preliminary estimates (i.e., compare with *Exhibit 1-8*). This was due to the expected the upward trend in expected problems if status quo PCs were not replaced.

Comparison of Buy and Lease-to-Own

Given the advantage of the two acquisition alternatives over status quo, three comparisons were made to help differentiate these two alternatives:
1) Breakeven analysis
2) Savings-to-investment ratios (SIR)
3) Cash flow

Breakeven Analysis

Breakeven refers to the time required to achieve payback of 'get in' acquisition funds due to savings from reduced PC downtime. *Exhibit 1-19* graphically shows the accumulation of cost savings over the 36 months of the forecast horizon. Costs of acquisition were compared with estimates of cumulative savings. Cumulative savings surpass the *present value* costs (i.e., the breakeven point) of the lease alternative ($28,677) in the 23rd month, and in the 24th month for the buy alternative ($29,727).

Note that breakeven points for both the buy and lease-to-own alternatives are within the 36 months (i.e., three years) of economic life that the subject matter expert predicts for reliability of replacement PCs.

Exhibit 1-19

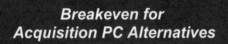

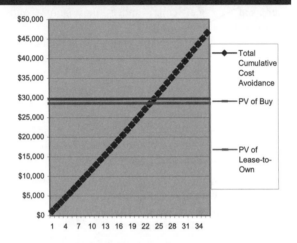

Savings-to-Investment Ratios (SIR)

The purpose of the savings-to-investment ratio differs from that of breakeven analysis. Where breakeven analysis computed the time period for payback, the SIR computed magnitude of payback. The larger the SIR, the greater the payback amount for the investment. A SIR value of one (i.e., unity) or higher is required for minimum savings to at least equal acquisition costs.

The total benefits due to cost avoidance for new PCs (i.e., both acquisition alternatives) was calculated (from values in *Exhibit 1-17*) at $66,487 - $16,622 = $49,865. The investment requirement for each alternative was calculated at $29,272 for *buy*, and 28,677 for *lease-to-own* (see *Exhibit 1-3*).

From these values, for the three-year period of expected benefits, the savings-to-investment ratio (SIR) for the *buy alternative* calculated to be 1.68

(i.e., \$49,865 $_{\text{cost avoidance}}$ ÷ \$29,727 $_{\text{cost to acquire}}$). Similarly, the calculated SIR for the *lease-to-own alternative* is 1.74 (i.e., \$49,865$_{\text{cost avoidance}}$ ÷ \$28,677$_{\text{cost to acquire}}$), which is a slightly higher payback amount than for the buy alternative.

Cash Flow

A final consideration for comparing relative advantages between the two acquisition alternatives was *cash flow*. As illustrated in *Exhibit 1-20*, cash flow compares out-of-pocket acquisition costs to cost avoidances due to savings.

Exhibit 1-20

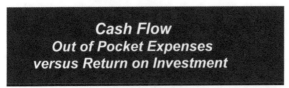

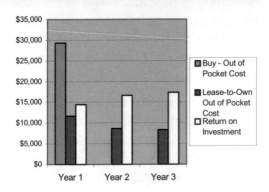

The *buy* alternative (the blue column) expends the total investment for new workstation PCs at the time of purchase, then recoups benefits (the yellow column) over future periods. It is essentially 'in the red' for nearly two years. The *lease-to-own* alternative (the red column) spreads the cash outflow into three increments. This allows benefits to exceed total expenditures before the end of the first year. It is essentially 'in the black' over most of the three years.

Evaluation of Indicators

Both the *breakeven period* and the *SIR* indicators marginally favor the lease-to-own alternative. However, the *cash flow* indicator significantly favors the lease alternative.

Assessment of Risks

Risk—the treatment of *uncertainty* of forecasts—is inherent in all estimates of potential future events. Uncertainty results from both imprecision of the underlying data and of modeling assumptions. OMB Circular A-94 advises:

> ...Probabilities [of uncertainty] should be used when possible [to assess the] nature and magnitude of potential biases to estimates.... Insights into probabilities can sometimes be gained by relative outside indicators, such as market interest rates, private insurance rates or [stochastic] simulations.

To Jim it seemed that the analysis of risk to evaluate chances of investment payback was a good idea. To better understand how to evaluate this risk, he again called the operations research analyst for advice. The O.R. analyst explained to Jim that variation around the fitted regression line is the first step to understanding risk. The second step is to recognize that forecasted values are merely *projections of historical pattern*, and that confidence intervals around past events may or may not be similar to *prediction intervals* of forecasted values.[xiv] Jim then followed advice

---

[xiv] *Prediction Intervals* are statistical boundaries within which *forecasts* are expected to fall—similar to *confidence intervals* for fitted *historical data*.

to once again review statistical forecasting references concerning risks and estimates of predictive intervals. He went over his notes from the forecasting text, and then attempted to incorporate what he learned in his BCA narrative, as follows:

Assessment of Risks

There are several areas of risk for the estimation of potential payback from new PCs. Forecasts for potential savings due to new PCs depend on the potential variability of forecasts. Risks for estimates in this BCA were as follows:

1) *Limited data history*: The forecasts for 36 months of expected service calls were extrapolated from the 12-month historical trend figures. Three years of forecasts from one year of historical data exceeds desirable forecast horizons recommended in forecasting literature. To augment chances of validity, the subject matter expert generally supported the projection as likely to continue increasing at the forecasted rate of 9.7% per year.

Discussion: The forecasting literature suggests that mathematical reliance for twelve months history is somewhere around three to six months.[2] The literature further indicates that 'mechanical' forecasts augmented by subjective forecasts from subject matter experts (SMEs) can sometimes improve validity of long-range forecasts.[3]

To help gain additional confidence about the savings forecasts and projected trend, Jim had again interviewed the service call supervisor. She was asked if, in her opinion, the service calls would continue to increase at the current rate of approximately 10% over the next three years if not replaced with new workstations. She indicated that the projection was seemingly accurate, and if anything, might understate the deterioration rate of the older PCs. She was considered a knowledgeable subject matter expert.

> 2) *Data variability*: The variability of Service Call Hours, the historical 12-month figure, is relatively high, around an average of 23.8 hours, ± 10 hours per month (see *Exhibit 1-21*).

Exhibit 1-21

	Service Call Hours	Fitted Trend Line	Errors (Service Call Hours – Fitted Values)	Errors Squared	Step 1 (Errors Squared)
Month					
1	22	22.6	-0.6	0.4	
2	12.5	22.8	-10.3	106.1	
3	22.1	23.0	-0.9	0.8	
4	31	23.2	7.8	60.8	
5	33.7	23.4	10.3	106.1	
6	27	23.6	3.4	11. 6	
7	21	23.8	-2.8	7.8	
8	25	24.0	1.0	1.0	
9	22	24.2	-2.2	4.8	
10	21	24.4	-3.4	11.6	
11	15	24.6	-9.6	92.2	
12	33	24.8	8.2	67.2	
	23.8 = *Average*		**±10.3**		**Step 2** *Sum of Squared Errors*
				470.4	
				6.9[xv]	**Step 3** *Standard Error*

[xv] The standard error is calculated by taking the square root of the average error (i.e. 470.4 ÷ 10 (i.e., degrees of freedom: 12 - 2 months).

Discussion: While the variability around the fitted trend line is 'noisy,' examination of the 'misses' of the forecast equation (i.e., the error plot around the zero error line in *Exhibit 1-11*) shows no consistent *bias*. That is, historical data are nearly evenly distributed around the zero error line. This in- dicates that the forecast equation is not consistently calculating predictions too high or too low.

An examination of the possible influence of this 'wobble' around the average trend line was ana- lyzed statistically using spreadsheet software. The *standard error* for the 12 months of service calls was computed to be 6.9 hours. *Exhibit 1-21* shows this calculation. Next, confidence intervals were calcu- lated to assure probability of success. This is a statis- tical *confidence interval*. *Confidence intervals (CIs)* are then combined into confidence bands of 85%, 90%, and 95% for the service call hours. This is illus- trated in *Exhibit 1-22*.

Exhibit 1-22

**Confidence Intervals (CIs)
for Historical Service Call Hours**

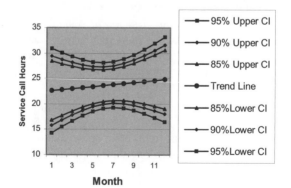

These confidence bands are keys for assessing the amount of risk that is inherent from the wobble of historical data. Consider the historical service calls. The monthly average was about 24 (actually 23.8) service call hours (*Exhibit 1-6*), and the calculated standard error of about 7 (actually 6.9) hours (*Exhibit 1-21*). Given this, there is 68% statistical assurance that a randomly observed value will not exceed ± 7 hours; or that a new observation will fall between 17 and 31 hours. If a higher assurance is needed, the CI is widened for acceptable values. For example, to attain an 85% confidence, one can expand the acceptable range of potential outcomes to ± 10 hours (i.e., 1.44 x standard error); for 90%, ± 12 hours (i.e., 1.65 x standard error); and for 95%, ± 14 hours (i.e., 1.96 x standard error).[xvi]

Also note, at the average point in time of all the months (i.e., at month 6.5), the confidence bands are the tightest fit, and expand for months further away. This is because of the mathematics of the time series regression model.[4] It implies that the forecast periods, from month 13 onward, will have even more expansion of CIs (and more uncertainty, if the statistical calculations alone are relied upon). This was a primary reason for using the expert opinion of the service call supervisor to help ensure the mathematical forecasts make sense and are reasonable.

3)   *Subjective estimate of savings*: The estimates of potential savings were based on the subjective estimation of the information technology subject matter experts (SMEs).

Discussion: In addition to the subjective opinion that the estimated value for the long forecast horizon seems about right, other subjective opinions were also used. Key among these were the estimates

---

[xvi] These values are derived from standard normal probabilities where: ± 1 standard error ≈ 68% of the area under the normal curve, ± 1.44 standard errors ≈ 85%, ± 1.65 standard errors ≈ 90%, and 1.96 standard errors ≈ 95%.

by office workers that they spend about 70% of their productive hours using computer workstations, and that PC downtime hours would be reduced by 75% of current rates if new workstations are acquired. Subjective estimates are unavoidable where historical data are limited or not available. They also can be used to supplement suspicious data, and help validate use of almost any data. These estimates were based on several SMEs' opinions, and were assumed to be fair estimates of these factors.

At this point, Jim wondered, "Just how do I translate the current *confidence intervals* into meaningful estimates of *predictive intervals* to assess risk at the estimated 24-month breakeven point?" (See *Exhibit 1-19.*) The operations research analyst had advised that future forecasts were indeed subject to increasing uncertainty, and—the longer the forecast horizon, the more the uncertainty would increase, as was implied in *Exhibit 1-22.*

He then offered Jim rule of thumb that might help develop reasonably accurate confidence intervals for the 36-month forecast horizon. He referred Jim to empirical studies that have indicated typical inaccuracies of forecasts across many tests, as measured by the *Mean Absolute Percent Error (MAPE)*, have tended to be around 7% in one year, 10% in two years, and 16% in three years.[5] The SME suggested that Jim could use the 10% MAPE as a benchmark, since his breakeven point occurs at the 24-month (two-year) point.

The MAPE is useful for measuring the percentage 'spread' of errors. As a percentage (i.e., a 'dimensionless' measure), it can help distinguish the relative uncertainty across different scales or magnitudes of time series data. Therefore, by measuring the current MAPE, and using 10% as a rule of thumb of minimum expected forecasting error, Jim could develop a reasonable estimate of the MAPE at two years into the future, when breakeven was projected to occur.

The operations research analyst showed Jim some relatively simple techniques for converting the MAPE into an approximation of the *standard error*. With an estimate of the MAPE at the two-year forecast horizon and conversion of that value to a *standard error*, it would be possible to use standard statistical methods to estimate, say, a 95% confidence value that forecasted savings would be attainable. Using these guidelines, Jim's BCA narrative continues:

Sensitivity of Forecasts due to Risks

To assess risk, a statistical estimate of required savings was calculated to assure *at least* a 95% confidence of sufficient funds to cover acquisition costs of new computers (i.e., for Alternative 3 (buy) or Alternative 4 (lease-to-own). The risk assessment used statistical analysis to determine the required amount of savings.

The first step toward calculating the 95% assurance level was to estimate an expected standard error for the predicted breakeven values (i.e., $28,677 for the lease-to-own alternative, and $29,727 for the buy alternative). The forecasting literature generally indicates that accuracy of long-range forecasts (i.e., long range is usually considered as over six months) is difficult to achieve by mathematical models alone. This is especially true with limited historical data, such as the 12 months of service call data.

However, one authoritative text reported that studies of accuracy from extrapolation forecasts have shown a *Mean Absolute Percent Error (MAPE)* of about 10% to be reasonable for the two-year forecast horizon.[xvii] This is useful, since the estimated breakeven point for the acquisition alternatives occurs at

---

[xvii] Makridakis & Wheelwright (1989), p. 350. Typical size of MAPE growth is at 7%—1 year, 10%—2 years, 16%—3 years, 18%—4 years, 25%—6 years.

approximately two years. It allowed use of the current MAPE value as an anchor for estimates of the standard error. The basic assumption was that the current MAPE (from the 12 months of history) is the same magnitude as the expected MAPE (at the two-year forecast point). Then, an approximation of the *Mean Absolute Deviation (MAD)* was calculated. [xviii] From the MAD, it was possible to compute the approximate *standard error* using a well-known mathematical relationship where 1.25 x MAD=SE.[6]

Using the predicted standard error for the two-year forecast horizon, a new level of savings, a 'safety level,' was calculated to provide the 95% assurance. This notion of additional savings to provide the 95% confidence is similar in concept to a safety level, often seen in inventory models.

Calculations for 95% Confidence

Exhibit 1-23 illustrates the calculations for the MAPE from the data for historical service call hours. The computed MAPE of 23.6% is calculated from the variation of service calls from the regression line over the 12 months of history. This is a dimensionless value since it is a percentage of the value, rather than the actual value. As such, the percentage can be taken of the future breakeven value, which is assumed to have proportional uncertainty to the observed history. This percentage was then converted into dollar values to calculate definite savings requirements.

The forecasting reference indicated forecasts of annual data have been shown to have MAPEs of around 10% after two years. However, the higher (more conservative) calculated MAPE of 23.6% was used for this study. This resulted in a higher savings requirement to achieve 95% confidence.

[xviii] The MAPE and MAD are closely related for data with small trend (and identical where there is no trend).

Exhibit 1-23

Computation of Mean Absolute Percent Error (MAPE)
(historical data)

Month	Savings (75% of Costs— Exhibit 1-7)	Fitted Trend Line	Error	Absolute Error	Absolute Percent Error
	X	F	X – F	$\|X - F\|$	$\frac{\|X-F\|}{X}*100$
1	$1,069	$1,098	-$29	$29	2.7%
2	$608	$1,108	-$501	$501	82.4%
3	$1,074	$1,118	-$44	$44	4.1%
4	$1,507	$1,128	$379	$354	23.5%
5	$1,638	$1,137	$501	$467	28.5%
6	$1,312	$1,147	$165	$154	11.8%
7	$1,021	$1,157	-$136	$136	13.3%
8	$1,215	$1,166	$49	$45	3.7%
9	$1,069	$1,176	-$107	$107	10.0%
10	$1,021	$1,186	-$165	$165	16.2%
11	$729	$1,196	-$467	$467	64.0%
12	$1,604	$1,205	$399	$372	23.2%
Sum	$13,866	$13,822		$2,841	283.4%
Means	$1,155	$1,151		MAD = $236	MAPE = 23.6%

The MAD values of the forecasted break-even points were estimated (using the historical MAPE) to transform the percentage into dollars. This allowed calculation of dollar estimates of the *standard errors* for the *lease-to-own* and *buy* alternatives. The *standard error* was then used to calculate the 95% confidence value for required savings.

The calculations were as follows: First, the MAPE is converted to an approximate estimate of the

MAD. Using advice from the operations research analyst, this was accomplished by multiplying the MAPE value times the breakeven value (for *lease-to-own*). The approximate MAD was calculated as:

$$MAD \approx \$28,667 \times 23.6\% \approx \$6,765.$$

Note that the forecasted value of the MAD (i.e., $6,765) is higher than the historical MAD of $4,248 due to the higher trended value forecasted two years into the future.[xix] This is a reasonable estimate, since the trend is relatively flat.

The mathematical relationship between the MAD and the standard error has been shown to be:[7]

$$1.25 \times MAD \approx \text{Standard Error}$$
$$1.25 \times \$6,765 = \$8,456 \approx \text{Standard Error}$$

Finally, to relate the estimate standard error to the 95% confidence level, the 'safety factor' is calculated at 1.65 standard errors:

$$1.65 \text{ standard errors} \times \$8,456 = \$13,952.$$

This dollar value is the calculated additional safety factor of required savings to assure a 95% chance that initial acquisition costs will be recouped by forecasted cost avoidance savings. That is, cumulative savings of $28,677 + $13,952 = $42,629 are required to assure, at 95% confidence, recouping of

---

[xix] The historical MAD of $4,248 (i.e., which was calculated from *Exhibit 1-23 (i.e.,* $236 MAD $_{\text{for a single PC}} \times 18 _{\text{PCs}} =$ $4,248). This is due to the trend of the forecasted values. Because of the trend, this is a more conservative estimate (i.e., higher required savings to achieve the 95% confidence). If the trend is too acute, the 'inflation' of the safety factor can become too high, and subjective opinions from SMEs may help determine what is reasonable. Also note that now, 1.65 x standard error = 95% for a one-tailed test (rather than 1.96 previously used for a two-tailed test—see *Exhibit 1-22*). This is because we are interested in achieving *at least* the breakeven savings—we do not care if we go over. Therefore, 5% risk (i.e., 5% of the area) is all on one end of the normal curve.

acquisition for the *lease-to-own* option. *Exhibit 1-24* illustrates the concept.

Exhibit 1-24

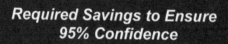

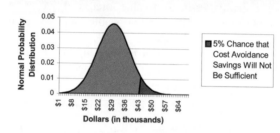

Shown is the 95% probability of having sufficient savings—the blue area (i.e., $28,677 assures 50% confidence, plus $13,952 additional to increase confidence to 95%).

The impact of this upon the breakeven point is to shift the time to achieve breakeven savings from approximately 23 months to 33 months for the lease-to-own alternative. This is illustrated in *Exhibit 1-25*.

Exhibit 1-25

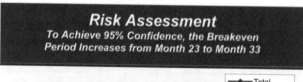

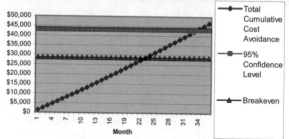

Similar calculations for the buy alternative compute to $ 29727 + $13,952 = $43,679. The break-even period increases from month 24 to month 34.

Subjective Evaluation of Forecasts

To help gain validation that these savings forecasts were reasonable, the service call supervisor was asked if, in her opinion, the approximately 10% per year increase in service call hours observed in the 12-month history seemed reasonable for future years. She estimated that the trend would likely continue over the next couple of years if the older PCs were not replaced.

She also confirmed that the variability of about 24% around average service call hours seemed reasonable (i.e., the 23.6% MAPE). She stated, "As service calls tend to rise, the technicians usually find 'gremlins' such as software viruses, and fix them. Then the service calls diminish until other 'gremlins' surface and again to increase the maintenance and re-pair hours."

The forecasts and breakeven evaluations were accepted as valid for this study based on the subjective confirmation.

Jim felt confident that he had captured the essence of the cost and breakeven comparisons among the three alternatives. He closed up shop for the evening, ready to develop conclusions for the study on the morrow.

Day 7—The Summary, Conclusions and Recommendations

Just one week before, Jim had been given this assignment to justify acquisition of new workstations for his office. He had probably worked harder than any time he could remember—but the time had gone swiftly, and he felt a sense of satisfaction at having both learned a lot and having pieced together a coherent analysis to support the case.

He now prepared the Summary and Conclusions section to 'bring it all together.' His narrative follows:

Summary and Conclusions

Summary

This study evaluated potential alternatives for a growing problem of expensive computer workstation downtime for an office of 18 workers. The problem was shown to have substantial cost consequences. For example, by keeping existing workstations (i.e., Alternative 1: the status quo alternative), the cost of use was estimated to be $66,487, forecasted over the next three years. These costs were derived from technician service call records provided by the information technology office. Conclusions were validated by interviews with *subject matter experts* from information technology, operations research, and the affected office where workers use the PCs.

To solve this problem, four alternative solutions were considered:

1) Status Quo (do nothing)
2) Upgrade existing PCs
3) Buy new PCs
4) Lease-to-own new PCs

The alternative for upgrading the older computers was dismissed as infeasible due to expected additional problems of calibrating new components in the aging and obsolete PC infrastructure. Costs and potential savings from the acquisition alternatives were then analyzed and compared with the status quo alternative.

'Total costs of ownership' were used as the criteria for comparing the status quo and acquisition alternatives. This is comprised of three costs: the *cost of acquisition*, the PC *selling price*, and the *costs of use* of status quo and new PCs.

Status Quo vs. Acquisition of New PCs

Acquisition Costs

Acquisition costs were zero for Alternative 1 (status quo). Acquisition costs of new PCs were comprised of two costs: costs of procurement and costs of the purchase price of the PCs.

The *present value* of unit purchase price was $27,000 for 18 PCs under Alternative 3 (buy), and $25,950 for 18 workstations under Alternative 4 (lease-to-own). The purchase price was less for lease-to-own due to discounting, which allows partial payments in 'cheaper' future dollars.

Procurement costs were estimated to be 10.1% of the unit price for both acquisition alternatives. This percentage was derived as a combination of 7.6% of unit price from company policy, and 2.5% for receiving and order closeout not accounted for by company policy. The 10.1% was calculated to be $2,727 of the face value of the contract unit price of $27,000 for both the buy and lease-to-own alternatives.

Adding the cost of acquisition and purchase price computed to total costs of $29,727 and 28,677 for the buy and lease-to-own alternatives, respectively.

Savings and Cost Avoidance

Benefits were calculated using expected *cost-of-use* savings, based on expert opinion that new PCs would incur 75% fewer service calls. The expert also predicted that these savings would be attainable over an economic life of three years.

Total ownership costs for continued use of the older machines were projected to be $66,487 over three forecasted years. Forecasted present value of total ownership costs for Alternative 3 (buy) were $46,349, and for Alternative 4 (lease-to-own) were $45,299 (see *Exhibit 1-18*). Net costs for both acquisition alternatives are less than expected status quo costs, and are considered more cost efficient. This eliminated Alternative 1 from further consideration.

Analysis then continued to determine the relative advantages of the two acquisition alternatives.

Buy versus Lease-to-Own

Benefit-cost relationships showed a breakeven for investments for new workstation PCs at 23 months for the *lease-to-own* alternative; 24 months for the *buy* alternative. Forecasted savings (see *Exhibit 1-17*) were $49,865 of the three years of economic life for the investment. The savings-to-investment ratio (SIR) slightly favored the lease alternative, at *1.74* (i.e., $49,865 $_{\text{cost avoidance}}$ ÷ $28,677 $_{\text{cost to acquire}}$), versus *1.68* (i.e., $49,865 ÷ $29,727) for the buy alternative. Both of these indicators favor the *lease-to-own* alternative, though only marginally.

A third consideration was the *cash flow*. The *buy* alternative expends the total investment for new computers at the time of purchase, and then recoups benefits over 24 months. It is essentially 'in the red' for nearly two years. The *lease-to-own* alternative spreads the cash outflow over three increments. This allows savings to accrue to exceed expenditures during the first year, and for cash flow to be 'in the black' thereafter.

Conclusions

The analysis clearly shows that acquisition of new workstation PCs is economically preferred to the continued costs of older PCs, therefore eliminating Alternative 1, Status Quo.

Further comparisons showed the lease alternative to be more cost efficient using three comparison indicators. Both a shorter breakeven time and a larger savings-to-investment ratio (SIR) marginally favored the *lease-to-own* alternative. However, the cash flow indicator was a major factor in favor of this alternative.

Recommendations

Review of *total costs of ownership* showed significant advantages for acquisition of new PCs, eliminating the *status quo* (no change) alternative.

Potential savings from replacement of the existing PCs, even after accounting for administrative acquisition and purchase price costs, were significant. Net savings due to expected cost avoidances were forecasted to approach $50,000 over the three years of expected economic life for new PCs.

For the two remaining acquisition alternatives, the *lease-to-own* alternative was marginally more cost efficient than the *buy* alternative for *break-even time* (i.e., 23 versus 24 months), and the savings-to-investment ratio (i.e., 1.74 versus 1.68) for the lease-to-own alternative. Additionally, *lease-to-own* is significantly favored for the *cash flow indicator*.

Lease-to-own is the recommended alternative. However, should policy requirements dictate, such as uncertainty of availability of funds during the lease years, the *buy* alternative (Alternative 3) is a practical second choice.

Given the recommendation for the lease-to-own alternative, a draft plan of action is included for suggested implementation steps. A Gantt chart for the plan of action is included in *Exhibit 1-26.* [8]

Exhibit 1-26

Recommended Plan of Action Acquisition of New PC Workstations									
Procure PCs	Start	End	%	No. of	Oct	Nov	Dec	Jan	Feb
Description	Date	Date	Com-plete	Days					
Brief Budget Committee	15-Oct	15-Oct	0	0	◆				
Procure Workstations	16-Oct	29-Oct	0	14	▪				
Receive and Install	30-Oct	03-Nov	0	5	▪				
Monitor Service Calls	04-Nov	01-Feb	0	90		▬			
Report Problems	02-Feb	02-Feb	0	1					▪
Close Project	03-Feb	03-Feb	0	0					◆

Day 8—The Final Report and Presentation

At this point, Jim prepared a draft final report and presentation for his boss and the budget committee. For all practical purposes, these are the final study documents. However, he awaits feedback for any needed corrections and changes after which, he will produce copies as required. An example of Jim's final presentation is shown in the last chapter of this book.

As can be seen, the 8-Day BCA study was relatively intuitive. Jim relied upon the help of technical references and experts to get the 'mechanics' of the study figured out. He also frequently queried subject matter experts to provide a sense of validity to the study assumptions and findings. Inherent in the study were numerous underlying *concepts* and *techniques*, many of which were not explicitly stated. It is important to review these in more detail to help broaden understanding of the example. Moreover, these concepts and techniques are especially important for understanding and appreciation of the capabilities of more comprehensive studies, such as those that deal with process reengineering, enterprise resource planning, outsourcing, supply chain management, inventory and so forth. The remaining sections of this book review these in much greater detail. Many of the key study considerations for performing credible BCAs are presented next in Part II (*concepts*) and Part III (*techniques*). Finally, in Part IV, actual *procedures* for developing your business case analysis are presented.

[1] B. J. LaLonde and P. H. Zinszer (1976). Customer service: Meaning and measurement. Cited from D. P. Herron, *International Journal of Physical Distribution and Materials Management,* 10 (8), 481–505. Based on research data of American merchandising companies for consumer and industrial goods. Specific cost of distribution, as a percentage of inventory value, is 11.1%. Costs include transportation, 7.4%, administration, 1.2%, receiving and shipping, 0.6%, packaging, 1.2%, and order processing, 0.7%.

[2] J. S. Armstrong (1985). *Long-Range Forecasting: from Crystal Ball to Computer.* New York: John Wiley & Sons, p. 167.

[3] N. Sanders and L. Ritzman (2001). Judgmental adjustment of statistical analysis forecasts. Cited from J. S. Armstrong (2001), *Principles of Forecasting* (pp. 405–416). Boston: Kluwer Academic Press.

[4] M. Berenson and D. Levine (1989). *Basic Business Statistics: Concepts and Applications (*4th ed.). Englewood Cliffs, NJ: Prentice Hall, pp. 580–583.

[5] S. Makridakis and S. C. Wheelwright (1989). *Forecasting Methods for Management.* New York: John Wiley & Sons, p. 350.

[6] R. G. Brown (1967). *Decision Rules for Inventory Management.* New York: Holt, Rinehart and Winston, pp. 282–283.

[7] Ibid.

[8] H. Gantt, developed circa 1917. Concepts were a basis for modern PERT (Program Evaluation and Review Technique) charts in 1958.

Art and science have their meeting point in method.
Baron E.G. Bulwer-Lytton (circa 1860)

II

CONCEPTS

**The Logic Behind Good
Business Case Analysis**

2—The History
3—The Technical
4—The Social
5—The Situation
6—A Sociotechnical View
**7—Implications for Business
   Case Analysis**

It is a shameful thing to be weary of inquiry when what we search for is excellent.

Cicero (circa 53 B.C.)

The History

=== **2**

History gives us a kind of chart.

Sir John Buchan (circa 1935)

If no use is made of [history], the world must always re-main in the infancy of knowledge.

Cicero (circa 40 B.C.)

    Most of what we know about analysis of business situations has been learned within the past century. There is, however, a brief, sketchy history of business and commerce as far back as 5,000 years when Sumerian priests invented a script to record inventory. Greeks recorded rudimentary finance, logistics and manufacturing activities as early as 400 B.C. This was followed by a gradual change in accounting and material control techniques through the next two millennia. Approximate origins of various business functions before the 20th century are as follows:

Exhibit 2-1 (a)

Business Functions in Antiquity		
3200 B.C.	*Egypt / Sumerians*	*Writing—tax / inventory records[9]*
1100	*Babylonia*	*Money—½ oz silver ingots*
400	*Greeks*	*Management is an art.[10]*
350	*Plato*	*Specialization principle*
325	*Alexander the Great*	*Staff principle*
175	*Romans*	*Distribution logistics[11]*

Business Functions in Antiquity
(Exhibit 2-1 (a) continued)

20 A.D.	*Jesus Christ*	*Unity of command; golden rule*
1340	*Genoese*	*Double entry bookkeeping*
1450	*Germans, Koreans*	*Movable type; Gutenberg press*
1456	*Venetians*	*Cost accounting, Inventory control*
1760	*Europe/America*	*Industrial Revolution*
1776	*Adam Smith*	*Specialization*
1799	*Eli Whitney*	*Scientific method; American system of manufacturing with interchangeable parts*
1832	*Charles Babbage*	*Division of labor; time and motion study; 1ˢᵗ computer*

Compare this with the crescendo of management innovations during the twentieth century. *Exhibit 2-1 (b)* illustrates many of these beginning management and organizational theory developments. While the list is not all-inclusive, it is representative of many of the most important management innovations.

Exhibit 2-1 (b)

Selected Management Innovations During 20ᵗʰ Century

Decade	Color Codes—Green: Management Science Red: Social Science Blue: Integrated Approach		
1900	Frederick Taylor —Scientific Management	Frank Gilbreth —Automated Time and Motion Study	Henry Gantt —Gantt Charts
1910	Hugo Munsterberg —Father of Industrial Psychology	Harrington Emerson —Efficiency Engineering	First Scientific Management Conference
	Ford Harris —EOQ: Economic Order Quantity	Henry Fayol— Principles/Functions of Management	

Selected Management Innovations During 20th Century
(Exhibit 2-1 (b) continued)

Decade	Color Codes—Green: Management Science Red: Social Science Blue: Integrated Approach		
1920	W. A. Shewhart —Statistical Sampling	R. A. Fisher —Statistical Experimental Design	Elton Mayo —Business Sociological Concepts
1930	James Mooney – Universal Principles of Organization	Chester Barnard —Need to Inform All People and Levels	
1940	Max Weber —Bureaucratic Organizations	Rensis Likert —Participative Management	Chris Argyris —Learning Organizations
	WWII —Operations Research	Norbert Weiner —Computer Systems	Claude Shannon —Communication Theory
1950	Kurt Lewin —'Action Research' in Organizations	Herbert Simon —Management Decisions often must 'Satisfice'	Robert Schlaifer —Decisions under Uncertainty
	Tavistock Studies —Sociotechnical Systems Theory		
1960	Joan Woodward —Types of Technology	James D. Thompson —Environmental Complexity	Blake and Mouton —Managerial Grid
	Burns and Stalker —Mechanistic and Organic Processes	Alfred D. Chandler —Structure follows Strategy	Katz and Kahn —Organizations Adapt to Environment
	Tannenbaum & Schmidt —Boss Centered vs. Employee Centered Management		
1970	Self Regulating Work Groups	Louis Davis —Sociotechnical Job Designs	Kast and Rosensweig —Systems Approach to Management
	Lawrence and Lorsch —Integration and Differentiation	Lorsch and Morse— Contingency Management Theory	Deming —TQM: Total Quality Management
1980	PCs —Microcomputers	Peters —In Search of Excellence	Japanese— Just in Time Processes; Rapid Customer Response
	Schein— Organizational Development & Culture	Kets de Vries —The Neurotic Organization	

Selected Management Innovations During 20th Century
(Exhibit 2-1 (b) continued)

Decade	Color Codes—Green: Management Science Red: Social Science Blue: Integrated Approach		
1990	Internet	Globalization	Loh—Most Reorganizations Unsuccessful
	Hammer and Champy —BPR: Business Process Reengineering	Peter Senge—The 5th Discipline: Most Problems Grow Gradually from Needed Process Adaptations	Michael Hammer —Fragmented Processes, not People, the Culprit
2000	Information Integration – Supply Chain Management (SCM) & Enterprise Resource Planning (ERP)		

Note that the business management innovations have been color coded to indicate contributions from two basic themes: management science and social science.

Management science is comprised of objective, measurable techniques, such as the quantitative tools used in operations research.

Social science deals with how humans behave and perform in organizations—tools of psychology, sociology and cultural anthropology are adapted to organizational settings. Social science applications are generally found in management literature under organizational behavior and organizational development topics.

As can be seen from the color-coding scheme, management innovations have been about evenly split between management science and organizational behavior and development. The graph in *Exhibit 2-2* illustrates the historical cumulative count of management innovations over the 20th century.

Exhibit 2-2

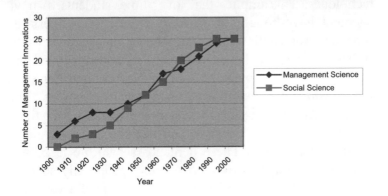

Cumulative Growth of 20th Century Management Innovations

This historical view supports an integrated approach to management analysis, using an eclectic combination of elements from both management science and social science. One of the earliest integrated approaches originated in the 1950s with the early British studies in *sociotechnical systems theory* that focused on group behaviors in technical work situations. This concept was later mirrored by Robert Blake's and Jane Mouton's *Managerial Grid* (1966)—with focus on management and leadership styles. Blake and Mouton theorize that management consists of two primary forces: concern for production and concern for people. On a scale of 1 (low) to 9 (high) for each, a '9-9 manager' is considered best. Effective managers motivate through both high concerns for job performance and for workers' welfare. Best results are theorized to result from "Work accomplishment...from [socially] committed people [and technical] interdependence through a 'common stake' in the organization."[12]

It is obvious from *Exhibit 2-2* that there has been a close race between both techniques of management science and of social science in the search for better organizational techniques. This implies that, over time, students of management have sought to develop successful business approaches from both, either individually or in combination. A brief review of the development of both technical and social aspects of management can be useful for understanding constituent elements for business case analyses. This review sets the stage for understanding total organizational needs. It starts with needs to consider the demands placed on the organization. These demands set up the task environment. Given the task environment, potentially successful responses are elicited from combinations of a variety of technical and human (social) resources. Our examination of both the technical and social aspects begins with studies of *the technical,* found in the *management science* literature.

---

[9] W. Durant (1935). *The Story of Civilization, I*. New York: Simon and Schuster, Inc., p. 228.

[10] Unless otherwise noted, approximations are adapted from C.George (1968). *The History of Management Thought*. Englewood Cliffs, N.J.: Prentice-Hall, Inc., pp. xiii–xvii.

[11] J. Roth (1999). *The Logistics of the Roman Army at War (264 B.C. – A.D. 235)*. Boston: Brill.

[12] R. Blake and J. Mouton (1966, July). Managerial facades. *Advanced Management Journal,* p. 31. Cited from: F. Luthans (1973). *Organizational Behavior.* New York: McGraw-Hill Book Company, p. 533.

CHAPTER THREE

The Technical

=== **3**

One good measurement is worth a thousand opinions.
Grace Hopper (circa 1980)

Quantitative business case analysis techniques have gradually evolved over the centuries, with many of the most used techniques 'blossoming' in the late 20th century with the advent of economical information processing. Numerous methods and models have origins in military activities. One of the earliest recorded instances of mathematical modeling of military action dates back to 212 B.C., when Archimedes devised methods to break the naval siege of the Romans on the City of Syracuse. Using "catapults able to hurl large stones to a considerable distance; their rain of projectiles was so devastating that [the Romans] retreated...."[13]

Statistics and Probability

A slow, cumulative buildup of management quantitative techniques continued through the centuries. One of the most important enabler tools was *statistical probability theory,* which was developed in the mid-1600s by French philosophers/scientists Blaise Pascal and Pierre de Fermat. Their concepts, found in unpublished correspondence, dealt with a problem in gambling. Dutch scientist Christiaan Huygens followed up these remarkable observations with a publication on probabilities in dice games in the 1600s. By the early 1700s, probability theory had important applications in the rapidly developing insurance industry.[14]

An important extension of statistical probability concepts was the development of *statistical inference* theory. Statistical inference allows the analyst to speculate about the reliability of estimated characteristics about a *population* by examining *samples* believed to be from that population. The smaller number of observations in samples can be more easily gathered. In fact, samples are often the only options. Proper use of these statistical techniques, following guidelines of the *scientific method*, can often produce highly reliable estimates of the larger population.

The Scientific Method

Significant correlations, using standard statistical methods among observations, do not necessarily prove cause and effect. To help bolster confidence that observation 'a' causes 'b,' certain rules are imposed during scientific experiments. These rules, generally known as the *scientific method*, can greatly enhance understanding about the likely cause and effect relationships. Steps for application of the scientific method are shown in *Exhibit 3-1*.[15]

Exhibit 3-1

The Scientific Method

1. *Define the problem.*
2. *Develop a mathematical model.*
3. *Derive alternative solutions from the model. Find values of the variables that maximize effectiveness.*
4. *Compare model solutions to real world outcomes.*
5. *Establish controls to ensure solutions are feasible.*
6. *Implement feasible solutions.*
7. *Observe feedback—repeat the steps as necessary.*

Linear Regression

One of the most useful 'cause and effect' statistical approaches is *linear regression*. This method automatically calculates the correlations between two or more variables (i.e., observations of events), and can 'weight' the relative contribution of each 'predictor' variable's explanatory power for estimating behavior of the 'predicted' variable.

Linear regression is used for many different types of analysis. It is commonly used to forecast future events using past trends over time. This approach, *time series regression,* develops an equation of the mathematical relationship of the event's values to sequential time periods. Regression can also be used to develop an equation of the relationship between events other than time periods. Using correlations between/among single or multiple predictor (independent) variables, an equation can be developed to predict the predicted (dependent) variable, given values for the predictors. This approach, *relationship regression,* can provide valuable information for, say, the link between advertising dollars spent and sales, or between training costs and increased worker productivity—and so forth.

Interestingly, there are some sophisticated extensions of the linear regression techniques, including various polynomial (nonlinear) regression equations. However, these more elaborate equations have generally been found less reliable in forecasting outcomes than simple linear equations, perhaps because their complicated interrelationships are more difficult to understand.[16]

Calculus

Another very important mathematical discovery of the 17th century was Newton's discovery of *differential and integral calculus* (circa 1666). Joint credit for the discovery of calculus goes to German mathematician Gottfried Leibniz, who independently discovered calculus some eight years later, and was first to publish. Newton had not yet published his discovery. Leibniz's notation systems, such as *dx*, are used today in the calculus.[17]

Differential calculus determines the exact point on a curve, given its shape. This point is determined by what is called the *derivative*. For example, suppose, from past experience, it has been observed that as advertising increases, sales follow a pattern similar to an S-shaped logistic curve function.[xx] Suppose further that customer surveys indicate that the market will support a maximum of 20,000 units sold weekly. It is also known that 1,000 units per week are sold with no advertising, and 4,000 units are sold with $2,000 advertising. Differential calculus can be used to calculate (the point on the curve) of sales for a given amount of advertising.[18] If, say, the advertising budget is $5,000, the expected number of unit sales can be determined.

Integral calculus, sometimes called the *anti-derivative*, enables determination of the cumulative *area under the curve* between points on the curve. For example, for the marketing problem above, suppose that $2,000 in advertising increased sales to 4,000 units per week. Integral calculus allows calculation of how much additional advertising is needed for some additional sales target, such as 12,000 units sold per week.[19]

Scientific Management

Given these early mathematical innovations, along with the 200-year accumulation of Industrial Revolution infrastructure, the time had become ripe for combining

---

[xx] A logistic curve has a stretched 's' shape—it starts slowly, rapidly builds, then flattens. Its shape closely resembles the cumulative normal curve.

systematic measurement techniques with industrial management practices. By the beginning of the 20th century, rational approaches to management were developed under the umbrella known as *scientific management.*

Scientific management was developed and popularized primarily though the works of *Frederick W. Taylor,* known as the Father of Scientific Management. This was a time when the industrial revolution was maturing, and standardization was becoming possible in industry due to repetitive large-scale production and manufacturing.

Scientific management fostered ways to dramatically boost productivity of work crews. For example, at Bethlehem Steel, circa 1898, Taylor was able to quadruple the rate of manual loading of iron ingots onto rail cars. He demonstrated these techniques by selecting a worker, given the pseudonym Schmidt, and then closely supervising his work and rest breaks. He stressed the importance of proper selection of workers suited for the demanding manual labor, and appropriate scheduling of work and resting time. Interestingly, only about one-eighth of the original 75 men in the ingot loading section were physically able to keep the new pace. [20]

In other experiments, shoveling iron ore and rice coal, Taylor found greater productive efficiency by having the company provide special shovels. He did away with the practice of workers bringing their own shovels, and built a storeroom that stocked company owned shovels designed to carry a 21-pound load.

He also performed time-and-motion studies to determine potential savings, and estimated the new techniques would save over between $75,000 and $80,000 per year (in circa 1900 dollars).[21]

Frederick Taylor's work became widely publicized after he reported findings to a United States Congressional committee in 1912. He reported that:

> Scientific management is not [merely] an efficiency
> device... [but] in essence, involves a complete men-
> tal revolution...on the part of working men... and...
> equally... on the management's side ... toward their
> workmen...and daily problems. [22]

Two other prominent contributors to early scientific management were *Frank and Lillian Gilbreth*, made famous for developing refinements to time and motion study. Frank could analyze a person's motions and determine wasted movements down to 1/2000 of a second. This was done by filming a microchronometer clock (that he had invented) in the background while hand cranking motion pictures of work. As an example of precision, the Gilbreths were able to categorize all hand motions into 17 basic motions, such as 'grasp,' 'hold' and 'position.' Such motions were called 'therbligs,' Gilbreth spelled backwards with the 't' and 'h' transposed.[23]

Henry Gantt developed his famous Gantt chart in 1917. The chart provides a simple planning and control technique. The concepts were so effective that they were later used as a basis for developing the more sophisticated *Program Evaluation and Review Technique (PERT)*[xxi]. PERT, and a more Gantt-like method, the Critical Path Method (CPM), are used today for planning and controlling many kinds of programs in business and government, from small to very large.

Harrington Emerson, the 'High Priest of Efficiency,' introduced productivity methods that were forerunners of modern business process reengineering and integrated supply chain management. In 1910, appearing before the Interstate Commerce Commission, he estimated

---

[xxi] The *Program Evaluation and Review Technique (PERT)* was used by the United States Navy in planning and coordinating its Polaris Missile Project in 1958.

that the railroads could save one million dollars a day by adapting scientific management principles. Among his 'Twelve Principles of Efficiency' are the need for reliable, timely and accurate records; standardization of instructions and operations; and effective production control and scheduling techniques.

By World War I (1914–1915) there were beginnings of large-scale military applications for many of these techniques. Englishman *F.W. Lanchester* derived equations relating the chances of success in battle given both relative troop strengths and firepower. Also, American *Thomas Edison* developed a statistical 'war game' to assess the probable merits of 'zigzagging' as a merchant ship countermeasure against submarines.

Quantitative methods were also evolving in commercial applications. In 1917, Danish mathematician *A.K. Erlang*, working for a telephone company, introduced early *queuing theory* formulae that would not be fully developed until almost half a century later, with modern 'waiting line' theory. This provided a foundation for *mathematical simulation*.

One of the first significant elaborations of statistical probability into *statistical inference* was the introduction of quality control charts by *Walter Shewhart* at Bell Telephone Laboratories in 1924. Shewhart's coworkers, *H. F. Dodge* and *H. G. Romig,* developed the technique of *statistical sampling* in connection with quality control.

During the mid-1920s, the work of *Sir Ronald Fisher* further developed many of the methods used in *applied statistical theory* today—including chi-square tests, Bayesian statistics, sampling theory, and experimental design.

Inventory theory and development of the *Economic Order Quantity (EOQ)* algorithm is credited to *Ford Harris*, who described his model in 1915. The model calculates optimal trade-offs between holding costs and ordering costs to determine lowest total inventory costs. R. H. Wilson popularized the EOQ in his 1935 Harvard Business Review article.[24] The EOQ model is still referred to as the '*Wilson Q*' by management scientists.

Harold Hotelling developed early application theories about economic capital and interest, in 1925. Break-even charts were developed in the 1930s.

Operations Research

It was not until World War II (1940–1945) and after, that most of the large-scale applications of scientific management were realized. The war, and the coming computer revolution in the decades thereafter, set the stage for significant advances in combined measurement techniques. This opportunity for wide scale, eclectic combinations of different disciplines enjoyed a jump start when the first *operations research* groups were formed in England during WWII. One of the first O.R. groups, 'Blackett's circus,' was comprised of "…three physiologists, two mathematical physicists, one astrophysicist, one Army officer, one surveyor, one general physicist, and two mathematicians."[25]

Operations research groups expanded the repertoire of techniques to help measure all physical phases of private and public business enterprise. Evolving techniques developed applications using statistics, multiple linear regression, network theory, forecasting, inventory, linear programming, queuing and simulation, to name some of the more important areas.

Then came the beginnings of the computerized information technology explosion. This started with the development of the first electronic computer, ENIAC, in 1945, followed by the UNIVAC computer, used by the United States Census Bureau in 1951.

Management Science

The advent of the modern computer exponentially expanded the practical application of early math and measurement techniques. The growing ability to measure, record and interpret massive amounts of data helped transform early *scientific management* into what is known today as *management science*. Older mathematical techniques have come into routine, widespread use for day-to-day business activities, and newer approaches have been developed. Important tools enabled by the tremendous new calculation capabilities include linear programming, analysis of distribution networks, statistical forecasting, and increasingly sophisticated inventory management calculations.

Linear Programming

Linear programming has been hailed as one of the most important inventions for business management. In 1980, management expert Eugene Lawler wrote:

> [Linear programming] is used to allocate resources, plan production, schedule workers, plan investment portfolios and formulate marketing (and military) strategies. The versatility and economic impact of linear programming in today's industrial world is truly awesome.

Linear programming was first used to mechanize optimal allocation of resources for training, logistical supply and deployments.[26] It is one of the most widely used techniques today for allocation and distribution calculations.

The core mathematical breakthrough came with development of the *simplex method* by George Dantzig in 1947. At that time, he was a mathematical advisor for the United States Air Force. The simplex method is one of the first effective algorithms to perform *linear programming*.

Dantzig was modest about his invention. He observed:

> The tremendous power of the simplex method is a constant surprise to me. [27]

The technique is mathematically simple, yet tedious when more than a few variables and constraints are required. Fortunately, with the speed of modern computers and advances in the mathematical algorithm, extremely large problems can now be solved. For example, today the food industry can calculate optimal production inputs and outputs for problems with 600,000 constraints and seven million variables.[28]

Networks

Development of effective *network algorithms* for planning and tracking progress of very large scale scheduling programs was another significant development. One of the most prominent examples is the Program Evaluation and Review Technique (PERT), developed for the Navy Polaris Missile Program in 1958. The Critical Path Method (CPM), developed for commercial uses such as construction projects, does similar scheduling of interactions between activities and bears more of a resemblance to the early Gantt charts.[29] Also, a number of rule of thumb (i.e., heuristic) techniques were developed for smaller network problems, especially for distribution and assignment problems.

Forecasting

One of the biggest quantitative measurement advances for business analysis came with the publication of the first comprehensible and readable book on *business forecasting* by Spyros Makridakis and Steven Wheelwright in 1973. In the Preface to the fifth edition (1989), they recall:

> When the first edition of *Forecasting Methods for Management* was published in 1973, only a handful of books on forecasting were available. Those books tended to be mathematical and to provide in-depth coverage of only a few forecasting techniques. We wanted to present an overview of a broad range of forecasting techniques ... without requiring [managers] to have a substantial background in quantitative methods.[30]

Dozens of other forecasting books followed. Forecasting the future depends on examination of the past and present situation, searching for patterns and trends, and projecting these patterns as estimates of future activities.

There is nothing magic about past patterns, however. And there is no assurance they will continue into the future. Nor is there any assurance that managers will heed 'systematic' information about likely future events. In fact, the old adage, if we could know the future we would be rich, is not necessarily true. For example, in the movie *Back to the Future,* when the young 'Bif' actually acquired a World Almanac from the future—with all the sports outcomes—he was too daft to grasp the potential of knowing such information before, say, placing bets on sports events.

Forecasts, lacking feedback from the 'not yet happened future,' attempt the next best thing, to interpret and project the past. Basically two types of 'mechanical' forecasting approaches have been developed: relational and extrapolation. *Relational forecasting*, such as time series linear regression, develops mathematical equations of patterns for two or more variables. Expected future values of predictor variable(s) are then used to forecast a predicted variable. Presumably, the future values of the predictor variable are known (e.g., such as time increments). Forecasting using *extrapolation* depends *only* on the past behavioral pattern of the predicted variable. It is related only to itself. Examples of extrapolation techniques include moving averages, weighted moving averages, exponential smoothing, Holt-Winters (that measure trend-cycles), and Box-Jenkins ARIMA (*a*uto-*r*egressive *i*ntegrated with *m*oving *a*verages (of the residuals)).

A third forecasting approach, judgmental forecasting, uses subjective estimates from humans. These can be both forecasts of their opinions, and/or of their intentions. In recent years, researchers have increasingly explored the potential benefits of combining statistical (mechanical) with subjective forecasting methods.[31]

Simulation

Queuing and *waiting line theory* (based on averages) and *Monte Carlo simulation* (based on probability of variations around the averages) have become the bases for comprehensive simulation models. Queuing equations, based on Erlang's formulations (1917), and calculation of probabilistic outcomes (from Fermat and Pascal, circa 1650) offer opportunities to test impacts of alternative business process scenarios *before* actually risking company assets on promising programs. In this sense, simulation is a sort of forecasting approach, using a contrived history and current situation based of laws of probability. It implies that, if the model can accurately mimic current conditions, the simulated results from changed conditions will be representative of the hypothetical new situation.

Inventory

This topic is particularly important, since some of the biggest cost savings opportunities in manufacturing and logistics organizations lie in efficient inventory policy.

During the 1940s and 1950s, labor was the largest component for cost of goods in industrialized countries. However, 50 years of refinements in how to cut labor costs, from shop floor efficiency to inexpensive offshore operations, has changed the cost landscape. [32] Increasingly, labor has become a relatively smaller part of costs. In the 1990s, as the average costs of material for an enterprise rose to around 60 to 80% of total costs, it is not surprising that focus has shifted to managing these costs. [33]

In this book we shall examine the recent management science techniques for optimizing inventory levels. Enabled by information automation, economic order quantity calculations had become increasingly more elaborate and comprehensive by the 1960s, as did other inventory requirements computations. Computers allowed mechanization of many manufacturing and distribution processes to help seek 'optimal' stockage policies for inventory both in production processes (i.e., *material requirements planning,* or *MRP*), and in supply chain holding points. Perhaps the most profound advances, however, were for inventory support of the often-erratic processes of maintenance and reconditioning of reparable items.

Inventory for Maintenance and Repair

Conventional inventory models are often adequate for stable or planned requirements, such as the repetitive stocking for production runs for new item manufacture. Steady state conditions, such as forecasting a relatively constant rate of consumption for a production run, can enable accurate MRP. [34]

Maintenance activities, however, such as repair of machines and vehicles, can be highly dynamic and non-routine. Repair scenarios present vastly more complex logistics problems than manufacture of totally new items. In new manufacture or retail supply chain operations, the uncertainty can be narrowed to the final estimate of output (i.e., customer demand), then systematically back-stepped to develop requisite process activities and supporting inventory requirements. But maintenance tasks often do not lend themselves easily to routine, repeatable processes. This adds complexity when calculating supporting inventory requirements for maintenance and refurbishment. Large commercial manufacturing and transportation companies, as well as public organizations such as the U.S. defense department and other governmental agencies, spend billions of dollars per year reconditioning machinery and vehicles. Particularly costly is the inventory requirement for replacement of recoverable (also known as reparable) items that are worn beyond economic repair (i.e., condemned).

For example, aircraft items subject to either refurbishment or replacement require inventory management of millions of parts. Further, most recoverables require relatively infrequent (and often unknown) reconditioning actions as they undergo preventive or corrective maintenance. When new parts are required, there can be long lead times when manufacturers must initiate nonstandard shop setups and worker rescheduling.

There is ample incentive for management of recoverable items, since reconditioning and repairs can reduce overall costs significantly. The U.S. Air Force has found that around 90% of recoverable items can be economically repaired rather than replaced for aircraft systems.[35] Repaired items can often generate savings of 40% or more over the purchase of new items.[36]

Recoverable items are often comprised of subcomponents (subindentures) that are likewise reparable. This adds greater inventory management complexity due to both the relatively low frequency and high variability in repair tasks, and the often-sporadic inventory support for repaired or replaced subcomponents. This led the U.S. Air Force and their consultants at the Rand Corporation to develop more sophisticated inventory models to help manage the billions of dollars of spares in their inventory.

Beginning in the 1960s, breakthrough inventory models were developed by the Rand Corporation and other consultants for the Air Force. These models represented a new focus. Rather than calculating minimum aggregate inventory ordering and holding policies, such as EOQ type models, these techniques calculate requirements item-by-item, and then marginally cost-weight buy lists. These reparable models, also called *S-1, S models*, calculate expected backorders for each item, and then compare relative benefit-to-cost ratios among items (i.e., marginal reduction of backorders per dollar).[xxii] Sophisticated computer programs allow the prioritizing of buy lists among multiple end items and indentures of subcomponents, for supplying multiple locations. Further elaborations can account for multiple sources of resupply. Time and costs can be factored in for resupply from multiple echelons of repair (i.e., local repair, intermediate repair, and depot). The items are first rank-ordered to minimize expected backorders, then added to a shopping list based on their relative bang-for-the-buck (i.e., benefit/cost ratios).[37]

One of the first S-1, S recoverable item inventory models can be traced to the Rand Corporation's *Base Stockage Model*, developed in 1963.[38] This model

---

[xxii] Inventory systems for expensive reparable items are frequently modeled using an (S-1, S) inventory model. This works as follows: An initial inventory of serviceable items is provided. A failed item is then put into a 'repair cycle.' If a replacement unit is available, it is put into service; otherwise the consumer must await the next repair. In this process there are 'S' units, randomly split between serviceable units in stock and units in the repair (or replacement if condemned) cycle. These models are described in greater detail in Chapter 14, Inventory.

calculates fractional expected backorders—item-by-item—and incrementally adds them to a shopping list to reduce the total backorders, up to a given budget constraint. The Base Stockage Model was followed by *METRIC*[xxiii] (1966)[39], the first model to be widely implemented to calculate reparable requirements for Air Force budget exercises. METRIC elaborates the original model to include resupply from and to multiple locations as well as through supply chain echelons. *Mod-METRIC* (1973)[40], a further elaboration, optimizes inventory of subcomponents for higher assemblies.

Additionally, in 1973, the Logistics Management Institute, also working for the Air Force, developed the *Aircraft Availability Model (AAM)*. This model calculates marginal contributions, item-by-item, up to a probable average availability of serviceable aircraft, given a budget constraint. A primary contribution of the AAM is to help ensure that global budget allocations provide adequate support across different *fleets* of machines/vehicles, allowing each to seek target availabilities required by management while seeking to avoid under funding of one at the expense of another.

Inventory for Readiness

In addition to steady-state budgeting models, near-term *readiness* is of keen interest. Budget processes to acquire inventory are often far into the future. Readiness concerns near-term inventory availability, given existing inventory. This fundamentally shifts the focus to calculation of *performance requirements first*, then development of the *budget requirements second*. These concerns led to development of the *Dyna-METRIC* model in 1982.[41]

[xxiii] The METRIC acronym stands for <u>M</u>ulti-<u>E</u>chelon <u>T</u>echnique for <u>R</u>ecoverable <u>I</u>tem <u>C</u>ontrol.

Dyna-METRIC computes marginal improvements to fleet readiness, given incremental additions of inventory items. Its equations can be used compute peak requirements for given dynamic scenarios, such as surges in utilization rates, delays in resupply due to deployments, interruptions in repairs, and so on.[42] Dyna-METRIC can also consider 'cannibalization' of spares from other higher assemblies which can dramatically change the expected mission accomplishment rate. The model still incorporates many of the features of earlier METRIC steady state models— multi-location, multi-item, multi-echelon and multi-indenture.

Finally, in 1993, Rand analysts developed Dyna-METRIC Version 6, completely refocusing the computational approach from analytical, calculus type equations to Monte Carlo simulation. The simulation version gives up some of the features of earlier analytic versions (i.e., the ability to compute spares levels to specified performance goals). But it makes possible other needed assessment calculations, such as considering the effects of lateral resupply between locations, lateral repairs, and queue balking of lower priority repairs.[43]

Inventory Macro Models and Budgets

Perhaps the biggest problem with most of the METRIC and AAM calculations has been their vulnerability to long-term dynamics that can occur between large-scale calculations and actual receipt of budget funds. This was discovered in the early 1980s during an extremely erratic set of economic and political circumstances that were impacting prices and budget projections. There were significant price spikes for items, exacerbated by larger environmental influences including an international oil crisis, double-digit inflation, and economic recession. The METRIC type models performed poorly as out-year budget predictors due to their strong dependence on more recent data (i.e., item demand history has been found to be valid for only about six months to a year).[44]

These models often depend on four quarters of item demand history. This limits their forecasting accuracy range to near-term outcomes. Additional problems come from data instability. For example, studies of both consumable and recoverable items have shown that generally about 75% of U.S. Air Force inventory items are dormant (i.e., have had no demands over the past six months to a year). However, about 25% of the items that become active within the next year are generated from among those previously dormant items.[45] This item 'churn' places great demands on any forecasting system. METRIC and AAM type models depend on item-by-item demand history. Long-term accuracy of forecasts suffers as new items rapidly replace previously active items over the budget execution forecast horizon. This is especially true in times of dynamic changes for technology or prices.

To deal with these multi-year forecasting problems, the U.S. Air Force introduced macro inventory budget forecasting models. POSSEM, the first macro-model (1983), and was replaced by the ALERT model a year later, in 1994.[xxiv] ALERT uses a totally different type of recoverable spares budget requirements forecasting approach than METRIC based models.[46] Aggregate level forecasts of ALERT were found to be a significant improvement of METRIC models alone for aggregate out-year budget estimates.[47] The macro forecasting model takes advantage of the three rules of forecasting:

1) Forecasts are always wrong.
2) Forecasts are more wrong farther in the future.
3) Forecasts are more wrong in detail.

[xxiv] ALERT stands for A̲ir L̲ogistics E̲arly R̲equirements T̲echnique.

The ALERT model forecasts large, aggregated numbers for the distant future (2–7 years) that are inappropriate for forecasts at the detailed item-by-item level. ALERT reverses the telescope, from 'bottom up' (i.e., item-by-item aggregations up to a total budget) to 'top down' (i.e., accuracy of aggregate inventory budget forecasts). Using linear regression techniques, it develops statistical equations of relationships between original budget forecasts (the predictor variables) and the actual budget expenditures that eventually occur (the predicted variables). The multiple predictor variables can include, in addition to aggregate METRIC calculations, other predictors such as estimated age and value of the fleet. Interestingly, the model found that planned utilization rates (i.e., flying hour programs) did not correlate highly with need for replacement parts. This is understandable due to the high churn rate of items entering and leaving active demand status over two years or more between budget requirements estimation and execution.[48]

ALERT calculations are computed individually for several major aircraft systems (e.g., the B52, C141, F15, F16, etc.), and then combined into a total budget estimate that is usually comprised of the 17 or so sub-budgets. Combined forecasts have been found to be more accurate in many situations.[49]

Technical Concepts Today

By the 1970s, there was a more realistic understanding by managers and management scientists about what can and cannot be accomplished using management science/ operations research techniques. Businesses paid more attention to getting facts and applying quantification techniques where feasible. There was less attention to finding optimal answers, more to developing and adapting flexibility of processes to help evolve to changing circumstances.

Since the 1980s, the information revolution has had a monumental influence. Computers have become very fast, with enormous storage capacity, and can easily and cheaply communicate with other computers around the world over the Internet. Many of the management science tools are now more fully employed, and practical use of algorithms has improved. Sophisticated management information systems and decision support systems make possible sophisticated, automated collection of transaction data and its transformation into suitable information for each level of enterprise. All business processes can benefit from better decision support, including shop and retail activities, mid-level operations, and top-level strategic planning.

More comprehensive data, along with nearly real time, automated business success and cost indicators, has fostered unprecedented opportunities for business analysis and planning. For example, in manufacturing and commerce, information technology is enabling practical applications of total asset visibility, just-in-time inventory, and precise scheduling of multiple events using material requirements planning (MRP). MRP systems compute net requirements for inventory items, allowing 'just-in-time' phasing of acquisition based upon step-by-step process requirements.[50]

For ongoing supply chain activities, a variety of management science tools have been continually improved. These include improvements in process planning such as Enterprise Resource Planning (ERP), resource allocations (using linear programming), network tools (using PERT/CPM), and a variety of inventory models for management of consumable and recoverable items.

For office and administrative processes, off-the-shelf business process reengineering software and faster computers have enabled quick, efficient simulation of office document flow scenarios. These techniques use a variety of management science techniques, including queuing theory, statistical approximations of events, and Monte Carlo simulation.

Also, many mechanical methods to mimic complex human decision processes have evolved, including artificial intelligence, data mining, neural networks and 'fuzzy' logic. These methods seek to infer existence of hidden coalitions of seemingly disparate facts, often too complex for singular analytical or simulation models.

Research analysis itself has increasingly undergone an elaboration—from deductive hypothesis testing to inductive hypothesis development. This inductive method takes advantage of the tremendous growth in information management, and is called *grounded research*. Grounded research differs from the typical deductive approach, based on generalizing from the specific hypotheses toward general conclusion. A grounded research study starts with the examination of many general clues. Then, cumulative collections of raw data are searched for redundancies and categories, followed by generalization of underlying situations into hypotheses.[51]

Given the complexity of modern corporate enterprise, combinations of both inductive (to objectively develop hypotheses) and deductive (to choose best alternatives) may be useful, depending where one begins the analysis effort. A combined approach of inductive and deductive analysis can perhaps provide for a bridge in understanding the relationships between the objective measurements of management science and the qualitative measurements of behavioral science.

With the more recent development of business process innovation and reengineering in the 1990s has come awareness that quantitative methods, to be useful, must be realistically applied. Despite some impressively sophisticated analytical and simulation approaches, this type of understanding has more to do with the 'human side' of enterprise—the interpretation of situations, applying decision support tools that make sense to practicing managers and workers. Perhaps the biggest clue to extreme importance of this phenomenon is the high failure rate of mergers and restructuring projects in the 1990s. More than 85% of Fortune 1000 companies that downsized or restructured still had overhead costs significantly over their best global competitors.[52]

No matter how accurate the quantitative measures are, it is *human behavior* that ultimately dictates company policies and procedures. Human beliefs, value and behaviors will ultimately dictate how well the enterprise works, and how flexible and adaptable it will be when changing conditions necessitate. This helps explain why, over the past century, efforts to improve analysis of the human side of the organization have matched efforts to understand the technical side (see *Exhibit 2-2*). With this background, it is now appropriate to review the contributions of *behavioral science* toward understanding the human influences when conducting business case analyses.

---

[13] W. Durant (1939). *The Story of Civilization: 2*. New York, MFJ Books, copyright renewed, 1966, p.632.

[14] INFOPEDIA 2.0 (1995). Mathematics. Cambridge, MA: Softkey Multimedia Ind., a subsidiary of The Funk & Wagnalls New Encyclopedia.

[15] R. Ackoff (1956, June). The development of operations research as a science. *Operations Research*, pp. 265–266. Cited from C. George (1968), *The History of Management Thought* (pp. 149–150). Englewood Cliffs, N.J.: Prentice-Hall, Inc.

[16] T. Stewart (2001). Improving reliability in judgmental forecasts. Cited from J. S. Armstrong (ed.), *Principles of Forecasting: a Handbook for Researchers and Practitioner* (p. 84). Norwell, MA: Kluwer Academic Publishers.

[17] Ibid.

[18] B. Kolman and C. Denlinger (1992). *Calculus for the Management, Life, and Social Sciences.* New York: Harcourt Brace Jovanovich College Publishers, p. 385.

[19] Ibid.

[20] F. Taylor (1911). *Principles of Scientific Management.* New York: Harper & Brothers Publishers. Cited from R. Hodgetts (1974), *Management: Theory, Process and Practice,* (pp. 29–31). Philadelphia: W.B. Saunders Company.

[21] Ibid.

[22] Ibid., p. 32.

[23] R. Hodgetts (1974). *Management: Theory, Process and Practice.* Philadelphia: W.B. Saunders Company, p. 33.

[24] R. Wilson and W. Mueller (1935). A new method of stock control. *Harvard Business Review,* 5, 197–205.

[25] C. George (1968). *The History of Management Thought.* Englewood Cliffs, N.J.: Prentice-Hall, Inc., p. 154.

[26] J. O'Connor and E. Robertson, *George Dantzig,* URL http://www-history.mcs.st-andrews.ac.uk/history/References/Dantzig_George.html.

[27] Ibid.

[28] R. McBride (1998, Mar–Apr). Advances in solving multicommodity-flow problems. *Interfaces,* pp. 32–41.

[29] R. Hesse and G. Woolsey (1980). *Applied Management Science: A Quick and Dirty Approach.* Chicago: Science Research Associates, Inc., p. 117.

[30] S. Makridakis and S. Wheelwright (1989). *Forecasting Methods for Management.* New York: John Wiley & Sons, p. v.

[31] J. Armstrong (ed.) (2001). *Principles of Forecasting: A Handbook for Researchers and Practitioners,* Boston: Kluwer Academic Publishers, pp. 387–388.

[32] C. Ptak (2000). *ERP: Tools, Techniques and Applications for Integrating the Supply Chain.* New York: St. Lucie Press, p. 117.

[33] Ibid.

[34] Ibid., pp. 227–228.

[35] J. Masters (1983). *Inventory Management,* AFIT Course LM 6.28. Wright-Patterson Air Force Base, OH: Air Force Institute of Technology.

[36] Author's personal experience with U.S. Air Force repairs of expensive aircraft jet engine components.

[37] J. Masters (1993). Determination of near optimal stock levels for multi-echelon distribution inventories. *Journal of Business Logistics,* 14 (2), 165–195.

[38] G. Feeney, J. Petersen, and C. Sherbrooke (1963). *Memorandum RM-3644-PR: An Aggregate Base Stockage Policy for Recoverable Items.* Santa Monica, CA: The Rand Corporation.

[39] C. Sherbrooke (1968a). METRIC: A multi-echelon technique for recoverable item control. *Operations Research*, 16, 122–141.

[40] J. Muckstadt (1973). A model for a multi-item, multi-echelon inventory system. *Management Science*, 20 (4), 472–481.

[41] T. Hillestad (1982). *R-2785-AF: Dyna-METRIC: Dynamic Muli-Echelon Technique for Recoverable Item Control.* Santa Monica, CA: The Rand Corporation.

[42] G. Crawford (1981). *R-2750-RC: Palm's Theorem for Nonstationary Processes.* Santa Monica, CA: The Rand Corporation.

[43] K. Isaacson and P. Boren (1993). *R-4214: Dyna-METRIC Version 6, an Advanced Capability Assessment Model.* Santa Monica, CA: Rand, p. v.

[44] G. Feeney, J. Petersen, and C. Sherbrooke (1963). *RM-3644-PR: An Aggregate Base Stockage Policy for Recoverable Spare Parts.* Santa Monica, CA: The Rand Corporation, p. 12; J. Lu and R. Brooks (1968). *RM-5678-PR: An Aggregate Stockage Policy for EOQ Items at Base Level.* Santa Monica, CA: The Rand Corporation, p. 14.

[45] Ibid.

[46] J. Brannock (1987). POSSEM-ALERT: the search for a requirements forecasting system. *Air Force Journal of Logistics*, XI (2), 31.

[47] Personal correspondence between the author and Air Force budget personnel, circa 1987.

[48] Ibid.

[49] S. Armstrong, M. Adya, and F. Collopy (2001). Rule based forecasting: using judgment in time-series extrapolation. Cited from: J. S. Armstrong (ed.), *Principles of Forecasting: A Handbook for Researchers and Practitioners*; and S. Makridakis (1990). *Forecasting, Planning, and Strategy for the 21ˢᵗ Century.* New York: The Free Press, p. 261.

[50] J. Coyle, E. Bardi, and C. Langley (2003). *The Management of Business Logistics: A Supply Chain Perspective.* Mason, Ohio: South-Western, p. 251.

[51] I. Bouty (2000). Interpersonal and interaction influence on informal resource exchanges between R&D researchers across organizational boundaries. *Academy of Management Journal,* 43 (1), 50–65.

[52] M. Loh (1995). *Reengineering of Work.* Hampshire, England: Gower Publishing Limited.

CHAPTER FOUR

The Social

4

No social system will bring us happiness, health, and prosperity unless it is inspired by something greater than materialism.
Clement Richard Atlee, circa 1950

The Nature of Organizations

Edgar Schein, a prominent organizational development consultant, illustrates the cultural complexity of two real organizations for which he consulted over a number of years, from the mid-1960s through the early 1990s. His pseudo-names for them were the *Action* and *Multi* corporations. The following narrative is adapted from his book, *Organizational Culture and Leadership (1992)*, and his Cape Cod Institute seminar on *Organizational Therapy* (summer 2002).

Action Company

Action was an early leader in the international race to invent, develop and market electronic equipment. Its founders prized, above all, a casual, confrontational atmosphere among its employees. Being 'right,' having a better idea, was valued above being a 'team player.' Also, mistakes were tolerated in the risky pursuit of the unknown, of new things that might work. Power and prestige evolved from successes; rank and 'corner office with a view' were not so important.

The working environment at Action was informal and egalitarian. Power and prestige were more tied to successful ideas and interventions by individuals than to formal approval by higher authority. The organization was loosely structured, with divisions having a great deal of autonomy in their respective areas of competence. Meetings took place at impromptu tables in common areas—closed offices were not the norm.[53]

Multi Company

Multi was a large multidivisional international chemical products company.[54] Its artifacts included private, closed offices, hierarchical decision structure, and business rules that fostered conformity and loyalty to the organizational structure.

The working environment at Multi Corporation was formal. Top echelons expected top down decisions to be followed, and the structure was highly bureaucratic with specialized subgroups in charge of product areas. 'Do not disturb' placards outside individual offices indicated when occupants might be available.

Organizational Cultures

Action Company had an overall culture, embedded by its founder, which viewed the world as an unpredictable, changing place. Maximum value was placed on ingenuity and a 'good idea.' Chances were taken and failures accepted as the normal process in search of the few good ideas. Using sociologist Talcott Parsons' categorization of social systems, Dr. Schein categorized Action as *emotionally charged* (informal confrontations allowed), *specific* (people related to one another in official roles, versus broader family or other cultural ties), particularistic (specific expertise of the individual was important, versus stereotyping, such as an 'all computer folks are alike' mentality), highly *achievement oriented* (rewards, status and rank were assigned based on performance rather than birth rights, proper school attended, etc.), and *self oriented* (norms fostered individual competitiveness versus team playing).

Multi Company was more bureaucratic with its emphasis on scientific research, systematic measurements and adherence to hierarchical status and rules. It was categorized as *emotionally neutral, specific*, somewhat *universalistic*, and somewhat mixed on *status rewards* (both achievement and the right credentials, such as family background and education, were important). It was also somewhat mixed concerning values placed on individual, self-made decisions versus collective decisions. The general assumptions encouraged team play. The implied value system was that if everyone did their individual best, the results would turn out better for the company as a whole.

Discussion

These examples illustrate that there is a great deal of latitude for cultural and social traits among different companies, with different primary tasks, goals, and cultural settings. Also, prevailing world views of environmental complexity and coping with uncertainty are illustrated. Action saw the world as a 'dangerous place' with no sure way to manage. Only by continual probing could better products be found. Multi envisioned the world as knowable, and embraced the notion that their competitive edge could be maintained through methodical, scientific research.[55]

Both companies were very successful for a number of years. Their cultures reflected their underlying assumptions. A good deal of influence concerning their choices of management structure and processes could be attributed to the personalities of their founding leaders—followed by cumulative learning about what worked or did not work over years of operation.

Culture and Adaptability

Both companies later had significant 'growing pains' as mature organizations.

Action Company eventually became too decentralized and democratic. Upper management became indecisive when choosing from among 'best ideas' of strong subgroups and individuals. This resulted in difficulty committing to specific strategic initiatives. All projects tended to be well represented, but resources were scarce for new ventures. The general attitude, "nobody can be sure of the next star product," resulted in ambiguity and indecision.

When Action eventually merged with another electronics/computer company, there were severe problems in trying to integrate the two corporate cultures. The merged company was more formally structured, with regimented rules and a vision that they knew 'what the product was.' Their vision of a path for continued success was to make incremental, systematic process improvements, and not to depend so much on the continual search for new products. This clashed with Action's view, its *espoused values,* of the need for flexibility and confrontational decision processes. To Action, a decentralized, discretionary management style was needed to develop flexible production and needed new products for an uncertain world.

Eventually, Action 'missed the boat' on a strategic level. It failed to embrace the new world of PCs until too late—the market shifted to other entrepreneurs with new core competencies for that dynamic task environment. Action's decentralized management approach had focused on tactical opportunities, and when the strategic 'playing field' technology shifted, long-time resistance to centralized focus prevented the company from collectively seeing the bigger picture.

Multi Company's cultural milieu was different. Its prevailing corporate attitude was one of grandeur—the prevailing view was that Multi somewhat arrogantly 'knew' what was best for the customer. This underlying attitude was due to their self-image as a cutting edge innovator for pharmaceuticals and chemical research due to their scientific experimentation and expertise. 'Build it, and they will come!'

However, a bitter pill came to their collective ego when top management effected a merger with another chemical company that was completely incompatible with Multi's self-view. The new company produced household cleaning products. The merger was perceived as an insult to the lofty cultural attitudes at Multi. Merging with this mundane business challenged Multi's espoused values as a cutting edge developer of prestige pharmaceuticals.

The merger was fraught with problems. The two company cultures clashed. Multi treated the new associates as inferior with their perceived 'low level technology' for common cleaning products. Significant cultural exchange problems could have been expected, given that the existing cultural and social value systems were so challenged.

Discussion

Description of Action and Multi illustrates the complexity and diversity of the cultures of two companies, both successful for a long time. They are but two examples of an infinite variety of potential business organizations—each with particular visions, goals, and niches in their local and global economies. It took years to form the essential nature of these companies, and would take years more to change their basic cultures toward new goals.

This bodes well for caution when conducting business case analyses. Any organization will have a complex social infrastructure. It is important that examination of problems and recommendation of potential alternatives keep this in mind. The best technology will fail, and the most promising changes will be thwarted, if not embraced by the folks who do the job. It is the analyst's challenge and task to systematically gather such information where alternatives might substantially challenge or cause change to the social system.

Gathering Information on Social Processes

For deeper understanding of the social nature of the organization, a *process consultation approach* can help. The visible clues about how organizations function can be seen in their *artifacts* (i.e., observable processes and surroundings). These include such things as the arrangement of the offices (e.g., open areas or closed office doors), formality of processes (e.g., open conferences or 'behind-doors' sessions), formality of business meetings (e.g., pecking order for who can speak versus free interchange of ideas from all), and so forth.

How open or closely held these observable events are can reveal much about organizational *values and belief systems*. This, in turn, can lead to insights about the organization's deeply held *assumptions*. *Assumptions* form the essence of the collective mentality used for establishing the mission, goals and allocating resources.[56] And, while much operational information can be gathered from company sales and financial records, this is often of little use when trying to determine how to change processes and organizational structure for more effective future performance. Over 85% of the 'real' information about the organizations is still not in computers.[57]

As illustrated in the historical developments chart, the quest for increased productivity of scientific management has been paralleled by equally impressive research on the human behavior part of the equation (see *Exhibit 2-2*). Systematic, scientific consideration of human behavior in organizations can be traced back to early studies in organizational behavior, including *industrial psychology*, group dynamics, leadership and management, and human decision processes.

Industrial Psychology

As early as 1912, Hugo Munsterberg, known as the Father of Industrial Psychology, challenged scientific management as virtually ignoring the psychology of workers in economic tasks. He sought to rectify this in his studies of psychological demands placed on individuals in various jobs.

One of his earliest experiments studied the psychological characteristics of trolley car drivers involved in accidents in various cities. After ruling out most obvious causes of accidents (e.g., poor vision, slow reaction times), he defined the real problem. He shifted focus from physical to mental ability—the ability to recognize dangerous situations from people moving around and near the cars with the potential for crossing in front. He was able to test prospective drivers with illustrations of potentially dangerous situations, then verify later that those who chose correct responses also had safer and more efficient records on the job.

Munsterberg further developed and expanded vocational testing methods to other work groups, from ship's officers to telephone operators. The central objective was to test whether or not the person was psychologically fit to do the job. He believed that safety and efficiency depended on the worker's ability to concentrate only on the direct element of the job. For more complex situations, such as the trolley car driver's, an extended field of concentration was needed. For other jobs, a narrower field of concentration might be useful. He popularized industrial psychology by showing how vocational testing could be useful for any and all levels in an organization.[58]

Group Dynamics

Elton Mayo, an industrial researcher at Harvard, popularized the use of sociology in organizational settings. From an early experiment in a Philadelphia textile mill in 1923–1924 he diagnosed low morale (what he termed as 'pessimistic reverie') due to chronic fatigue as a cause of high turnover in the 'mule spinning' department. Turnover was over 40 times the norm, and efficiency low, despite offers of incentive pay.

Mayo and his associates introduced simple work breaks—two ten-minute breaks in morning, two in the afternoon. During breaks the men were encouraged to lie down and to sleep if possible. The results were astounding. Morale improved, turnover decreased and productivity remained the same, despite the work breaks.

Suddenly the work breaks were terminated due to a greater demand for output. However, output immediately declined, and workers again became gloomy and pessimistic. Breaks were restored—but the workers were by then skeptical and remained melancholy. Only after control was delegated to the workers of when to take work breaks was morale improved. Then, productivity soared to all-time highs.[59]

Perhaps the most familiar Elton Mayo experiments took place at the Western Electric Company's Hawthorne plant, near Cicero, Illinois. They were conducted between 1924 and 1932. The most famous and widely cited outcome is known as the *Hawthorne Effect*—the effect of group reaction to merely being paid attention to. The Hawthorne Effect was first observed when manipulating the lighting levels in the relay assembly test room. Two groups were separated—one receiving more illumination, the other less. To the puzzlement of researchers, productivity increased in *both* groups. Later, different groups were observed under other changed conditions, including manipulation of work places, rest pauses, length of working day, methods of payment, and a free midmorning lunch. There were continuing increases in performance.

During the experiment, the women workers were pretty much left on their own to set the pace and joined by friendly, supportive observers. In later interviews they consistently mentioned "freedom" and the "nice way they were treated" as explanations for their attitudes and behavior. The initial effect of increased productivity was first thought to be merely the result of paying attention—making the workers feel important—but was later observed to continue over the four-year period of the study.

In a different experiment, in the bank terminal wiring process, *just the opposite was observed*. Here, *workers purposely restricted the number of completed units*. Careful analysis showed that supervision and the working climate for the bank wiring room experiment were different. First, there was an adversarial relationship between workers and management. Workers did not agree with management about production requirements. Second, management seemed to reinforce distrust of the workers by posting regular department supervisors to maintain order in the test room.

It was noted that the supervisory arrangement produced an inhibiting atmosphere. Also, the outside observer played a disinterested role—unable to answer questions or provide feedback. This was different from the relay room experiments, where observers were supportive and may have been perceived as pseudo managers.

After four years of observations and thousands of interviews, there were still many unanswered questions about the complex, dynamic reactions of workers at the Hawthorne plant. There were some indications that supported the belief that attention and feeling of worth enhanced production in the relay assembly test room (i.e., supportive management, semi-autonomous, participative work scheduling). Other explanations helped in understanding the restricted production in the bank wiring room. For example, there was general disagreement of production requirements. Also, there was an informal group that resisted authoritative management oversight. The common threads between the two situations, according to one management theorist, were supervision and working climate.[60]

In retrospect, the Hawthorne studies are credited as one of the first instances that an intensive, systematic analysis was made of human group dynamics in the business work environment.[61] The results gave important insights into the complexity and dynamics of individual and group behaviors in the work environment. They also pointed out that supervisory and work climate can be important motivators.

Early Supervision and Leadership Studies

University of Iowa Studies (1937–1938)

By the late 1930s, University of Iowa researchers Ronald Lippitt and Ralph White were to uncover basic insights about the effects of supervision that generally supported the findings of Mayo. These studies were under the general supervision for Kurt Lewin, recognized as the Father of Group Dynamics. They were from an entirely different setting than previous organizational studies: hobby clubs of 10-year-old boys. These findings helped illustrate the universality of supervision on subordinate motivation. The Iowa studies manipulated supervision of different groups using three supervisory styles: authoritarian, democratic and laissez faire.

They found that the boys generally reacted to the *authoritarian leader* in either of two ways, aggressively or apathetically. In the 1937 study, reviewing films and recording detailed records, the researcher observed that hostility occurrences were 30 times more frequent for autocratic than democratic climates. In a second experiment a year later, they found four out of five groups had extremely nonaggressive, apathetic behavior patterns with an *autocratic leader*—but exhibited outbursts of behavior when the leader left the room. Group reactions to *democratic leaders* fell between the two extremes of aggressive and apathetic behavior.

The findings of the studies generally support earlier notions about the potential effects of directed versus democratic leadership styles. However, the historical value of the studies is that they were the first to analyze leadership from a systematic, scientific perspective—and showed that different styles can produce different, complex reactions from the same or similar groups.[62]

Ohio State University Leadership Studies (1945)

In addition to implications about supervision style, observed behaviors can also reflect perceptions about the overall organizational climate in its relationship to individual behavior. For example, in highly motivated, learning organizations, there is generally believed to be a connection with the proper balance of rules (need for central coordination) and discretion (need for individual worth and growth). These beliefs can be traced to the 1945 Ohio State studies where statistical factor analysis was used to separate two consistently occurring factors relating to performance.

For example, in studies of Air Force bomber crews *consideration* (i.e., a trusting, friendly relationship between crew and commander) and *initiating structure* (i.e., well-defined, prescriptive operating rules) accounted for 83% of the explanatory power for behavior.[63] These factors were subsequently verified in multiple follow-up studies. Many models, such as Blake and Mouton's Managerial Grid model (1967), assume similar determinants of behavior (i.e., 'concern for people' *(consideration)* and 'concern for production' *(initiating structure))*.[64]

University of Michigan Leadership Studies (1945)

At about the same time, a study by Rensis Likert, conducted under a grant from Office of Navy Research, extended one of the findings from the Hawthorne Studies— the productive effects of *worker participation.*

There are good reasons to expect *participation* will yield more enthusiasm. Lower level needs from Abraham Maslow's theory of motivation are likely to be somewhat satisfied in modern organizations. For example, *basic needs* (e.g., pay) and *security needs* (e.g., seniority, unions, severance pay) are generally satisfied as terms of employment. This is not necessarily so for higher needs, such as feelings of *belonging, esteem,* and *self-actualization.*

Likert and his associates at the University of Michigan, after many years of research, developed a model of potential management systems, from authoritarian to participative, to test their effectiveness. The idea, widely accepted, is that workers will tend to buy in and be more highly motivated if given a chance to help set up work methods—which in effect, bolsters their higher needs.

The focus of study for the Michigan studies was to determine what effects active involvement *participation* has on *both* productivity and employee satisfaction. In research conducted at the Prudential Insurance Company,

Likert separated departments into highest and lowest producers. He then asked hundreds of managers to describe the management styles at the highest and lowest. It was found that *participative* managers (supervisor discusses, receives inputs) and *democratic* managers (complete trust and joint decision making) had consistently higher-producing sections than more autocratic leaders.[65] Benefits from participative management have been found in hundreds of similar studies in a wide variety of industrial, hospital, governmental and other organizations.

Yet, Likert recognized that there are many ways to apply a participative system—depending on such things as the situation, industry tradition, values and skills of a particular company.[66] People are pretty smart. They will tend to know, given the situation, when trust and support are appropriate and due credit given. Smart managers will likely be aware of this also. If sincerity in management-employee relations is missing, new programs will have more difficulty in achieving buy-in from organizational stakeholders. Such situations should be noted as risks for new policies and programs during business case analysis.

Human Decisions and Bias

Spyros Makridakis, in his 1990 book on forecasting, planning and strategy, observes:

> ...the human memory is a superb organ...[its] complexity is estimated to be ... sixty times that of the entire U.S. telephone system, and its capacity 500 times that of the entire *Encyclopedia Britannica*...yet [it] would be filled to capacity in a few days ... [if it could not organize] what to remember and what can be ignored.
> ... The difference between memory and judgment is that ... we accept limitations of memory [and write things down] ... [but] rarely ... remedy the deficiencies of our judgment, mainly because we are unaware

or unwilling to accept that our judgment can be faulty or biased ... yet empirical evidence demonstrates beyond all reasonable doubt their existence and their negative, damaging consequences.

... Judgmental biases do not mean stupidity ... their presence is clearly discernable among highly intelligent people ... rather, they result from the way the mind operates [to reconcile] conflicting objectives.[67]

Through our day-to-day experience we all form beliefs and opinions about what works and what doesn't. These patterns of judgment become deeply embedded in our minds, and allow us to function and make decisions. For routine decisions, there are programmed responses that require little mental efforts. This leaves our minds relatively free to parse out the few significant new situations that require us to expend mental energy. It is with new information that we must decide to believe or not, or to change our opinions, beliefs and ways of doing things because of it.

Human decision bias shows up consistently in cognitive psychologists' studies. One researcher found that *90% of the information we seek aims toward supporting preconceived beliefs and notions*. We generally do not seek disconfirming evidence. For example, the marketing department may be convinced that a promotional campaign is the cause of increased sales—but there are so many factors, such as the economy or the product, that it may be impossible to prove the campaign was the main cause. Disconfirming evidence (i.e., stop promotions and advertising) may be the only way to prove their effectiveness—though this may seem impractical for most companies.[68]

Another bias seems to follow from generally seeking only confirming evidence of our beliefs—it will tend to reinforce preconceived notions and lead to *overconfidence* that we were right in the first place. This is further complicated by the findings that we tend to remember con-firming evidence better. Studies have shown that believers in a situation remember 90% of confirming evidence and only 40% of negative material.

Sensing this, subordinates may tend to pass 'good information' up the organization, and it will tend to be re-membered. Negative information, contrary to manage-ment's perceptions but necessary for adapting processes, is often ignored. Disconfirming evidence should be sought to enable awareness for the need of innovative decisions when previously routine conditions have changed. Sometimes the 'devil's advocate' is an essential role. Jay Forrester of MIT remarked that the hallmark of a great organization is "how quickly bad news travels upward."[69]

Inconsistency is another human bias—changing our minds when there is no need. This is the opposite of hold-ing onto beliefs and behaviors despite changed conditions, and can be just as damaging. Studies in the 1950s showed that production managers often alter monthly production amounts with apparently no supporting feedback. When decisions were formalized, reduced production costs im-proved profits. These findings have been reproduced in a great number of studies. It seems people are often inconsis-tent because they lack appropriate guidance, forget, are in-fluenced by mood, are bored, or wish to think things have changed.[70]

One amazing discovery, given human bias in deci-sions, was the observation by Meehl (1954), and quoted often in forecasting literature, that *simple statistical models*, using few predictor variables, *generally make more accu-rate forecasts than people*.[71] This might be because these structured models (e.g., regression based expert systems) can consistently apply the predictive weight of all variables simultaneously. Humans tend to pick only a few, based on their mood, recent information, and other factors, and lose the added information value of the several.

There is also evidence that bias can be amplified during *group decision making*—an omen, since most organizational decisions involving changing policy are probably made in daily/weekly staff meetings. These meetings are routine and often not structured for systematic examination of issues (i.e., history, successes in similar situations, and so on). This problem can become exacerbated due to *group think*—a phenomenon that develops when group members become supportive of the boss and each other, and tend to avoid conflict and dissent during meetings.[72] This also offers anonymity to individuals for risky decisions. But perhaps the biggest danger in unstructured meetings, where nobody speaks up, is the general tendency toward a consensus solution that nobody wants. This has been called the Abilene Paradox.[73]

Conventional wisdom, often based on unfounded truisms or myths we have grown up with in our culture, can also lead to bias. A few of these myths are:[74]

> 1) *More information is always better.*
>
> Not so. Numerous studies have shown that beyond a minimum amount of factual information, additional information tends to bias judgments—either through information overload, or over confidence (i.e., we accept mostly supporting data).
>
> 2) *We can distinguish useful from irrelevant information.*
>
> Not so. Empirical research indicates subjects supplied with 'good' and 'bad' information cannot distinguish—will likely use both, decreasing decision quality.

3) *We assess chances of failure fairly accurately.*

Not so. We are overly optimistic. For example, most new businesses expect to succeed—and someone decides to take the risk. Yet, 70–90% of new businesses fail in the first few years.

4) *We know when to quit.*

Not so. Many projects are prolonged far too long because of the tremendous investment so far—rather than cutting losses for failed efforts and considering the past as sunk costs.

Obviously decisions made at one point in time will need to be adapted as the situation changes in task environment changes. This implies the need for a learning organization—by definition, one that monitors effectiveness of processes, makes mistakes, and adjusts current rules that are no longer useful. It also implies a need for stability and consistency, as long as current rules are appropriate. These dual influences, the need to adapt as the situation changes while simultaneously seeking consistency where possible can bias decisions if not properly recognized. A partial list of biases, some indicating too much faith in change, some too little, is shown in *Exhibit 4-1.*[75]

Exhibit 4-1

Biases Found in Future Oriented Decisions	
Gambler's Fallacy *(Jarvik, 1951)*	*Seeing five 'heads' tossed from a coin and betting a 'tail' is more likely next — wrong interpretation of the law of averages—odds are still 50-50.*
Hindsight Bias *(Fischoff, 1975)*	*The 'I knew it all along' effect—tendency to exaggerate how accurate one's past predictions were or would have been.*

Biases Found in Future Oriented Decisions
(Exhibit 4-1 continued)

Availability Heuristic
(Tversky and Kahneman, 1973)

The 'I saw it in the news' effect—example question—"Which is more common in the United States, homicide or suicide?" Many would answer homicide—it is frequently reported in the news—yet, statistics reveal suicides outnumber homicides by thousands.

Anchoring
(Tversky and Kahneman, 1974)

Tendency to accept beginning values without question—shows importance of reasonable beginning estimates to improve decision accuracy. For example subjects were asked what percentage of nations in the United Nations were African. A beginning value was selected by spinning a wheel of fortune. Those starting with 10% made predictions averaging 25%; those starting with 65%, predicted 45%. (p.s.: actual value was 29% in 1974).

Optimism
(Hayes, 1936)

Wishful thinking beyond supporting evidence. For example, 84% of voters who intended to vote for Hoover in the 1932 presidential election thought he would win—only 6% of Roosevelt voters believed Hoover would win.

Conservatism
(Webster, 1965)

Failure to change (or changing slowly) one's mind in light of new information. For example, interviewers of prospective new employees tend to form opinions in the first 30 seconds and stick to them.

The Neurotic Organization

Manfred Kets de Vries, an organizational psychoanalyst, amplifies another theme of possible dysfunctional decision processes. Works of behavioral theorists Wilfred Bion and Sigmund Freud had implied that organizations, as well as individuals, might also have a 'personality.' Kets de Vries expands this notion, and hypothesizes an organizations can be viewed as having psychoanalytic nature. He suggests that the 'collective mind' of organizations, like individuals, can exhibit mild neurotic traits such as shyness, depression, irrational fears, and suspicion. As an organization matures, it develops a collective corporate image and identity about company origins, growth, and hardships faced, promotion and reward systems, and so on. This image is, of course, made up from the composite of organizational members, and influenced by various subgroups and cultures. But, to Kets de Vries, it manifests in collective form.

Healthy organizations will have a broad enough variety of individuals, subgroups and coalitions to prevent any to unduly influence the organizational personality. However, for 'sick organizations,' the mild effects of broadly dispersed neuroses can manifest more acutely, especially if the dominant power coalition (i.e., formal or informal leaders) has become overly neurotic. In this heightened form, needed organizational adaptive behavior can be severely hampered.

Kets de Vries outlines symptoms for five general types of organizational neurotic styles that lead to dysfunctional behavior, as adapted in *Exhibit 4-2*.[76]

Exhibit 4-2

Five Dysfunctional Styles of Organizations

Neurosis Type	Symptoms	Behaviors
Paranoid *(fear of hostile and dynamic external environments)*	Overly suspicious and 'on guard'	*Constant vigilance*: -primary emphasis on organizational intelligence - sophisticated MIS - Institutionalized suspicion - 'reactive' focus impedes 'proactive' strategies
Compulsive *(seeking to avoid internal surprises to avoid outside controls)*	Perfectionism; preoccupation with trivial details	*Rule Laden*: - formal organization rules - preprogrammed decisions - emphasis on conformity - narrow focus impedes needed change

Five Dysfunctional Styles of Organizations (Exhibit 4-2 continued)		
Neurosis Type	**Symptoms**	**Behaviors**
Dramatic *(CEO has egocentric, narcissistic personality)*	Directives overly aggressive or impulsive; primitive management structure and information systems	*Boss centered:* - autocratic - little input from others - decisions from hunches versus facts - attempts to 'enact' rather than 'react' to environment - top down focus impedes information about needed operations adaptations
Depressive *(feeling of impotency and incapacity for change)*	Very bureaucratic, hierarchal, position based on position rather than expertise	*Pessimistic:* - control by formal programs rather than leaders - just follow the rules - inhibitions to action - needed changes resisted -can only survive in protected, stable environment
Schizoid *(detachment; safer to remain distant)*	Leadership vacuum, power shift to second tier managers who 'game' top leader for their individual goals	*Drifting:* - top leader insecure, withdrawn, no consistent policy - individual politics prevent consistent strategy - alienated subordinates - real barriers to objective information about performance impede recognition of need for change

Conclusions

There are many reasons why status quo operations and strategies become maladapted or need change. The external environment can change—causing a shift in needed or allowable outputs. Also, the internal environment can become out of step with productivity and social needs.

Additionally, organizations come in all sizes, shapes and abilities.

We have gotten a flavor for the variety and complexity of internal social dynamics with Edgar Schein's description of Multi and Action companies. Systematic application of social sciences to the study of organizations can be traced to as early as the 1910s for industrial psychology, and 1920s for group dynamics. By mid-20th century, important principles concerning industrial psychology, group dynamics, leadership and supervision styles were becoming better understood. Generally, people are more motivated when the climate is supportive (Lewin, 1937), there are clear parameters about what is expected (Ohio State studies, 1945), and they perceive they have participation in conducting the processes (Likert, 1945).

Finally we examined many ways that organizational change needs can be overlooked. One source of misinterpretation is through normal human bias. This can happen either by faulty logic (e.g., 'the gambler's fallacy'; undue optimism; anchoring; availability heuristic) or inappropriate selection or acceptance of information (e.g., hindsight bias; conservatism). At the organizational level, we examined potential collective neurotic behaviors. These included neurotic types of paranoid (fear of outsiders), compulsive (fear of insiders), dramatic (too authoritarian), depressive (too bureaucratic), and schizoid (aimless withdrawal and detachment).

With knowledge of these behavioral and management science observations, it becomes apparent that there are many ways to develop successful organizational improvement strategies. However, given specifics about the culture and task requirements, some organizational forms might have more success than others in certain situations. It is now appropriate to examine in more detail the influences of the task *situation* on types of organizational form.

[53] E. Schein (2002, August). *Organizational Therapy Seminar*, Eastham MA: Cape Cod Institute.
[54] Ibid.
[55] Ibid.
[56] E. Schein (1992). *Organizational Culture and Leadership* (2nd ed.). San Francisco: Jossey-Bass, p. 17.
[57] T. Davenport (1993). *Reengineering Work through Information Technology.* Boston: Harvard Business School Press, p. 71.
[58] R. Hodgetts (1975). Philadelphia: W.B. Saunders Co., pp. 66–70.
[59] Ibid., p. 71.
[60] F. Luthans (1973). *Organizational Behavior.* New York: McGraw-Hill Book Company, p. 32.
[61] Ibid.
[62] Ibid., pp. 34–35.
[63] Ibid., pp. 35–36.
[64] R. Blake & J. Mouton (1966, July). Managerial facades. *Advanced Management Journal.* Cited from F. Luthans (1973), p. 533.
[65] F. Luthans (1973), pp. 525–526.
[66] R. Likert (1967). *The Human Organization.* New York: McGraw-Hill Book Company, p.192.
[67] S. Makridakis (1990). *Forecasting, Planning, and Strategy for the 21st Century.* New York: The Free Press, pp. 25–26.
[68] Ibid., p. 31.
[69] P. Senge (1990). *The Fifth Discipline: The Art and Practice of Learning.* New York: Doubleday, p. 226.
[70] S. Makridakis (1990), p. 34.
[71] P. Meehl (1954). *Clinical Versus Statistical Prediction: A Theoretical Analysis and a Review of the Evidence.* Minneapolis: University of Minnesota Press.
[72] Janis, I. (1972). *Victims of Group Think.* Boston: Houghton Mifflin, 1972.
[73] The Abilene Paradox states, "When nobody speaks up, the chosen solution will be one that nobody wants." Source unknown.
[74] S. Makridakis (1990), p. 40.
[75] Primary sources include studies cited from: J. Armstrong (2001). Extrapolations for time-series and cross sectional data. Cited from: *Principles of Forecasting: A Handbook for Researchers and Practitioners*, J. S. Armstrong (ed.); and Makridakis, S. (1990). *Forecasting, Planning, and Strategy for the 21st Century.* New York: The Free Press.
[76] M. Kets de Vries (1985). *The Neurotic Organization.* Washington: Jossey-Bass Publishers, pp. 24–25.

CHAPTER FIVE

The Situation

═══════════════════════════════════ **5**

Lots of folks confuse bad management with destiny.
Frank McKinney (Kin) Hubbard (circa 1925)

We have begun to appreciate the significant impact of both the technical and social aspects of organizations. But perhaps more important for business case analysis is how they interact in specific task setting. In management, a universal dictum is that 'it all depends on the situation.' This chapter explores the complexity of the task situation, and how successful organizations are likely to adapt their technical and social processes to it.

External Influences—The Technological Imperative

In the 1950s, British researcher Joan Woodward conducted one of the first comprehensive studies of the external task environment as an influence on types of organization. She concluded that a *technological imperative* greatly influences how organizations are formed. Up to the time of Joan Woodward's study, popular management literature viewed the formal organization as being composed of structure and possibly a group of processes.[77] Technical complexity of the task situation was not considered an integral part of the formal organization, but as merely a set of limiting constraints. Woodard asserted that technology might actually be the key to understanding how successful organizations were formed.

Woodward's classic study concerned types of organizations she found among 100 manufacturing firms in the London suburbs. Her observations were made between 1953 and 1957. She concluded that the technical complexity of each firm's task environment was a primary determinant of the organization's structure and processes.

To make her point, she classified the 100 firms into three groups: *unit/small batch, mass production* and *process production*. She speculated that these general task situations fell along a complexity continuum. Simpler processes were represented by unit/small batch production. Mass production was somewhat more complex, but with controllable steps. Continuous flow process production required very complex coordination steps.

Interestingly, she found organizational structure and process similarities between the simpler (*unit/small batch*) and more complex (*process*) firms. Both groups tended to require more decentralized decisions. In contrast, *mass production* firms—in the middle complexity range—tended to develop more formal decision procedures. Borrowing from concepts of her contemporary management theorists Tom Burns and G. M. Stalker, she classified the management systems requiring more decision discretion as 'organic,' and those requiring more standardized control of process steps as 'mechanistic' management systems.[78]

Woodward speculated that the reasons for similarities in decentralizing decisions (i.e., having more organic decision processes) were partially due to allow needed flexibility for nonroutine problems. *Unit/small batch* production requires frequent shifts in routines due to a large variety of products. Decisions require tailoring each production activity to unique, changing customer needs. *Continuous processes* require quick, informed coordination and solution for problems at activity levels for highly interrelated system processes. Delays at any point can cause excessive delays for the total system. *Mass production* systems, Woodward surmised, have less complexity (i.e., more routine tasks than unit/small batch; more flexibility/time to correct and coordinate activity problems than continuous process production). It makes sense, therefore, to have more formal (though less flexible) management structure and processes to avoid unwarranted deviations from the relatively well-established, routine production standards.

There were critics of Woodward's conclusions. They basically argued that technology itself is probably only one of many determinants of how firms are organized. Other influences, such as local culture, leadership style, firm size and age, and nature of competition, can also affect the structure. However, in a broad sense, Woodward's work found support among many studies of the period.

For example, Charles Perrow, another prominent management analyst, found similarity among organizations based on how predictable the task is and how much variety exists in production. More formal routines make sense where tasks are analyzable and stable (such as steel mills). And, more decision discretion is required where processes are more complex (i.e., where there is higher variability of tasks, or where quick adjustments may be needed for problems among highly interrelated steps).[79]

Other researchers, Fremont Kast and James Rosensweig, found comparable arrays of organizational types. More organic systems (i.e., those having more decentralized decisions) were found where task variety and instability were high; and more formal (mechanistic) ones were found where process steps were stable and routine.[80]

Internal Influences—Process Integration

James D. Thompson, in his seminal work, *Organizations in Action* (1967), speculated that organizations are probably structured by necessities to handle process interdependencies. He categorized three broad types of technology, based on process interdependencies that seemed to be widespread and sufficiently different from one another. These are *long-linked, mediating,* and *intensive* types of technology.

Long-linked technology exists where many steps are required, but they are well prescribed—outputs are a *standard, repetitive product,* and criteria for work and resources are clear-cut. *Mass production* represents this kind of technology. Technical competences, especially through development of management science techniques, have made great contributions to productivity for these types of organization.

Mediating technology, Thompson's second category, departs from the industrial technologies presented by Woodward, et al. The primary functions of these processes involve the *linking of customers* who seek interdependent activities. Banks, telephone companies, the post office, and employment agencies mediate such links. Complexity comes from the large variety of customer needs that are to be matched with the large variety of outputs. Standardization permits a common set of rules to limit required input and output behaviors—thus making linking of common needs possible. Impersonal, *bureaucratic techniques* are considered the most beneficial here.

For *intensive technology,* Thompson's third type, there is great complexity of tasks, but standardization beyond a minimum level is difficult. Each situation requires unique handling. Hospitals, research facilities, and the construction industry are examples. The nature of the input determines the number and variety of skills required, and output services are customized from combinations to suit a particular customer. *Discretionary, creative decisions* are needed.[81]

A decade after Thompson's theory was published, Denise Rousseau suggested that the three categories could be interpreted along a continuum, each category requiring increasingly sophisticated decisions.[82] For example, for tasks in *long-linked technology* environments, such as mass production manufacturing, problems can routinely diagnosed and solved. In *mediating technology* environments, such as banks or insurance companies, task diagnosis is more complex, but once accomplished, solutions are standardized. *Intensive technology,* as found in hospitals, presents the most complex environment due to the enormous range of both diagnosis and accomplishment functions.

This begs the question, also, that a fourth category may exist—technologies where diagnosis is routine but accomplishment is complex. This could be the case where organizational processes have become fragmented, or functions and departments have become overly independent, and do not share overall company values.[83]

Structure Follows Strategy

Along the same theme that technological complexity (i.e., either from the external *technological imperative* or *internal process interdependencies*) dictates the appropriate formal and informal organizational cues, Alvin Chandler (1966) introduced the thesis that organizational structure follows management strategy.

To test this hypothesis, Chandler examined records and reports, and made interviews at four large corporations and found that they all had migrated from centralized to decentralized management structures—but for different reasons. DuPont had decentralized to create more creativity for product diversification. General Motors—to remedy stifling 'rule laden' management among its diverse products, partially replaced the early founder's authoritarian leadership style—keeping centralized control, but decentralizing operations. Standard Oil of New Jersey had similar problems for needed flexibility—but decentralized over time, incrementally, rather that by abrupt overall change. Finally, Sears, Roebuck started out decentralized, became centralized to attain clear channels of communication and authority, then decentralized again as needed flexibility was lacking. In each case, structure followed strategy.

Strategy is a primary function of corporate leaders. This implies that leaders need to understand and define strategic goals, monitor performance, and provide resources to support their achievement.[84] Consequences of inappropriate management strategy, especially where deep change in company values is needed, can result in failed programs. Developing such strategies depends heavily on understanding both internal and external complexities, and the ability to adapt appropriately relative to efficiencies and resource needs.

However, world dynamics are changing operating environments at an exponential rate for commercial and governmental organizations. Significant changes to the playing field have been introduced by both local and global political and economic development, technology, and new competitive strategies.[85] Perhaps the most significant social realization for management strategy has occurred only in the past decade of so—the concept that the customer is supreme. This view is reinforced by modern competitive on-demand production systems and efficient customer response (ECR) management systems. For example, flexible production processes allow Toyota Motors to produce custom automobiles to suit customer on-demand preferences in a day or two. Also, in the fast moving fashion industry, The Gap can transmit point-of-sale information directly from retail stores to offshore factories to initiate reorders for replacements of hot selling clothing items, by size and style.

Such competitive strategies imply the need for continual surveillance and feedback to both understand customers' buying habits, and inventory availability and response needs. Internal supply chain customers, such as intermediate manufacturers, require comparably demanding communications and flexible business processes to adjust to ultimate demand processes.

Developing this awareness and being able to change to new process demands presents different challenges to different organizations. This is partially due to the technical nature of the processes, and partially due to the internal maturity and complexity of the organization's social and cultural systems. For example, Edgar Schein theorizes:

> Organizations are often characterized by their history and age. In *young organizations*, original founders still run the place; by *mid-life*, leadership passes to 2nd and 3rd generations of managers. And in *mature organizations*, professional managers and multiple subcultures have replaced original founders.

Understanding the age or maturity of an organization can be an important first step in understanding problems and potential improvement strategies that fit their existing culture and social system.

> *Young organizations* are dynamic and flexible. The founding leaders define their purpose.

These 'alpha' leaders guide the effort to establish a purpose, operating rules, and behavioral rules about how to treat customers and each other within the company.

Over many trials and errors, the stakeholders learn what works and what doesn't. Learning accumulates, and eventually shared concepts become the 'way we do things around here.' Shared concepts are defended, and operations are perceived as the 'right way.' These embedded habits and relationships are rarely critically evaluated, so long as general business seems on course. These learned habits and relationships become the business rules that in combination represent the culture of the organization. This culture is defined by shared patterns of beliefs, thoughts, feeling and values. [86]

Networks of human activities support and perpetuate what works, and help identify and adapt what doesn't. Change of normal operations becomes necessary when outputs get 'out of step.' At this juncture, leaders must redefine the purpose and managers set new goals and means of operation. Warren Bennis, a prominent management consultant, is credited with defining this as "managers do things right, leaders do the right thing."[87] Continuing with Schein's observations about organizational culture:

> *Mid-life organizations* tend to shift from the rather conservative philosophy of the 'father' to the more liberal worldview of the 'son.'

As the organization strives to grow, expand, diversify, nonfamily members are brought in, eventually to outnumber the founders' original 'organizational family.' The 'cultural glue' that has grown over the early years has now been embedded in day-to-day operations, and newcomers pick up preexisting shared patterns of beliefs, thoughts, feelings and values about how things 'ought to be.'

These organizations continue to grow, diversify and become increasingly complex. Various functions and product areas have become elaborate, requiring specialized subcultures to evolve for their management. These subculture groups eventually become the basis of evolution in new directions.[88]

> In *mature organizations*, non-related professional managers eventually replace original owners and founders.

Continual elaboration of business processes requires more emphasis on integration of overall functions in *mature organizations*. Corporate leaders are selected for cultural traits that promote internal harmony and unify against external threats. Subcultures that represent the embedded traits thought responsible for past successes tend to anchor belief systems about what it takes to grow and be successful. For example, success in moderate to complex task environments may be attributed to 'individual initiative' as a top quality. Where the organizational tasks are more predictable and mechanistic, bureaucratic rules may have been institutionalized.[89]

Change Strategies Depend on Both Social and Technical Factors

So, it appears that development of successful change strategies will require analysis of *both* the task complexity (i.e., the 'technological imperative') and the social state of the organization (i.e., adaptability of the structure and processes). Many organizational forms can work for the same or similar situations, but may have difficulty in adapting to required change. This was apparent in Schein's depiction of Action and Multi companies. These companies had been successful in the past, but were significantly challenged when change became necessary. This puts a pall on the 'golden grail' of management—the search to find better (if not best) ways to manage. Such a quest might be illusive. Yet, management literature has developed some promising insights about change interdictions that might be useful certain situations. These are found in the basic nature of the business task. The implication is a need for awareness about potential organizational forms that accommodate the dual needs for needed creativity and overall system coordination, given task complexity.

Complexity—Task Variety and Stability

There are indications that certain management processes may be more appropriate, given the complexity of the situations. Joan Woodward's work indicated that external task demands influence appropriate organizational structure and processes. Task variety of output for unit/small batch processes and tightly sequenced process steps for continuous processes required greater decision flexibility at production levels. More structured, mechanistic management was found in mass production to help control coordination costs, possibly at the expense of needed flexibility.

James D. Thompson's work also implied that management approaches might be tied to task complexity. His work extends Woodward's by illustrating that task *variety* and *stability* are probably universal factors, applicable to service industries as well as manufacturing. A related notion, derived from the work of Kurt Lewin (1947), is that organizations will simultaneously seek needed flexibility (i.e., less variety—to reduce lost opportunity costs) and needed controls (i.e., increased stability—to reduce coordination costs).[90]

These and other studies of organizations imply that ingredients of successful organizational form and function might be contingent upon degrees of task complexity. Task complexity can be operationally defined as the cumulative effects of task variety and stability.

Thompson's observations suggest that the degree of complexity, based on levels of task variety and stability, can help determine likely organizational forms that will be compatible with the task situation. *Exhibit 5-1* is adapted from his concepts:[91]

Exhibit 5-1

Task Complexity and Organizational Form

Organizational Forms

Task Stability

		Stable	Shifting
Task Variety	**Low**	- few functions - similar departments - standardized rules - centralized control	- variety of functions - departments match outside counterparts - strategic planning - decentralized control
	High	- variety of functions - dissimilar departments - flexible operations - centralized control	- variety of functions - differentiated departments - continual surveillance and feedback - decentralized control

Sources of Task Complexity

British Tavistock Institute researchers Fred Emery and Eric Trist, in their classic article *The Causal Texture of Organizational Environments* (1965), delineated four ideal types of environment that will influence the types of organization tasks required for success. These types range from simple to complex. Type I is the *placid-randomized environment.* It represents the simplest organization; rewards and costs are relatively unchanging and randomly distributed. Economically, Type I organizations exist in 'perfect competition.' Many small organizations can exist. Planning is tactical, not strategic.

In Type 2, the *placid-clustered* environment, organizations become serially related and more specialized, with specific roles in overall production processes. Strategy evolves to determine what services the network needs, and where to locate resources and logistics. Distinctive competence develops. Organizational processes elaborate hierarchically and horizontally.

The Type 3 environment is *disturbed-reactive*. Here the existence of a number of similar, large organizations becomes the dominant characteristic of the environmental field. Each organization must shift from accounting for other organizations meeting at random to explicitly considering strategic competitive factors. *Strategy* evolves into search for desired objectives—where one wants to be at a future time—and *tactics,* a matter of selecting immediate actions from existing capabilities that aid getting there.

Operations, a term adopted from German and Soviet military theorists, appears in the disturbed-reactive environment as an intermediate level of organizational response. An operation consists of a campaign involving a planned series of tactical initiatives, calculation of competitors' reactions, and planned counteractions. Needed flexibility puts a premium on quality and speed of decisions, and encourages some decentralization.

Also, under a disturbed-reactive environment, it becomes convenient to define the organizational objectives more in terms of power and ability to control the environment—through takeovers, mergers, and cooperative ventures—in addition to the more traditional measures of location and position. Conditions are too complex for unilateral control. When coming to terms with significant others, such as competitors, interest groups and governments, one has to know when not to fight to the death.

Type 4, *turbulent fields,* is the most complex situation. Like Type 3, it requires dynamic changes in modus operandi (unlike static types 1 and 2). Unlike 3, however, dynamic properties arise not only from competitive forces among significant others, but also from the larger environment field, involving a total industry and its relations with the wider society. The 'ground is in motion.'

Three conditions lead to Type 4 environments:

1) Linked networks of organizations so large and controlling that, in combination, can cause change in, as well as be affected by the larger environment.

2) Deep interdependence between the economic and other facets of society, fostering increased controls in legislation and public regulation.

3) Increased reliance on research and development to meet competition, resulting in continual change in the environmental field.

What becomes precarious for Type 4 conditions is how organizational stability can be achieved. The need is evident for emergence of values useful to all organizations of the field—no one organization, however large, can adapt alone. Unable to trace consequences of their individual actions, organizations collectively seek to reduce uncertainty with value-based rules that to provide ethical guides to action. Values are neither strategies nor tactics, but allow stability to keep things under control.

Whether this is good or bad depends upon how appropriate restrictions may be for needed environmental requirements. Also, there needs to be some overarching form of organization. Basic needs of constituent members are positively correlated. In Type 3 organizations, fates of similar organizations are somewhat negatively correlated, due to competition. But in Type 4, the turbulent environments of dissimilar organizations are positively correlated, where no one dominates and whose collective fates depend upon overall cooperation.

In these situations, matrix type ruling bodies, regulated by, say, professional standards, permit overall stability and allow individual members to carry on Type 3 fashion, but now subject to upward limits imposed by collective values. These collective values translate into universal rules, and organizations become *institutions*. Institutions can be defined as organizations that have embodied values that relate them to wider society.

Institutionalized organizations now must consider dual strategic objectives: goals that are congruent with both their own character and that contribute to the stability of other relevant parties. This implies need for a change in overall orientation of organizations; a trust in the better nature of other organizations, similar to Douglas McGregor's Theory Y assumptions about individual people in organizations.[xxv]

Developing interorganizational rules of engagement and standards to ensure mutual trust can take a long time. It requires developing systems that allow accurate feedback of how the organization is faring (a technical attribute). It also necessitates that the feedback satisfy expected performance and behavior values among the technically related companies (a social attribute). Similar to the long gestation period that influences a single organization's culture, this macrocultural view on industry scale can be expected to take many decades to reach maturity.

[xxv] Douglas McGregor, in his classic management text, *The Human Side of Enterprise* (1960), categorized management assumptions about employees as Theory X (people will comply but must be controlled) and Theory Y (people seek to contribute and should be allowed to make decisions).

Organizations as Open Systems

From Emery and Trist's conceptualization of environmental complexity, it can be argued that over time, in order to be successful, organizations will adapt core task capabilities to deal with their respective task environments. This, in turn, implies that they will be able to adapt their organizational forms (i.e., structure and processes) to be compatible with the complexities of their task.

This ability to adapt and change is different from earlier management thought that essentially viewed organizations as 'closed systems.' Under a closed system view, organizational structure and processes remain relatively static, and react to outside contingencies the best way they can, making incremental changes as efficiency measures dictate. Once formed, the primary adaptive mechanisms become the measurement of its processes for efficiency.

Shirley Terreberry (1968) questioned the assumption that organizations are merely closed systems with limited, incremental adaptive mechanisms. She viewed organizations as living, open systems capable of larger changes in response to environmental complexities. She realized that in very complex situations, efficiency measures might not be enough. This is especially true if the enterprise outputs have become out-of-step with required new environmental needs. If only incremental adaptations are made until such changes are no longer sufficient, the organization's viability might depend on the need for radical reengineering of the core competencies. At this juncture, rational decision-making is replaced by 'disjointed incrementalism.'[92] If the social and technical foundations are malleable enough to withstand radical reengineering, a fundamentally new organization emerges to cope with task requirements. If changes come too little or too late, a sort of

Darwinian weaning takes place as organizations leave the game.

Practical Analysis Concepts

These management observations imply that organizations may need to adapt either tactically (incrementally) and strategically (radically), depending on their situational problems. Methods in recent management literature have been developed for monitoring both tactical (closed system) and strategic (open system) organizational change requirements. Techniques for systematic monitoring of day-to-day operations involve notions of incremental change, such as those of *Total Quality Management*. Strategic change has been addressed by innovations for *Business Process Reengineering*.

Total Quality Management (TQM)

TQM is perhaps the most recognizable contemporary name for an approach to monitoring and adapting to incremental change needs. It involves continual monitoring for discovery and correction of small performance aberrations. Statistical measurements are used to compare expected process efficiency to actual performance.

TQM fosters the notion of a need for continual improvements. It involves systematic monitoring of operations, evaluation of feedback, and incremental scheduling of improvements. Such innovation programs are concerned with aligning organizational activities within their basic processes. The approach requires rigorously tracing symptoms back to root causes and systematically adjusting for underlying problems.

Search for incremental adaptations implicitly assumes that the basic enterprise is sound, and has structure and processes closely aligned with its socioeconomic purpose.[93] Successful incremental process improvement strategies have been reported to yield consistent benefits over costs in the neighborhood of 5 – 12% per year.[94]

Business Process Reengineering (BPR)

BPR, also known as radical business process reengineering, deals with major organizational restructuring. These include radical organizational programs such as downsizing, rightsizing, mergers, and outsourcing noncore processes. BPR techniques are required when gradual improvements are not enough; when the organization has been confronted with the need for significant change.

Business process reengineering is often the only viable way to cope when needed organizational processes have become too outmoded for the task situation. Reengineering generally involves changing the organizational structure and processes, which, even if successful, can have significant side effects on the fundamental culture of the enterprise. While more risky, successful BPR projects can result in effectiveness gains in the range of 50% or more.[95]

TQM and BPR Relationship

These approaches to organizational change, gradual and radical, are described by Michael Hammer, one of the founders of the reengineering movement in the mid-1990s. He, along with James Champy, wrote the influential book *Reengineering the Corporation* in 1993, espousing the needs for BPR. In his 1996 sequel, *Beyond Reengineering*, Hammer recants that radical reengineering may be too harsh a remedy in many situations due to social ramifications. He envisions implementation of general process innovation along a continuum, with continual TQM for small, incremental process changes, and BPR when the need for a radical reengineering initiative becomes apparent.[96] Hammer suggested that most successful organizations probably adapt over time using a variety of approaches, from gradual TQM to 'jump-step' BPR, as illustrated in *Exhibit 5-2*.

Exhibit 5-2

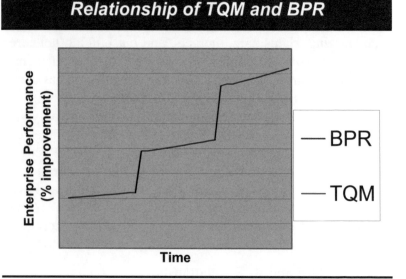

TQM improvements can help keep the enterprise on track for tactical and operational adaptations. But strategic monitoring is also required to keep the big picture in focus. Incremental adaptations may no long suffice if needed changes to business operations are too large. In that situation, radical reengineering may be the only alternative to 'unfreeze' time honored, but dysfunctional, organizations and make way for strategic change.

These approaches seem straightforward enough. Yet, there is ample evidence that they are not so simple to implement. Over 50 percent of the improvement initiatives from the 1990s wave of restructuring, downsizing and delayering failed to achieve goals.[97] Even so, a viable approach seems to be in place—use TQM for simple, day-to-day adaptations and BPR for major reorganizations. Due caution is advised, however, for likely social and cultural impacts.

Processes that people follow as they perform day-to-day work should be congruent with task complexity demands. In turn, organizational structure should be congruent with the processes to help enable needed flexibility and minimize coordination costs. To help understand these dynamics, we now introduce a third major theoretical management approach, sociotechnical systems theory.

---

[77] F. Luthans (1973). *Organizational Behavior: A Modern Behavioral Approach to Management.* New York: McGraw-Hill Book Company.

[78] T. Burns and G. Stalker (1961). *The Management of Innovation.* London: Tavistock Publications Limited.

[79] C. Perrow (1967). A framework for the comparative analysis of organizations, *American Sociological Review,* 32, 196.

[80] F. Kast and J. Rosensweig (1974). *Organization and Management: A Systems Approach* (2nd ed.). New York: McGraw Hill, Inc., p. 187.

[81] J. Thompson (1967). *Organizations in Action.* New York: McGraw Hill Book Company, pp. 15–17.

[82] D. Rousseau (1977). Technological differences in job characteristics, employee satisfaction, and motivation: a synthesis of job design research and sociotechnical systems theory. *Organizational Behavior and Human Performance,* 18, 18–42.

[83] J. Brannock (1981). *Socio-technical Systems Theory: A Study of the Degree to Which Organizational Structure, Process and Technological Complexity are Congruent in a United States Air Force Jet Engine Overhaul Facility.* PhD dissertation. Lincoln, NE: University of Nebraska, School of Business, p. 136.

[84] A. Hillman and T. Dalziel (2003). Boards of directors and firm performance: integrating agency and resource dependence perspectives. *Academy of Management Review,* 28 (3), 383–396.

[85] T. Davenport (1993). *Process Innovation: Reengineering Work through Information Technology.* Boston: Harvard Business School.

[86] E. Schein (1992). *Organizational Culture and Leadership,* pp. 305–317.

[87] E. Schein (1988). *Process Consultation.*

[88] E. Schein (2002).

[89] Ibid.

[90] E. Schein (1992), p. 298.

[91] J. Thompson (1967), p. 72.

[92] S. Terreberry (1968). The evolution of organizational environments. *Administrative Science Quarterly* 12 (4), 595–596.

[93] M. Hammer (1996).

[94] T. Davenport (1993). *Process Innovation*, p. 10.

[95] Ibid.

[96] M. Hammer (1996). *Beyond Reengineering,* pp. 81–82.

[97] M. Loh (1995).

CHAPTER SIX

A Sociotechnical Systems View

6

The margin between that which men naturally do, and that which they can do, is so great that a system which urges...initiative... is preferable, in spite of the wastes....

Louis Brandeis (circa 1940)

The evidence from management literature strongly suggests that successful business organizations rely on congruence of both the social and the technical aspects with the complexity of the task situation. This situational complexity manifests from both external and internal conditions of the task environment. How types and functions of organizations evolve to handle these complexities were shown in the works of Joan Woodward and James D. Thompson, respectively. They indicated that, in general, more complex tasks require more creative decisions (and, often, more flexible business rules). Alvin Chandler's assertion that "structure follows strategy" further extended our appreciation of the social influences of management vision and goals by pointing out that strategy (a social process) precedes structure (a technical state).

Accepting that social implications may be as important as technical ones, we now examine what is known about integration of social and technical resources to achieve situational demands. This involves a third general approach to management, sociotechnical systems theory.

A Combined Sociotechnical Approach

The basic question for business case analysis is not so much "Is there a best way to manage?" as "Are there better ways to manage for a given situation?" Other questions include: "Is it possible for the analyst to identify some measure of task complexity?" "If so, can inferences then be made about seeming incongruencies of organizational capabilities and task requirements?" And finally, "If incongruencies exist, can the organizations' existing social and technical capabilities be adapted to become compatible with the task requirements?" If such analysis is possible, it might provide a beginning point for recommending viable changes and alternatives. A blueprint for strategic improvement could be possible, followed by plans to enact needed TQM and/or BPR changes.

Sociotechnical systems theory can help offer a high level approach for such analysis. Its basic tenets prescribe the need to simultaneously consider requirements of both social and technical resources, given the demands of the situation.

Early Sociotechnical Studies

The British Coal Mines

The first landmark sociotechnical study was by Trist and Bamforth in 1951. Eric Trist, a scholar, and Kenneth Bamforth, formerly a miner with 18 years experience on the 'coal face,' reviewed the social and technical relationships of the coal mines for over two years—using 20 informants from various jobs in the process. They were able to observe a menagerie of management styles, from the early craftsman climate to post-1949 nationalized, automated mining processes.

For example, in earlier 'hand-got' processes, small three-man teams worked single independent shifts and had decentralized decision authority to line up contacts for needed inputs and outputs to the larger process. They had spontaneous feedback about the 'wholeness' or finished quality of a day's work.

The newly mechanized, centrally controlled 'long-wall' method disrupted many of the psychosocial factors. With the advent of mechanical coal cutters and conveyors, the technical complexity of coal mining was transformed from a craftsman atmosphere to a continuous process operation. Wholeness of the task was fragmented—three shifts now sequentially operated, carrying on continuous processes form one crew to the next.

Personal autonomy and responsibility were significantly reduced with the mechanized process. Previous job attributes such as self-selection of team members, local decision authority to solve work glitches, requirements for multiple skills for each worker, and a craftsman-artisan environment all but disappeared. With the sadly degraded social quality of the work-life, productivity failed to achieve expectations, group cohesiveness and individual satisfaction were low and sickness and absenteeism were high, despite higher wages and better amenities. After reintroducing minimal improvements to restore the lost social qualities, there were significant gains in performance and motivations.[98]

This early study exposed many of the underlying principles that would be later integrated into sociotechnical theory, and have remained popular in the general management. These include the importance of feedback (i.e., the sense of closure from seeing finished outcomes), and feelings of belonging and process ownership emanating from self-selection of team members, responsible autonomy for decisions, and the variety of multiple job skills.

Indian Textile Mills

A. K. Rice elaborated many of the sociotechnical implications found by Trist and Bamforth in his experiments at the Calico textile mills, in Amedabad, India (1953–1955). Rice, working as a management consultant, was the first to explicitly use the sociotechnical concept in the experimental design of a production system.[99]

Paraphrased extracts from Rice's notes set up the scenario for the first experiment at the *Jubilee automatic loom shed*:

> Automatic looms had been introduced in 1952, but productivity was no better than with non-automatic looms. Analysis showed individuals with confused task and role relationships. Workers were uncoordinated, with no stable internal structure. Also, under-worked higher-level supervisors micro-managed the over-worked [first line] supervisors. Further compounding the problem, there were no cohesive teams. Any change in complexity of the weaving job required change in team composition [individual worker skills were too specialized, not interchangeable]. Also, due to low turnover and pay status, as well as over-specialization, and job fragmentation, mobility between jobs was limited.

Rice described six sociotechnical conditions he believed were needed to improve the poor performance.[100]

> 1) Coordinate relations between interdependent tasks.
>
> 2) Promote team stability and cohesion for same loom operations.
>
> 3) Develop interchangeable skills for same loom team members.
>
> 4) Protect team boundaries to reinforce territorial responsibility.

5)   Reduce internal differences in opportunities to help promote internal team leadership.

6)   For dissatisfied members, permit movement of workers between work groups of similar skills.

Rice then designed and implemented the 'reorganization experiment' at Jubilee. He formed two groups, one responsible for keeping looms running through short stops (e.g., such as simple yarn breaks); the other responsible for getting looms weaving again after long stops (e.g., meal breaks, seven-hour intervals between second and first shifts). He further composed team size and composition requirements based on sort complexity (i.e., coarse, medium, fine weaving), and on the natural physical limits of the working space (i.e., groups of four to eight teams to proportionally match up with the 64 looms).

Upon presentation to management at Calico, Rice's planned reorganization was OBE'd[xxvi]. After seeing his plan, enthusiastic managers, supervisors and workers nearly spontaneously self-organized into four small groups of seven workers each, with a combination of long-stop and short-stop talent, and comprised of various and balanced skill grades. Performance results, monitored by Rice over the next two months, resulted in efficiency increasing to 95% (from the status quo of 80%), and reducing wastes due to damage by one-third of the pre-experimental rates. The experimental period ended upon introduction of third shifts in some areas, making additional comparisons nonrepresentative.[101]

A second experiment was conducted at the *Calico nonautomatic loom* shed shortly thereafter. At this work site, in the conventional system, weavers each

---

[xxvi] OBE = Overcome By Events.

independently ran two looms. They made frequent visits to other parts of the mill to obtain weft yarn and to deliver woven cloth. There was low output and high damage.

In the experimental loom shed work processes were reengineered to have small groups in control of setup and maintenance of 40 looms. Interdependent workers shared four roles: group leader, front loom worker, back loom worker and helper. The aggregate of 22 workers in the conventional system was replaced by an internally structured group of 11. Minimal pay rates were raised, and bonus was paid for both quantity and quality. Bonuses were paid to the group rather than individuals, at the group's request.

Over the 10 months of the experiment, both management and workers tested out each other's sincerity and willingness to cooperate. Gradually collaborative trusts built up. Sensitivity to the 'wholeness' of the operation was enhanced as all shifts attended work conferences. A minor setback toward progress came at about four months, with a citizens' backlash against 'rational' management, resulting in pickets outside plant gates and worker harassment. However, when some workers left the experimental program, there were more than adequate volunteer replacements.

After a very slow start, efficiency climbed, and eventually surpassed that of conventional loom sheds, despite antirationalization demonstrations from local workers and citizens. Also, quality of cloth, originally lower than that of other sheds, finally surpassed status quo. Due to higher prices obtainable for higher quality cloth, it became feasible to add a third shift. Overall results were a 21% increase in output, a 59% reduction in damages, and a 55% increase in earnings by group workers.[102]

15 Years Later—A review of what worked?

Eric Miller, a British consultant who had worked with Rice, conducted a follow-up review of the Indian textile mills in 1970, 15 years after the initial studies. He found mixed results. Substantial degradation had occurred in work group methods for the Jubilee automatic loom operations. Interestingly, however, for the nonautomated Calico experimental shed, he found the new group processes nearly intact from the original reorganization design.

Why? Miller examined the overall textile industrial environment. Though the automated operations had allowed Jubilee to become a competitive leader in higher quality cloth, governmental policies had placed two significant constraints on the industry. First, there was a tight import control on the quality of long staple cotton materials, mainly from Egypt, needed to produce the finer quality cloth. Second, governmental restrictions, protecting the existing hand-loom industry, prevented installation of additional power looms, as well as importations of replacement loom repair parts.

These environmental constraints had significant affect for the automated loom operations. Task interdependencies had become more complex. At the same time, government restrictions on the import of higher quality cotton from Egypt caused a shortage of input materials required for the higher quality cloth outputs. Quality declined and so did revenues. Forced to cope with lower standards of production and reduced profits, micromanagement returned to Jubilee to 'fix' the resulting lower quality, higher damage processes. Eventually, the new group reverted back to pre-experimental processes.

Analytically, Miller interpreted the regression of the automated group to smaller, more rigid subgroups as a response to the impossible problems resulting from larger society constraints. Inability to coordinate processes to produce higher quality cloth, over time, *destroyed the group social system's resilience to cope.*[103] It was beyond the group's control to influence the larger governmental and social policies. *This resulted in the social system retreating to former coping processes* that still worked, but that were not nearly as efficient or effective overall. Miller interpreted this as a loss of the system's capacity for self-regulation. The group social system no longer could provide supporting technical operations for which it had been designed, and its current form was abandoned.

In contrast, for the nonautomated plant, the successful reengineered group processes that had been introduced 15 years earlier were essentially the same (i.e., a moderate task complexity and a reliable market for the product). Miller speculated that the *task conditions had not changed* sufficiently to cause degradation loss of internal group resilience and cohesion. External forces were insignificant, as input materials of medium grade cotton and materials were locally produced and readily available. And, sales of the medium grade, moderately priced cloth outputs continued to provide adequate revenues for continued operations, preventing pressures by management to intervene.

The Intergroup Exercise

The following narrative is paraphrased from one of the earliest British Tavistock/Leicester group relations studies on sociotechnical systems in 1959. It illustrates the powerful relationships between rational task accomplishment and social ability to react to the situational circumstances:

> The overall task was to decide on a program to take place during the second week of the [two week] conference. The Exercise took place in a large ballroom of the hotel. Conference members were seated in an irregular [fashion]. The first phase [the

director explained] was to [divide the overall membership of 29 people] into three groups... [which] should take no longer than 15 minutes.

What happened in the next minute or so was unexpected and crucial.

[After two or three questions and requests for more guidance, a member, with] anger in his voice, [said they should have] advice and help from the staff. While he was speaking, a small group moved their chairs [closer] to the main body so they could participate. [Someone then] said in a loud voice, "Let's do it alphabetically." He was disregarded.

The general stir of movement suddenly increased and within seconds one group of people were heading towards one corner of the room while another [headed] for the diagonally opposite corner; in the middle [a] central group was made up mainly of those [who had initially moved their chairs to join the main group].

In this way, within 15 seconds, the division had been made without any conscious decision as to how it should be done.[104]

This nearly instantaneous formation of three groups from a larger group of 29, with virtually no direction, illustrates the tremendously sophisticated, yet subtle networking that occurs among people during group dynamics.

But what followed was more amazing. It illustrates how profoundly each of the three groups was affected by the seemingly insignificant events leading to their creation. Groups X and Z were the two groups that independently initiated formation in opposite directions, leaving the remaining Y group 'stranded.' Initially, Y members had the painful task of facing each other, perceiving themselves as being the conference rejects.

Group X members felt guilt at being responsible for Y, and early on sent envoys to ask if Y wanted to redo the initial group selection. This was not done, but it did serve to help bring Y out of its malaise, and to work with X to develop the task.

The third group, Z, also felt guilt for having stranded Y, but reacted in a totally different way. Members became insular and withdrawn, leaving the formative work for completion of the assigned task to the other two groups. In turn, Z absorbed the emotional energy resulting from the projected guilt of the other two groups. The researchers interpreted this as transference of emotional group maintenance work to Z. This allowed the other two groups to cooperate and concentrate on the rational work task at a higher level than would have otherwise been possible. They had been freed of the efforts to develop their own groups' emotional maintenance.

Bion's Theory

Stories about group dynamics, as illustrated by groups X, Y and Z, are fascinating. They can be, however, merely anecdotal without some theoretical sense of the underlying psychological and social relationships. To help understand the underlying behavioral dynamics of this example, Tavistock researchers used group psychotherapy theory, developed in the 1950s by their colleague, Wilfred Bion.

Bion's theory distinguishes between *two levels of activity* within a group: *emotional* and *rational*. The emotional aspect has elements that are conceptually similar to Maslow's hierarchy of needs for individuals, as well as Freud's work on underlying motivations. They consist of three basic instincts: *dependence, fight/flight,* and *pairing.*[xxvii]

[xxvii] Bion calls them basic assumptions. To aid exposition, we take liberties with the technical definition of 'instincts,' extending the general concept (from individuals) to groups. His original symbols were *baD (dependence), baF (fight-flight), baP (pairing),* and *W (work task).*

Dependence surfaces in most business environments—e.g., 'Someone tell me the job tasks, and I'll do them.' *Fight/flight* surfaces in new situations, where physical and safety needs are uncertain. Groups come together to strengthen positions for attack or retreat, as necessary. *Pairing* occurs when two members carry on secondary conversations that are tolerated and listened to attentively by remaining group members—believed to be a primitive group preservation mechanism.[105]

These three basic group instincts are theorized to provide a fundamental adaptive mechanism for group survival until successful group behaviors and new inner resources can evolve. It is theorized that the basic instincts will not conflict with each other in practice. As one instinct becomes active in combination with actual task work, the others are suppressed—somewhat similar to Maslow's hierarchy of needs theory. The group tends to employ the basic instinctual behaviors necessary for work task situations.

Interpretation of X, Y and Z Behaviors

The exercise as a whole was carried out using a *fight/flight-work task combination*.[106] The fight/flight-work task climate had been caused by the ambiguity of the task and the shock of the initial breakup. The emotional fight/flight instinct manifested itself several ways: in the initial aggression of the 'abandoned' group Y, in the attempt at appeasement by group X, and in the emotional withdrawal of group Z. X (who believed Z had initiated the injustice) and Y (the aggrieved) were able to sufficiently shed the emotional burdens by projecting guilt onto Z. In turn, Z willingly, though not necessarily consciously, accepted the debilitating acceptance of guilt and withdrew from active competition for task ideas.

In this manner, the three groups took an equal share in the work of the whole conference. There were two fundamental functions: the 'rational' planning task, and the containment of the basic emotional group instincts. X and Y were able to handle the primary work task through the 'fight' side of the *fight/flight* instinct assumption. Z carried the main emotional burden by 'flight'—by making no real contribution to the task—and by taking on the emotional burdens.

In most life situations basic instincts for group survival are theorized to coexist with task requirements. The social challenge is to find a way for allowing the emotional and work tasks to be carried on concurrently. This was successfully accomplished in our examples by separating these tasks by subgroup for this conference.[107]

Does an Organization Have a Personality?

Both Sigmund Freud and Wilfred Bion have implied, in their psychoanalytic studies, that individual and group psychology might constitute the same field of study.[108] Yet, individuals and groups are different. Individuals have independent, sophisticated personalities when entering groups. They have developed their views and concepts from experience. They have assimilated assumptions, beliefs and behavioral patterns that tend to work when coping with different situations. It is not likely that they 'forget' all they have learned when joining a group, and that they will become mere pawns subsumed in the initially primitive group mentality.

It is more likely, as inferred from Edgar Schein's work of organizational culture, that the group or organization develops its culture (i.e., its group personality) somewhat similar to individual development—but with much greater disparity among its components. As an organization grows and matures, it forms underlying assumptions about its purpose, and develops values and goals to help direct and coordinate activities. The organizational culture and group mentality will espouse values and goals that promote its welfare concerning its collective primary tasks. It will react to situational demands in ways that help preserve its survival and growth.

This does not imply that the organizational mentality replaces that of the individual members. Group behavior will almost certainly be different from that of individual members, each with their own agenda. Group membership is only a part of their psychological and social makeup. For complex issues, group decision may even seem irrational for the individual's perspective. While organizations are composed of unique individual members, those members can belong to many organizations.

Individuals, however, will likely tend to comply with the group mentality within reason (e.g., to preserve their employment, among other things). The implications are that organizational change alternatives should consider not only the potential impacts on the organizational culture (i.e., will the changes work), but also the limits individuals are willing to accept (i.e., will they leave or subvert innovation efforts for personal reasons).

Sociotechnical Principles

From the above studies and many others, several useful *sociotechnical principles* have been developed by Albert Cherns, shown in *Exhibit 6-1*.[109]

Chern's principles are, admittedly, not all-inclusive. For example, they do not deal directly with measurements of effectiveness and efficiency. Further, the principles do not help us gauge the degree of 'congruence' needed, or provide feasible quantitative measures of ranges of values among complexity, structure and processes. However, such scales, if developed, could have significant implications for business case analysis, as shown in Chapter 7.

Exhibit 6-1

Principles of Sociotechnical Design
(adapted from Albert Cherns, 1976)

Compatibility	Processes should match complexity. (e.g., more flexible for dynamic situations; more structured for routine, low variability situations).
Minimum Critical Specification	Ensure that essential tasks are identified. (but avoid micromanagement—strict compliance of too many rules can stop the entire process).
Sociotechnical Criterion	Control problems near their source. (e.g., quality folks advocate preventive rather than corrective inspections—encouraged by trust and good information).
Multifunction Principle	Redundancy of skills is often more efficient than fractionalized processes from overspecialization. (this principle enables *minimum-critical specification*)
Boundary Location	Effective activities have boundaries separating internal selective competence and external coordination. (effective groups optimize social and technical needs; managers help with boundary maintenance to protect activities and coordinate relationships between them).
Information Flow	Information should be appropriate to task roles. (e.g.. detailed transaction data for operations; executive summaries for top management).
Support Congruence	Organizational form should support complexity needs. (e.g., more decentralized decisions for complex tasks; more structured rules for simple, routine tasks).
Feedback	Motivation from meaningful work. (i.e., behavioral science shows greater support motivation when there is knowledge about overall value of the processes, individual responsibility and credit, and reinforcing feedback about outcomes).
Continual Improvement	Organizations are always changing (i.e., final design of structure and process requires continual, ongoing efforts).

[98] E. Trist and K. Bamforth (1951). Some social and psychological consequences of the longwall method of coal getting. *Human Relations,* 4 (1), 3–11.

[99] E. Miller (1975). Socio-technical systems in weaving, 1953–1970. *Human Relations,* 28, 349–386, in W. Pasmore and J. Sherwood (1978), *Socio-technical Systems: a Sourcebook* (p. 272). La Jolla, CA: University Associates, Inc.

[100] A. Rice (1955). Productivity and social organization in an Indian weaving shed. *Human Relations,* 6 (4), 309–310.

[101] Ibid., pp. 319–327.

[102] E. Miller (1975), p. 277.

[103] Ibid., p. 285.

[104] G. Higgin & H. Bridger (1990). The psycho-dynamics of an intergroup experience. Cited from: E. Trist and H. Murray (eds.), *The Social Engagement of Social Science: A Tavistock Anthology, Volume I* (pp. 199–202). Philadelphia: University of Pennsylvania Press.

[105] J. Sutherland (1990). Bion revisited. Cited from: E. Trist and H. Murray (eds.), *The Social Engagement of Social Science: A Tavistock Anthology, Volume I* (p. 121). Philadelphia: University of Pennsylvania Press.

[106] Higgin (1990), p. 218.

[107] Ibid., p. 291.

[108] Sutherland (1990), p. 129.

[109] A. Cherns (1976). The principles of socio-technical design. *Human Relations* 8, 785–791.

CHAPTER SEVEN

Implications for
Business Case Analysis

7

A favorite theory is a possession for life.
William Hazlitt (circa 1820)

It has been shown that the organization is subject to many influences, both internal and external. Contingencies from the work task establish the 'what' and 'how to' of needed organizational performance. These include the variety of skills and the stability of tasks. Additionally, organizations exist in larger systems and are influenced by the external environment. To survive, organizations must develop the ability to detect and interpret these internal and external environmental cues and to adapt appropriately.

The question becomes: What are the most promising adaptations? What are the strategic objectives, and what organizational programs are most likely to help foster movement toward improved performance? These are precisely the types of decisions that can be adapted to a socio-technical application. The key consideration is adaptation of the social system to be both aware and motivated to seek adaptive solutions.

The social system is defined herein as organizational *structure* and *process*. All social systems can be conceptualized to consist of patterned activities that are complementary or interdependent with respect to some common output. The degree to which these activities are repeated, relatively enduring and bounded in time is hypothesized to depend upon the complexity of the production task. The level of task complexity has significant influence on the stability of the patterns. By measuring the degree of complexity (i.e., the extent that patterns are repeatable and relatively enduring), tenets of sociotechnical theory indicate that appropriate levels of organizational *structure* and *process* can be adapted to improve effectiveness.

Structure

Structure is defined as the formalized, standardized, and officially sanctioned set of policies and procedures. Under 'norms of rationality,' organizations are hypothesized to codify procedures that will minimize required performance variations and associated costs.[110] As organizations seek to improve abilities for surveillance and control, they develop centralized rules over the activities that have become segmented and specialized. This *integration* of rules is necessary to ensure that key role occupants can get needed information to perform their subtasks. At the same time, most roles are limited to the prescribed needed behaviors—*structure* acts as a management tool to limit the individual's discretion.

But *differentiation* is essential for organizations operating in complex task environments. They tend to move toward a decentralization of rules to meet contingencies and attain required mobility and flexibility. This implies a need for increasing discretion for decisions made at sources closest to problem origins. This has implications for when, say, a highly decentralized management system makes sense, and when it might not. It implies that effective policies and procedures will be balanced to simultaneously seek required integration (more centralized structure) to control coordination costs, and required differentiation (more decentralized structure) to promote needed decision flexibility. *Exhibit 7-1* illustrates this notion. As the degree of task complexity increases, the requirement for decentralization and allowing more individual decision discretion also increases. The corollary is also implied: as complexity decreases, more bureaucratic structure is required to minimize coordination costs.

Exhibit 7-1

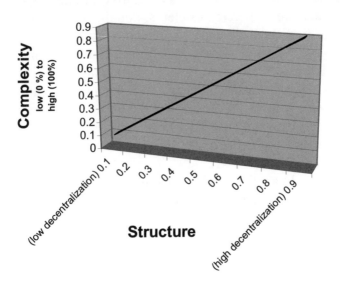

Required Structure Decentralization
(Increases as Task Complexity Increases)

There is evidence in the management literature to support this proposition. For example, D. S. Pugh, et al. (1968) studied the degree of *structure* in 52 manufacturing firms. They constructed 64 scales of organizational structural attributes to measure what were thought to be five primary variables of *structure*. These five variables are: (1) specialization (degree roles are prescribed), (2) standardization (extent that rules apply across all roles), (3) formalization (degree to which rules are written), (4) centralization of authority, and (5) management structure (line/staff ratios and administrative intensity).[111]

When tested, using statistical factor analysis of responses to the 64 scales, they actually found four dimensions of structure: the degree of role prescription, centralization of authority, standardization (degree of impersonal/written procedures), and relative size of support components (e.g., percent of clerks, nondirect labor, and so on) The first three dimensions explained two-thirds of the response variance. From this, presumably to handle complexities of various manufacturing situations, the researchers hypothesized taxonomy of potential organizational types—from very unstructured (unstructured rules, dispersed decision authority, decentralized control) to highly structured (structured rules, concentrated authority, centralized control).[112]

In another study of 19 manufacturing organizations, Bernard Reimann (1974) distilled three dimensions of structure from eleven core scales (including formality of rules, required functional specialization, degree of delegation of authority, amount of hierarchical control at each level, administrative density to line supervisors, degree of employee equity in dispersion of functional assignments, vertical span of control, and so on). The three structure dimensions were decentralization of authority, degree of required worker specialization, and formality of rules resulting in reduced decision autonomy.

Both studies indicate that social structure varies with the situation. Further, Joan Woodward's speculations that types of *manufacturing organizations* evolve in response to technology demands, and Thompson's for *services organizations* provide intuitive evidence that the nature of the organization's task (i.e., task complexity) is a key determinant of structural requirements.

Process

Structure thus far has been considered as the established pattern of relationships among components or parts of the organization. *Process* is considered as not so much the pattern, but rather the dynamic functioning between and among organizational subsystems—a separate and distinct function.[113] *Structure* provides the formal lines of authority and division of labor; assigns obligations, prerogatives, and responsibilities to organization members; facilitates certain kinds of communications and interactions; and channels human behavior.[114] *Process* takes place within the defined *structure,* and consists of interpersonal and intergroup types of behavior, including vertical and horizontal communications, face-to-face interactions, conflicts, power, formal and informal influences, and behavioral rewards. *Process* behaviors cement the patterns of relationships; behaviors that are anchored in attitudes, perceptions, beliefs, motivations, habits and expectations.[115]

While there is no consensus of what variables comprise *process*, several have consistently appeared, including decision making, coordination, control, leadership and motivation. All can be seen as influencing discretion to make decisions and interact with job tasks.

Process, in a manner similar to *structure*, is hypothetically related to task complexity. The situational conditions that influence policies and procedures also influence perceived trust, motivation and discretion of individuals who make decisions. It implies that collective behaviors of the *process* will adapt to and be constrained by implied acceptable behaviors for a given *structure*. As the degree of task complexity increases, the implications are that requirements for a process that allows more individual decision discretion also increase. *Exhibit 7-2* illustrates this notion.

The corollary is also implied: as complexity decreases, less individual decision discretion is required to minimize coordination costs.

Exhibit 7-2

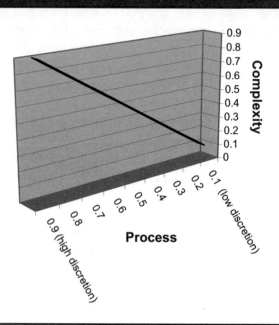

Combined Relationships of Structure, Process and Complexity

Work with the human side of the sociotechnical equation implies that effective organizations are only partially directed by a *technical imperative*. A *social imperative* might have an equally important role. Matching social system conditions (i.e., to elicit required human motivation and behavior) to task complexity requirements seems a promising approach for helping ensure successful organizational performance and adaptability.

When matching the organization's social system to the task environment, use of both structure and process are helpful. Organizational *structure* coordinates overall efforts and prescribes expected behaviors among workers and work groups. Organizational *process* consists of the set informal rules that workers generally abide by as they perform specific work tasks.

As implied above, *structure* and *process* will be related to the task *complexity* of the work situation. Complexity, of course, can emanate from both external and internal sources. For example, from the Indian textile mills research (see Chapter 5), the regression of Jubilee automated processes into more primitive forms due to governmental policies provides an example of complexity induced from external sources.[116] An example of internal complexity is the nearly infinite variety of task actions seen in modern hospitals. Another example is the very complex total system integration requirements of continuous manufacturing processes where total operations can be significantly disrupted by aberrations to small, tightly integrated process steps. Failure of any sequential step causes instability of overall throughput.

Given these relationships, it seems reasonable that the more successful organizations will seek to align appropriate organizational *structure* and *process* factors that complement task complexity. Where there is high task complexity, organizational structure and process become agile and flexible to prevent excessive lost *opportunity costs*. This implies the need for a more tolerant form of formal organization *structure* where rules are not set in concrete, honest mistakes are tolerated, and individuals are expected to 'buck the system' when convinced that things are wrong. This also implies need for *process* discretion that allows a requisite variety of responses to new problems. Perhaps this calls for decentralized rules and discretion to make decisions near the sources of problems.

Where tasks are more routine and predictable, more bureaucratic organizational structure might be appropriate to help reduce coordination costs. This implies a need for closer adherence to business rules and routines to ensure relatively smooth interfaces among sequential and parallel process steps. Centralized, mechanistic decision processes might be more appropriate to coordinate different aspects of operations. Also, the need for more comprehensive management information systems might be required to provide feedback on productivity.

Relationships among organizational structure, processes and task complexity are theoretically interrelated. Organizational structure and processes develop in response to complexity of technical demands. In turn, under the proper conditions, organizations can also influence the complexity of the task environment. These relationships are as follows.

The decision process provides the relatively informal responses to situational needs. Processes are partially controlled by the formal rules of organizational structure in order to ensure needed control and coordination. In turn, processes can influence structure when, over time, performance declines due to rules that are too stringent (i.e., the rules get in the way), or are too laissez faire.

Finally, both organizational structure and processes are influence by and can influence technical complexity. Internal complexity can sometimes be adapted to by enabling the technical processes with proper materials, training and scheduling. External complexity can sometimes be mitigated by a series of competitive strategies, including better technology, product innovations, and superior performance through bargaining leverage with suppliers and customers. Also, larger coalitions among organizations can evolve into institutional barriers to competitors due to capital requirements or close-held proprietary technology.[117]

The theoretical relationships among organizational structure, processes and task complexity are illustrated in *Exhibit 7-3*.[118]

Exhibit 7-3

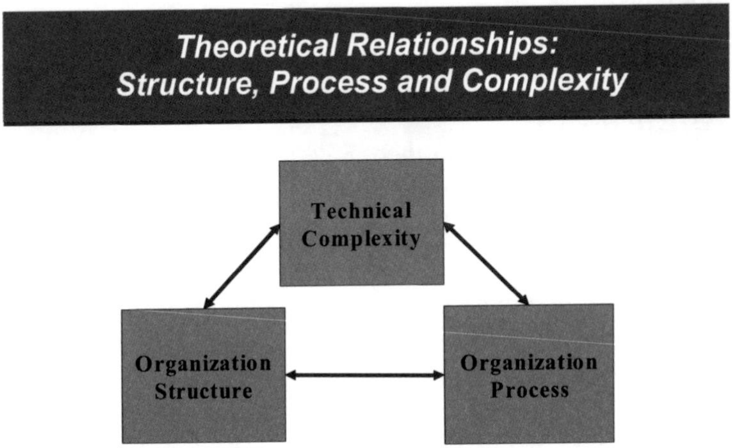

Theoretical Relationships:
Structure, Process and Complexity

Technical Complexity

Organization Structure

Organization Process

Given the integrative nature of these relationships, the question becomes how to establish measurements to calibrate these three factors. This is really a question of what level of effectiveness is appropriate, and what level of efficiency is achievable. *Effectiveness* relates to 'doing the right things.' For example, are the products and outputs needed, and within the technical range of this organization? Efficiency deals with 'doing things right.' The objective is to calibrate the efficiency and effectiveness goals so that costs of production are minimized for the required level and quality of output.

Exhibit 7-4 illustrates a model relating organizational effectiveness and efficiency, given environmental demands.[119]

Exhibit 7-4

A Model of Organizational Performance		
	Internal	*External*
Efficiency *Calibrate*	*Internal processes*	*Bargaining position: suppliers/customers*
Effectiveness *Maximize*	*Member motivation*	*Societal satisfaction*

Using the interdependencies of organizational *structure* and *process* with task *complexity* (i.e., *Exhibits 7-1* and *7-2*), and the model of performance (i.e., *Exhibit 7-4*), it is possible to develop a model of potentially successful organizations for various levels of situational complexity. Sociotechnical principles can help develop scales to measure existing (as is) organizational conditions, and provide insights on potentially rewarding directions for change toward (to be) ideal states. *Exhibit 7-5*, using a theoretical sociotechnical grid model, illustrates three hypothetical examples.

Exhibit 7-5

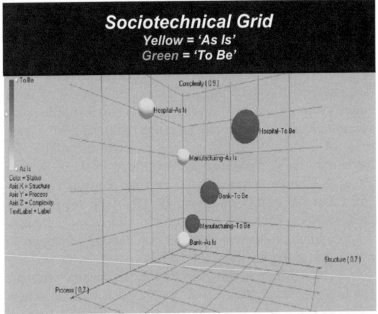

Type of Business	Structure 0%=Centralized 100%=Decentralized	Process 0%=Less Discretionary 100%=More Discretionary	Complexity 0%=Not Complex 100%= Very Complex
Manufacturing --As Is	20%	20%	70%
--To Be	33%	33%	33%
Bank --As Is	20%	20%	20%
--To Be	50%	50%	50%
Hospital --As Is	20%	50%	90%
--To Be	70%	70%	70%

These examples are adapted from the three organizational types described in Chapter 5 from Thompson (1967): long-linked (e.g., routine manufacturing), mediating (e.g., banks) and intensive (e.g., hospitals).

Sociotechnical Grid Model Interpretation

The three hypothetical types business represented in *Exhibit 7-5* are a *manufacturing* concern, a *bank* and a *hospital.* To illustrate the usefulness of a sociotechnical classification, suppose the 'as is' *complexity* conditions for *manufacturing* is measured as quite high (i.e., 70% on a scale of 0 %$_{(low)}$ to 100% $_{(high)}$). Subjective techniques for developing such measures are illustrated later, in Section III of this book. Assume that a process analysis has indicated that the sources of the complexity were due to inefficiencies like poor inventory control, micromanagement, inappropriate production feedback 'up the line,' fragmented processes 'along the line,' and so on.

Now, if a highly successful benchmark example (such as the successful Calico textile plant reorganization, from Rice's study) could be used, its successful features might serve to target improvements and repair the fragmented processes. Improvements to the structure (e.g., less micromanagement, better inventory control), and processes (e.g., better feedback and information to inform workers about situational needs) might help lower the overall system complexity.

Let us assume, by using appropriate measurement scales developed from sociotechnical principles, that the desired level of complexity for successful 'like-type' manufacturing is around 33%. Setting this as the new 'to be' goal, management adaptations might be planned and implemented to improve both structure and process problems. With these improvements, the 'to be' structure and process measurements might each be targeted to increase from 20%

to 33%, respectively. The plan might require adding more coordination rules and permitting less individual discretion. The working hypothesis would be that, given this intervention strategy, end-state system complexity would be reduced, hopefully toward a congruent goal of 33% (from the 'as is' of 70% for fragmented processes).

The results of these adaptations would be consistently monitored for both efficiency (resource consumption) and effectiveness (quality production standards). As progress is made toward reducing complexity, positive feedback would help reinforce that the new system makes sense. Over time, as workers buy into the new system, these measurements can become part of the culture of 'what works,' and become self-sustaining.

Similar analyses can be made for the other two cases illustrated in *Exhibit 7-5*. For *banks*, in the example, 'as is' situation, complexity is too low (i.e., 20%) relative to needed capabilities of 50%. This might impact customer relations due to such things as rude, bored bank tellers with too little incentive, lack of teller information about how to introduce customers to other bank services, or lack of training to handle account problems. More situational awareness training and decision flexibility might help increase the scales for process, structure and complexity up to, say, a benchmark target of 50% for all.

The *hospital* represents the most complex example in *Exhibit 7-5*. Complexity of the 'as is' is depicted as very high, yet management structure is depicted as too bureaucratic (at 20% there are too many rules), and processes too moderate (at 50% there is not enough discretion for professionals to make decisions, perhaps needlessly delaying patient processes). The need for a management innovation program to bring more flexibility to both structure and process (i.e., team training, technical training, management training, and so forth) is indicated.

The central theme is that examination of enterprise situational complexity can provide clues about what form of organization (i.e., concerning structure and processes) would be a good fit to help satisfy demands from its task environment. This type analysis can help determine the 'as is' starting point for business case analysis, and provide a conceptual benchmark for a 'to be' organization. The measurements of the 'as is' conditions can be matched against 'to be' objectives to establish plans for innovation projects. As plans are implemented, results can be monitored to determine progress toward 'to be' objective efficiency and effectiveness measures.

A key notion is the ability to measure both 'as is' and 'to be' situations, as well as feedback progress when developing a business case alternative. Management science/operations research techniques can provide many of the necessary tools for measurement of physical tasks such as efficient production, inventory and distribution techniques. Social science techniques can help capture subjective measures such as human decision processes (e.g., using Likert scales and expert systems). To provide insight for these measurement approaches, a comprehensive overview of such techniques is presented next in Section III, *Techniques and Applications*.

---

[110] J. Thompson (1967). *Organizations In Action*. New York: McGraw Hill Book Company, p. 78.

[111] D. Pugh, D. Hickson, C. Hinings, and C. Turner (1968). Dimensions of organizational structure. *Administrative Science Quarterly*, 13 (1), 73–76.

[112] Ibid., p. 115.

[113] F. Kast and J. Rosensweig (1974). *Organization and Management: a Systems View* (2nd ed.). New York: McGraw Hill, Inc., p. 207.

[114] D. Nightingale and J. Toulouse (1982). Toward a multi-level congruence theory of organization. *Administrative Science Quarterly*, 22 (2), 264–280.

[115] D. Katz and R. Kahn (1966). *The Social Psychology of Organizations*. New York: John Wiley & Sons, Inc., p. 33.

[116] E. Miller (1975).

[117] M. Porter (1980). *Competitive Strategy: Techniques for Analyzing Industries and Competitors*. New York: The Free Press, p. 4.

[118] D. Gillespie and D. Mileti (1977). Adapted from: Technology and the study of organizations: an overview and appraisal. *Academy of Management Review*, 2 (1), 13.

[119] D. Jacobs (1974). Adapted from: Dependency and vulnerability: an exchange approach to the control of organizations. *Administrative Science Quarterly*, 19 (1), 48.

He that will not apply new remedies must expect new evils.
Francis Bacon (circa 1616)

III

TECHNIQUES

Methods of Measurement

Waste not, want not.
Ben Franklin (circa 1780)

CHAPTER EIGHT

Economic Analysis

8

Take care of the pence, and the pounds will take care of themselves.

Benjamin Franklin (circa 1780)

Economic analysis provides fundamental quantitative tools for financial evaluations of business case alternatives. It provides a systematic approach for choosing how to employ scarce resources to achieve specific objects. Its purpose is to focus on cost-effective selection of the best alternative, given the several that are developed in the initial stages of the BCA.

In the 8-Day BCA exercise (Chapter 1), the economic analysis questions were relatively simple. In that example it became obvious that investment actions would become necessary due to the growing obsolescence of older PCs. The alternatives were: do nothing, try to refurbish the older machines, or acquire new ones. Refurbishment was ruled out for technical reasons; the older PCs were too out of date and refurbishment would not help much. This left two alternatives: do nothing (i.e., keep the status quo until another budget cycle or so) or acquire replacements. It was assumed that under the do nothing option (status quo), productive deterioration would continue at the same rate (i.e.,

10% growth per year). Further, it was determined (through expert opinion) that new PCs would improve reliability, thus reducing maintenance and lost productivity costs by 75%. The economic life of a new PC was determined to be approximately three years. Therefore, the financial focus was for payback or recuperation of investment in that time period. Calculations showed that improved reliability would generate breakeven savings within two years, and the additional benefits for the third year clearly favored acquisition of new PCs.

Finally, there were two options for acquisition: buy (cash up-front) or lease-to-own (cash outlays spread over 24 months). After shopping for best prices, the most competitive vendor offered a group purchase of PCs under two options, buy now, or lease-to-own with no interest if payments were completed in 24 months (i.e., 1/3 down, with two additional 1/3 payments in one and two years, respectively). Assuming a moderate discount rate of 4.1% (the present value of future payments in cheaper dollars, from OMB Circular A94), the lease buy was calculated to be marginally preferred.

The analytical steps that were used to make these calculations are surprisingly robust, and can be found at the roots of even the most complex business case analyses. They basically involve making quantitative evaluations of three key considerations: *profitability*, *sustainability* of operations, and the *hurdle rate* (opportunity cost of not investing elsewhere).

Profitability deals with assumptions that expected benefits exceed costs (a positive benefit/cost ratio), and will continue to do so in the future. As mentioned in the 8-Day BCA example, new PCs were determined, by expert opinion, to have approximately a three-year useful economic life.

Sustainability assumes that productive processes will remain competitive. As time goes on, investments are required for maintenance or replacements of facilities, machinery, worker skills, and so on, to avoid harmful deterioration of productive capacity. Again, in the PC example, it was assumed that the annual 10% deterioration rate would continue as the percentage of potential savings was calculated.

The *hurdle rate* provides the third key principle. Any ongoing business, in an economic sense, should be able to generate a higher *internal rate of return* than funds can generate if invested outside the concern. In the long run, keeping a business concern that provides less return on investment is not in the interest of investor, managers or workers whose contributions could be more handsomely rewarded elsewhere. For the PC example, this factor was considered in the dual notions of no interest rate charged for the leased time payments, as well as the implied external rate of return of 4.1% from the OMB circular.

Taken together, these three principles form the basis for determining the best economic alternatives for capital investment decisions. So long as the fundamentals of capital infrastructure (e.g., plants, machines, worker skills) can be developed and sustained at a competitive level to provide profits, a positive internal rate of return is supported. And, so long as the internal rate of return exceeds advantages of investing funds elsewhere (i.e., the hurdle rate), selection of a particular investment alternative makes economic sense. We now examine techniques for evaluating alternatives using these key factors.

Concept of Present Value

Estimating the internal rate of return on investments is the first step for comparing alternatives. To allow comparisons among alternatives, the notion of the 'time value of money' is almost universally used. As we saw in comparison of the

buy versus lease alternatives in the 8-Day BCA, the calculation of *present value* for each alternative was used. The
present value notion allows 'apples-to-apples' comparisons
of the different alternatives to evaluate total expected benefits and costs in *today's dollars*. This is essential, since
comparisons must be made 'today' that will be in effect
over the economic life of the chosen alternative. Using estimates of total net effects of future costs helps quantify
these comparisons of cash flows.

By the mid-1970s, nearly all major U.S. corporations had incorporated highly sophisticated analysis techniques using present value calculations to allow comparison of expected internal rates of return for alternative investments.[120] The theory is simple. A dollar invested today,
at 5% interest, will be worth $1.05 after a year. Conversely,
at a 5% rate, a dollar received a year from now is worth
only 1 ÷ $1.05 = 95.2 cents today. According to accepted
theory, the present value (i.e., the discounted value of future cash flows based on the expected interest rate) is the
appropriate way to compare future benefits with present
costs.[121]

This notion is easily extended to valuation of investments and the net present values of their future cost and
revenue streams. The alternative with the highest net
present value (e.g., benefit-to-cost ratio or savings-to-
investment ratio) is the preferred selection, assuming other
things (i.e., policies, strategic importance, and so forth) are
equal. The following examples help illustrate the value of
present value comparisons.

Specific Present Value Techniques

Present Value (PV): Equal Economic Lives

The 8-Day BCA illustration in Chapter 1 used this technique for the comparison of the buy and lease alternatives. These calculations were presented in *Exhibit 1-3* and are reproduced here in *Exhibit 8-1* in tabular form.

Exhibit 8-1

Present Value (PV) Projects: Equal Lives
Acquisition Costs for Buy and Lease Alternatives (18 PCs)
Cost = Purchase Price + Acquisition Expense

	Future outlays		PV discount	Present value of future outlays	
	Buy	Lease		Buy	Lease
Year 0	$29,272	$11,727 ($500 x 18 + $2,727)	* 1.0000 =	$29,272	$11,727
Year 1	0	$9,000 ($500 x 18)	* 0.9606 =	0	8,645
Year 2	0	$9,000 ($500 x 18)	* 0.9228 =	0	8,305
Totals				29,727	28,677

$PV = 1/(1+i)^t$

Lease PV Calculations

*Inital (Year 0) Payment: $PV = 1/(1+.041)^0 * $11,727 = 1.0000 * $11,727 = $11,727$*
*End of Year 1: Payment $PV = 1/(1+.041)^1 * $9,000 = .9606 * $9,000 = $8,645$*
*End of Year 2: Payment $PV = 1/(1+.041)^2 * $9,000 = .9228 * $9,000 = $8,305$*

Present Value (PV): Unequal Economic Lives

Assume now that the vendor also offers, in addition to the free first-year warranty, the option to purchase added warranty protection at 10% of the purchase price per year, renewable through the fifth year of ownership. The warranty premium is payable at the beginning of each respective year of coverage. Management is interested in purchasing additional warranty protection to ensure PCs are productive for five years. This makes sense, given the expected three years economic life without a warranty. Due to the unequal periods, management wants to know if the lease option is economically worth pursuing.

A quick method to compare the lease versus lease-with-warranty is to use the *uniform annual cost method,* as shown in *Exhibit 8-2.*[122]

Exhibit 8-2

| **Present Value (PV) Projects: Unequal Lives** |||||
| *Uniform Annual Cost (UAC)* |||||

| | **Future outlays** | | **PV Interest rate = 4.1%** | **Present value of future outlays** | |
	Lease	*With Warranty*		*Lease*	*With Warranty*
Year 1	$11,727	$11,727	* 1.0000 =	$11,727	$11,727
Year 2	9,000	11,700 = 9,000 + 2,700 (27,000 @ 10%)	* 0.9606 =	8,645	11,239
Year 3	9,000	11,700	* 0.9228 =	8,305	10,797
Year 4	0	2,700	* 0.8864 =	0	2,393
Year 5	0	2,700	* 0.8515 =	0	2,299
Totals				$28,677	$38,455
Average Annual Cost (UAC Weighted)				$9,946	$8,321

UAC Calculations

$$PV = 1/(1+i)^t$$

The UAC is calculated by:
1) Summing the discount rates for each total investment period.
   That is: a) for Lease, the UAC factor is 1.0 +.9606 + .9228 = 2.8834.
   b) for Lease with Warranty: 1.0 +.9606 + .9228 + .8864 + .8515 = 4.6213
2) Dividing the total discounted outlays by the UAC factor
   That is: (a) for Lease: $28,677 ÷ 2.8834 = *$9,946,*
           (b) for Lease with Warranty: $38,455 ÷ 4.6213 = *$8,321*

This allows computation of the average annual costs of each alternative over the unequal periods. Even with the additional cumulative costs of 10% per year for each additional warranty year, it is favored due to the lower average annual cost of $8,321 per year versus $9,946 per year without the warranty.

Breakeven Analysis

Breakeven analysis can be useful for determining relative payback periods among alternatives. Breakeven occurs at the point in time where present value of cumulative savings equals costs. Cumulative savings relative to the *lease-to-own* alternative are shown in *Exhibit 8-3*.

Exhibit 8-3

Breakeven Analysis			
Quarter	*Savings* (from Exhibit 1-17)	*Cumulative Savings*	*Breakeven Point*
1	$3,694	$3,694	
2	3,742	7,436	
3	3,839	11,275	
4	3,937	15,212	
5	4,034	19,246	
6	4,131	23,377	
7	4,180	27,557	} $28,677
8	4,277	31,834	

The breakeven value of $28,677 occurs somewhere in the 8th quarter. A breakeven chart graphical representation was presented in *Exhibit 1-19*.

Savings-to-Investment Ratio (SIR)

Using again the 8-Day BCA example, total savings over the three years of expected economic life for new PCs was calculated at $49,865 (see *Exhibit 1-17*). Total acquisition costs for the preferred alternative (lease-to-own) was $28,677 (see *Exhibit 1-3 (b)*). The SIR is calculated simply as $49,865 ÷ $28,677 = 1.74. In other words, this alternative will generate $1.74 cost savings for each $1.00 invested.

Benefit-to-Cost Ratio (BCR)

The benefit-to-cost ratio is a similar concept to the savings-to-investment ratio and distinctions are often not clear. If operationally defined, benefits can be thought of as expected increases in output from the existing resources. Similarly, cost savings can be defined as restoring lost efficiency for existing resources. Using these notions, benefit-to-cost analysis attempts to measure increased effectiveness (i.e., productivity), and savings-to-investment analysis attempts to measure increased efficiency.

An example might help. Assume, from the 8-Day BCA example in Chapter 1 that the 18 workers currently produce 100 widgets per month (1,200 per year). The term *widgets* can represent any type output, such as contracts, manufactured products, overhauled engines, completed customers orders, students trained, and so forth.

Assume further that the average fully loaded cost per worker is $34.67 per hour (see *Exhibit 1-5, Exhibit 1-7* and accompanying text). If 2,080 working hours are available annually per worker (i.e., 40 $_{hour\ week}$ * 52 $_{weeks}$), the total annual cost per worker is $72,114. This multiplied by 18 workers computes to a $1,298,052 payroll. Divided by 12 months, labor costs are approximately $108,000 per month. Considering labor costs only, the cost per unit produced is $108,000 ÷ 100 = $1,080.

Now, suppose acquisition of new PCs is estimated to increase productivity by 10%, to 110 widgets per month with the same labor force. The new cost per unit attributable to labor now becomes $982 (i.e., $108,000 ÷ 110). This represents a reduction in labor cost per unit of $98.

Finally, instead of increasing production to 110 units, management decides that there is only demand for 100 units per month. Planned annual production remains 1,200. But with the program improvements, 1,200 units can now be produced for $1,178,400 (i.e., 1,200 * $982). The status quo (before the program change) production costs attributable to labor are $1,296,000 (i.e., 1,200 * $108,000). The total cost savings is $117,600 per year, more than the cost of 1 ½ workers.

Now, let us compute the *benefit-to-cost ratio*. For the PCs example, the most cost efficient alternative was lease-to-own, with a total acquisition cost of $28,677 (from *Exhibit 1-3*). The BCR is calculated simply as $117,600 ÷ $28,677 = 4.10. In other words, this alternative will generate $4.10 cost savings for each $1.00 invested.

This is a very straightforward example of a benefit-to-cost ratio calculation. It is really too simplistic since it considers only labor costs and PCs as the source of improved outputs. But it does illustrate the power of estimating productivity enhancements. A business case analysis that convincingly estimates potential benefits can be most beneficial, indeed.

Payback Among Multiple Projects

Let's switch hats. Instead of the task of determining the best alternative to acquire PCs, suppose we are now on the other side, with the task of the budget committee in deciding which of multiple projects to fund with a limited budget. *Exhibit 8-4 (a)* shows a listing of several projects that have requested funding for the expected $80,000 budget:

Exhibit 8-4 (a)

Competing Projects

Project	Annual Savings	Present Value of Investment
A	$ 16,622	$ 28,677
B	$ 3,230	$ 13,000
C	$ 1,912	$ 6,000
D	$ 20,288	$ 32,000
E	$ 1,600	$ 9,000
Total Budget = $80,000		

As one indicator, the committee might favorably consider projects with shorter payback periods. This comparison can be made when the estimated savings are relatively constant throughout the economic life of the project. Dividing the present value of the investment by the estimate of annual savings approximates the relative payback periods. Projects can then be ranked based on the quickest payback using the appropriate present value (i.e., cumulative discount) factor.

For example, annual savings and investment costs for Project A in *Exhibit 8-4 (a)* are derived from the 8-Day BCA PC example. The average annual cost avoidance (i.e., savings) calculation is $49,865 ÷ 3 years = $16,622 (see *Exhibit 1-17*). The present value of acquisition cost is $28,677 (see *Exhibit 1-3*). The estimated payback period is calculated by $28,677 ÷ $16,622 = 1.73 years or about 21 months.[xxviii]

Next, the Uniform Annual Cost (UAC) payback factors are derived for continuous years using the 4.1% interest rate, as seen in *Exhibit 8-4 (b)*.

Exhibit 8-4 (b)

Uniform Annual Cost (UAC) Factors

Beginning of Year	Cumulative Discounts $PV = 1/(1+i)^t$							Implied Payback Value
1	1.00							1.00
2	1.00	+.96						1.96
3	1.00	+.96	+.92					2.88
4	1.00	+.96	+.92	+.89				3.77
5	1.00	+.96	+.92	+.89	+.85			4.62
6	1.00	+.96	+.92	+.89	+.85	+.82		5.44
7	1.00	+.96	+.92	+.89	+.85	+.82	+.79	6.23

Discount values for a continuous 4.1% interest rate.

Finally, in *Exhibit 8-4 (c)* the projects are rank-ordered by quickest payback ratios. These calculations are used similarly to the unequal economic life comparisons between alternatives, but are now generalized to multiple projects. Note that the Project A value of 1.74 falls between implied

---

[xxviii] This is slightly less that the detailed payback calculation of 23 months due to the averaging of the three years versus actual trend values, but allows for an accurate rule of thumb with other projects.

payback times of 1.00 and 1.96, or one to two years (from *Exhibit 8-4 (b)*). Similar calculations are made for other projects, which are then rank ordered according to the quickest payback criterion.

Exhibit 8-4 (c)

Rank Order Projects by Quickest Payback
Uniform Annual Cost (UAC) Calculations for $80,000 Budget

Rank	Project	Payback Factor	Payback between years:	Investment	Cumulative Investment
1	D	1.58	1 – 2	$ 32,000	$32,000
2	A	1.74	1 – 2	$ 28,677	60,677
3	C	3.14	3 – 4	$ 6,000	66,677
4	B	4.02	4 – 5	$ 13,000	79,677
5	E	5.62	6 – 7	$ 9,000	Not Funded

Total Budget = $80,000: Funding allocated to four of the five projects.	Project	Payback factors
	A	$28,677 ÷ $16,677 = 1.74
	B	13,000 ÷ 3,230 = 4.02
	C	6,000 ÷ 1,912 = 3.14
	D	32,000 ÷ 20,288 = 1.58
	E	9,000 ÷ 1,600 = 5.62

Direct Breakeven Calculation

Having developed the cumulative discount values, we can now demonstrate their use for another function, direct calculation of an investment breakeven value. In *Exhibit 8-1* we calculated the most cost-effective option between the buy and lease alternatives. The lease alternative was found to be the most advantageous. Suppose now that the vendor wishes to impose an interest charge, and you want to calculate if this additional cost elevates total acquisition costs for lease beyond that of buy, making the buy alternative the now preferred option. One way to achieve this is to find the breakeven point where the buy and lease alternatives are equal. Then, if the new interest charges for lease elevate its present value above the buy alternative, the recommended cost efficient solution would change to buy. Calculations are shown in *Exhibit 8-5*.

Exhibit 8-5

Direct Breakeven Calculation
Acquisition Costs for Buy and Lease Alternatives (18 PCs)

	Future outlays		PV discount	Present value of future outlays	
	Buy	Lease		Buy	Lease
Year 0	$29,272	$11,727 ($500 x 18 + $2,727)	* 1.0000 =	$29,727	$11,727
Year 1	0	$9,000 ($500 x 18)	* 0.9606 =	0	8,645
Year 2	0	$9,000 ($500 x 18)	* 0.9228 =	0	8,305
Totals				29,727	28,677

Recall from *Exhibit 8-1* (reproduced above) that the present value (PV) of the lease alternative was more cost efficient over the two-year payment schedule. We can calculate the exact breakeven point (i.e., how much the lease alternative cost can increase) to exactly equal the buy cost. This is the point that the present value costs of both alternatives are equal. The equations are:

Allowable total cost increase:
$$PV (_{lease}) = PV (_{buy})$$
$$\$28,677 + x = \$29,727$$
$$x = \$29,272 - \$28,677 = \$1,050$$
(This agrees with the tabular solution. See *Exhibit 1-3*.)

Allowable period (i.e., annual) cost increase:
$2,727 Acquisition Cost + Three Payments of $9000
$$PV (_{lease}) = PV (_{buy})$$
$$\$2,727 + (\$9,000 + x) * 2.8837 \text{ (cumulative discount factor)} = \$29,272$$
$$\$9,000 + x = (\$29,727 - \$2,727) \div 2.8837$$
$$\$9,000 + x = \$27,000 \div 2.8837$$
$$x = \$ 9,363 - \$9,000$$
$$x = \$363$$

So, annual lease costs can increase to $9,000 + $363 before exceeding the average annual value of the buy alternative.

Strategic Capital Investments

Few investments, such as the replacement of PCs in our 8-Day BCA example in Chapter 1, are intended as final solutions. Managers usually assume that at the end of a current investment's economic lifetime, another cycle of maintenance and upgrades will follow. Key decisions concern the long-term objectives of the organization. Long-term strategies can range from maintaining existing capabilities (efficiency), to enhancing capabilities (productivity), to phasing out certain operations that are becoming non-competitive. There are many strategic planning methods to assess a company's strategic goals. *Once these strategic goals are established*, there are economic analysis approaches to guide operations and tactics toward ultimate objectives.

Maintaining Existing Capabilities

Assume the strategy is to maintain current proficiencies. This implies a need for reinvestment in the capital infrastructure at a sufficient rate to sustain current productivity. Take, for example, the potential investment in new PCs in the 8-Day BCA. The present value total costs of the status quo alternative (i.e., no new investment in new PCs) yielded present value costs of $66.49 thousand over three years, or about $22.16 thousand per year (i.e., 66,487 ÷ 3: see *Exhibit 1-17*). This was the total cost of use with no new capital investments. New PCs were estimated to yield a cost avoidance savings of 75%, for an average of $16.62 thousand (i.e., $49,865 ÷ 3) per year over the economic life of the investment. This investment opportunity produces average savings (i.e., reduces cost of use) sufficiently to repay the acquisition capital investment of $28.68 thousand for the lease alternative in about two years (*Exhibit 1-25*).

The original 8-Day BCA analysis evaluated acquisitions based on the expected three-year economic life of the new set of PCs. With a couple of additional assumptions[xxix], the present value of $28.68 thousand could be considered as a perpetual annual capital stock investment requirement, for restoring and then maintaining lost efficiency. The implied replacement costs to maintain this continual renewal of the $28.68 thousand capital investment is $9.56 thousand ($28.68 ÷ 3). That is, since the PCs are replaced every three years at a present value cost of $28.68 thousand, the annual budget to avoid deterioration of productive capabilities implies a continual annual investment of $9.56 thousand as a maintenance cost.

We can now calculate the total return on investment for continually upgrading PC systems at $49,865 (*see Exhibit 1-17*). The current productive system, if maintained, yields annual savings of approximately $16.62 ($49.865 ÷ 3) thousand relative to non-upgraded systems. Subtracting the maintenance cost from the total savings yields a net savings of $7.06 thousand per year (i.e., $16.62 − $9.56). This is the amount of savings above that required to maintain the current system productivity, and represents avoided costs for system sustainability that can now be used for other purposes. Funds that would have been consumed can now be used a number of ways, such as offsets to other expenses or acquisition of other capabilities.

[xxix] Assumptions might include: 1) that the older PCs will have no net residual value after three years. This could happen if the cost of disposal equals the scrap value. 2) The present value of the replacement technology will remain relatively constant. PCs may continue to become cheaper for the same technology, but the assumption is that more and more sophisticated systems will be demanded, keeping relative costs per system relatively constant in present value dollars.

Considering these costs and savings as a continual investment scenario to maintain (versus increase or decrease) current system capabilities, the total discounted rate of future cash savings computes to total strategic savings of $149.11 (thousand) at the 4.1% discount factor. This is the total value of expected savings due to a policy of continual maintenance of current capabilities for 30 years. *Exhibit 8-6* shows the calculations.

Exhibit 8-6

Total present value of net savings
($ in thousands)

Year	Value of Work-stations	Cost Savings	Replace-ment Cost	Net Savings	Present Value Factor @ 4.1%	Present Value of Net Savings
1	$28.68	$16.62	$9.56	$7.06	0.961	$6.78
2	$28.68	$16.62	$9.56	$7.06	0.923	$6.52
3	$28.68	$16.62	$9.56	$7.06	0.886	$6.26
4	$28.68	$16.62	$9.56	$7.06	0.852	$6.02
5	$28.68	$16.62	$9.56	$7.06	0.818	$5.76
6	$28.68	$16.62	$9.56	$7.06	0.786	$5.55
7	$28.68	$16.62	$9.56	$7.06	0.755	$5.33
8	$28.68	$16.62	$9.56	$7.06	0.725	$5.12
9	$28.68	$16.62	$9.56	$7.06	0.697	$4.92
·	·	·	·	·	·	·
·	·	·	·	·	·	·
50	·	**Sum of Present Value Savings—50 Years**		·	·	**$149.11**

In this simple case, the **total** discounted present value (all investments into perpetuity) can be calculated directly, assuming that savings will continue to be invested at 4.1%.	Calculation of **perpetual value** of net savings (beyond 50 years to infinity) = $7.06 ÷ .041 = $172.20

Gradual Improvement in Capital Stock

So far, the analysis has only considered recouping lost efficiencies due to PC downtime and then maintaining current capabilities. It pays to invest toward this goal, since the net savings on internal investments is 25% (i.e., $7.06 ÷ $28.68) are considerably higher than the expected 4.1% rate of earnings savings could achieve using market investment rates.

In fact, since the internal rate is higher, management might consider investing *more* of the savings into the capital—to enhance 'normal' productivity. For example, the current reinvestment rate of savings is 58% (i.e., $9.56 ÷ $16.62). Suppose management decided to increase this investment up to 65%. *Exhibit 8-7* shows a table of expected enhanced of savings under this scenario, discounted at 4.1%.

Exhibit 8-7

	Capital Stock	Savings	Reinvestment at 58% of Savings	Reinvestment at 65%	Net Savings	Present Value of Savings (@4.1%)
Improvement of Capital Stock ($ in thousands)						
Year						
1	$28.68	$16.62	$9.56	$10.80	$5.82	$5.59
2	$29.92	$17.34	$10.06	$11.27	$6.07	$5.58
3	$31.13	$18.04	$10.46	$11.73	$6.31	$5.62
4	$32.40	$18.77	$10.89	$12.20	$6.57	$5.59
5	$33.71	$19.54	$11.33	$12.70	$6.84	$5.61
6	$35.08	$20.33	$11.79	$13.21	$7.11	$5.62
7	$36.50	$21.15	$12.27	$13.75	$7.40	$5.55
8	$37.98	$22.01	$12.77	$14.31	$7.70	$5.62
9	$39.52	$22.90	$13.28	$14.89	$8.02	$5.61
Etc.	.	.	.	.	.	.
.	.	.	.	.	.	.
.	.	.	.	.	.	.
Sum of Present Value Savings—50 Years						**$444.43**

The additional investments might be used to help pay for related PC improvements, including training, software, analysis of how to enhance processes (e.g., better coordination among workers' projects though networking and project control software), and so on. The 7% additional reinvestment (from 58% to 65%) result has an expected improvement of long-term savings (at 50 years) $444 thousand internal return on investment. This is nearly three times the expected rate of return for the status quo (at approximately $149 thousand) over the long run.

These calculations are admittedly simplistic (and simple—to a computer). In reality, the internal rate of return and the discount rate will certainly vary over such time periods, and in unpredictable ways. However, the computations do illustrate the usefulness of capital reinvestment when such rates can be relatively accurately forecasted. They can often be used as decision support tools to help managers choose when, or when not, to support capital improvement alternatives.

Gradual Phase out of a Program

The third assumption is that capital investments are more profitable than, say, investment in other ventures. This is the hurdle rate or opportunity rate.

Suppose that management plans to phase out a program. This presents the opposite proposition from the gradual improvement scenario. And, even for major technological or management process reengineering programs, it is not uncommon to keep the old systems or maintain parallel running systems until replacements are tested and verified. The effects of reducing required rates for sustainability could be easily calculated. For example, suppose the 58% sustainability rate for reinvestment (*Exhibit 8-7*) was reduced to 50%. The net discount degradation could be computed as a barometer for how fast productivity would be expected decline.

Summary

Economic analysis considerations depend on accurate operations and cost figures. We have reviewed several of the methods for comparing business case alternatives. A key calculation is the present value of investments. This allows comparison of apples-to-apples, even when projects have different cash flow, economic lives, or payback time periods.

While economic analysis techniques are essential for comparing competing business alternatives, the calculations depend on accurate and sufficient cost and income data to allow for adequate representation of business processes. These data are often the product of many other operations research and management science techniques. An overview of these quantitative techniques and models is presented in the following chapters.

---

[120] E. Brigham (1975, Autumn). Hurdle rates for screening capital expenditure proposals. *Financial Management,* p. 18. Cited from R. Gupta, R. (1996). *Managerial Excellence,* (p.51). Boston: Harvard Business School Publishing.

[121] R. Gupta (1996). *Managerial Excellence.* Boston: Harvard Business School Publishing, p. 55.

[122] Adapted from K. Larson (1990). *Fundamental Accounting Principles* (12th ed.). Boston: Irwin, p. 1136.

Although this may seem a paradox, all exact science is dominated by the idea of approximation.
Bertrand Russell (circa 1959)

CHAPTER NINE

Statistical Analysis

=====================================9

Statistics are no substitute for judgment.

Henry Clay (circa 1840)

Statistics has scared the *liven' bejesus* out of many a high school and college student—especially if required for graduation. And, perhaps more unfortunately, many who have had the formal courses walk away and rarely use the principles. This is regrettable—statistics can be a powerful ally in making a strong case for you analysis conclusions. And, understanding the basic assumptions can help make your BCA findings seem quite perceptive.

Let us return to our example 8-Day BCA. Recall that Jim calculated the projected breakeven value of savings—the point in time where cumulative savings (of more efficient new PCs) would equal acquisition costs (see *Exhibit 1-19*).

This projection relied on several assumptions. The first (implicit) assumption was that the projected breakeven point (i.e., $28,677 for the *lease-to-own* alternative) represented the 'expected value' for investment breakeven in the 23rd month. The expected value, in statistical terms, most often is the average or mean value.

A second unstated assumption was that the mean value of the breakeven estimate would be positioned exactly in the center of a normal (symmetrical) distribution. This is an important assumption, since statistical analysis generally depends on 'normality' of data distributions for making statistical inference about probabilities. Expectations are that most real world (i.e., empirical) observations will be more densely grouped at or near the mean. Statistical inference allows one to determine the chances of whether a new observation is close enough, by random chance, to be part of the 'family of observations' belonging to the mean value. If the disparity seems too far away (i.e., the difference of the mean value minus the observed value is too large), statistical analysis helps determine when an observed value is probably not part of that mean's family.

When the data distribution is not symmetrical, different measurements are used for estimates of the expected value. The *median* is the value of the observation where ½ of the other observations are above, and ½ below. The *mode* is simply the value of the most frequently occurring observation. However, more powerful statistical inference techniques can be used when a normal or nearly normal distribution exists.

Fortunately, the symmetrical form of the normal distribution comes close to fitting the actual observed distributions of many natural and social phenomena.[123] Observed events tend to cluster around a central average, and the 'outliers' are distributed in progressively fewer numbers, dictated by the shape of the normal curve. This is fortunate because of powerful inferences can be drawn about the accuracy of an observation.

One technique, using the 'central limit theorem,' even allows you to take repeated samples of a small number of observations of the event (say, random samples of 5 each from our observed 12 months of service calls), make averages of each of these sample's observations, and then *artificially form* a 'normal distribution' from these sample means, even if they originate in nonsymmetrical distributions.[124] Using these attributes, we now examine the relationship of risks using the normal curve.

Estimation of Risk Using the Normal Curve

We now return to the estimate of risk in the 8-Day BCA example, where we calculated a value of a 95% confidence (i.e., 5% risk) of needed additional savings to assure reaching the breakeven amount of $28,677. This 'safety level' of savings is shown in *Exhibit 9-1* (recreated from *Exhibit 1-25*.

Exhibit 9-1

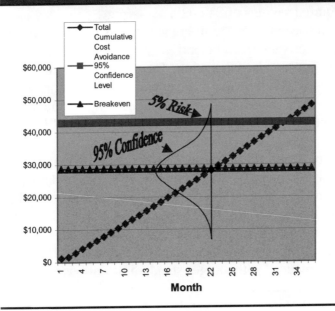

Superimposed is a graphic of the hypothetical normal curve, indicating the 95% area that represents 95%

confidence. The concept of the normal curve, and inference about confidence (or, alternatively, reduced risk) has been around for some time. Its discovery is now credited to DeMoivre in 1733[xxx] (though it was popularized by both Gauss and LaPlace a century later).[125]

The notion is, that by calculating a mean (the $28,677 breakeven point) and a standard error ($8,456—see page 69), a statistical factor (1.65 from statistical tables) can be used to estimate the total savings, represented by area under the curve, required for the 95% confidence that the break-even will be attained. Here we multiplied the standard error by 1.65 to attain a safety factor of $13,952. The total savings required for a 95% confidence that breakeven would occur were therefore $28,677 (the estimated *average* pay-back amount) plus $13,952 (the 95% confidence factor), for total required savings of $42,629.

Consistency of the inference is possible due two to key characteristics (parameters) of the normal distribution: the mean and standard deviation. The mean locates the center of the distribution, and the standard deviation represents the spread of observations around the center. For the same average, the area under the curve can be measured by the size of the standard deviation.

For example, *Exhibit 9-2* shows three normal distributions with a mean of 100, but with different standard deviations of 10, 20 and 30 (i.e. 10%, 20% and 30% of the mean, in this example). The shapes of these three distributions are normal. The only difference is the spread—taller and narrower for the small standard deviation (i.e., 10), and flatter and wider for the larger standard deviations. But, by

---

[xxx] Abraham DeMoivre, a transplanted Frenchman, was a math tutor and coffeehouse advisor to English gamblers—he is said to have predicted the day of his death (at 87) by noting that every day he required a few more minutes of sleep—and to have died the day his sleep requirement reached 24 hours.

the nature of the normal curve, the *area under each curve is the same*—and the percentage of area under each curve for one standard deviation away *from the mean* is the same, 34.13%. For two standard deviations it is 47.73%. For three it is 49.86%.

Exhibit 9-2

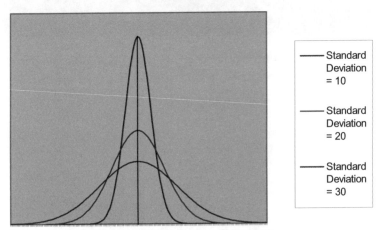

Shape of the Normal Curve with Standard Errors of 10%, 20% and 30%

Normal Distribution

Standard Deviation = 10

Standard Deviation = 20

Standard Deviation = 30

1 12 23 34 45 56 67 78 89 100 111 122 133 144 155 166 177 188 199

Mean = 100

Exhibit 9-3 illustrates the notion of the total area under the standard normal probability distribution, given the question "what is the area to the *left of the point of interest?*" We see that at one standard deviation, 84% of the area is to the left (i.e., 50% to the left of the mean + 34% to the right). At 1.65 standard deviations, this increases to

95% of the area under the curve. At two standard deviations, nearly 98% of the area is represented. At three standard deviations, nearly all (i.e., 99.9%) of the area is

covered. It is easy to see, for example, how rare it is for someone to score in the 99th percentile of a standardized test (i.e., about 2.33 standard deviations above the average test taker).

Exhibit 9-3

The Standard Normal Probability Distribution

Areas Under the Standard Normal Probability Distribution Curve

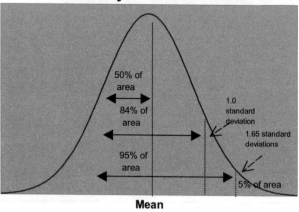

Linear Regression

Linear regression is one of the most used statistical analysis techniques. Regression analysis has been around for over 100 years, and its origins are attributed to an Englishman, Sir Francis Galton, a cousin of Charles Darwin. He is credited with the concept of statistical regression from his published paper, "Natural Inheritance" (1889). In it he described how characteristics of living organisms (i.e., size of sweet pea plants, heights of offspring, etc.) tend to revert, or regress, back to the mean sizes during later generations.[126]

There are numerous ways that 'relational' regression models can be useful. Among the most useful are their applications in forecasting likely future events for measured patterns of historical events.

Forecasting with Simple Linear Regression

Recall that in the 8-Day BCA example, a simple time series linear regression formula was calculated using PC spreadsheet software. Hard data were available from the information office log indicating the number and length of service calls per month for a 12-month period. Spreadsheet software was used to calculate the regression equation in *Exhibit 1-12*, which is reproduced below in *Exhibit 9-4*.

Exhibit 9-4

Simple Linear Regression Equation

$$F = a + bX + e$$
$$= 22.4 + .2X + e$$

Where: F = the forecasted value
(i.e., the dependent variable)
a = the Y intercept value
(a constant—where $X = 0$)
b = the month
(i.e., the coefficient by which the
X value is multiplied)
X = the calculated trend factor
(i.e., the independent variable)
e = random error
(i.e., error not explained by the equation)

The regression equation was developed to mathematically emulate the behavior of historical values with respect to time periods when projecting expected future values of the trend line. In this context, the equation is also known as a time series regression equation. *Exhibit 9-5* illustrates a graphical presentation of the fitted values from the historical linear equation. There it is easy to see the variation of the actual data around the average trend line.

Exhibit 9-5

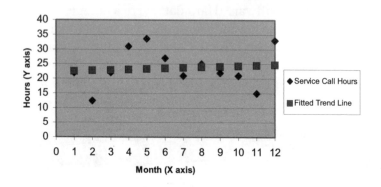

This illustration demonstrates a very simple use of linear regression—the fitting of a trend line through historical observations. Each observation is assumed to have occurred over equal time increments. Forecasted trend line values are then calculated by simply multiplying the time increment values by the equation coefficient. The underlying assumption is that the past trend represents a pattern that will continue into the future. Forecasting of expected future values is done by projection of the past trends derived from historical values.

While the simple regression technique forecasts very well in many time series situations, it is also very useful for developing equations for a wide variety of other kinds of relationships. Further, the basic techniques can be conveniently extended beyond the simple two-variable relationship using multiple linear regression.

Forecasting with Multiple Linear Regression

Sophisticated regression models using many predictor variables to estimate the value of a single dependent variable are quite common in daily business and economic situations, as well as other relationships in physical, biological and social sciences. Multiple linear regression is a similar mathematical model to simple regression, but uses several variables simultaneously to estimate the value of the one predicted variable.

For example, suppose measurements of children's sizes are as shown in *Exhibit 9-6*.

Exhibit 9-6

Multiple Linear Regression			
Data for Forecasting a Child's Weight from Height and Age			
Name	Age	Height	Weight
Jamie	6	43	55
Suzie	10	51	95
Todd	16	70	130
Kendal	14	61	113
Wyatt	12	54	100
Alexa	8	45	66

Using these data, we wish to calculate the expected weight of an additional child, given values for height and weight.

Note here that the linear regression equation now has two predictor variables instead of just one. Let X_1 represent the relationship of the Age variable, and X_2 the Height variable. Together, the additive relationship of the two to the forecasted variable F (i.e., Weight) can be calculated on a PC computer using regression software.

First, a new regression equation is calculated using the computer software, as shown in *Exhibit 9-7*.

Exhibit 9-7

Multiple Linear Regression Equation

$$F = a + b_1X_1 + b_2X_2 + e$$
$$= 8.3 + 7.1X_1 + .1X_2 + e$$

Where: F = the forecasted value
(i.e., the dependent variable)
A = the Y value (when X = 0)
b_1 *= the age*
(i.e., coefficient by which the X_1 value is multiplied;
b_2 *= the height*
(i.e., the coefficient by which the X_2 value
is multiplied
X_1 *= Age of new youngster*
X_2 *= Height of new youngster*
e = random error
(i.e., error not explained by the equation)

The equation is then used to predict the weight of a new youngster, given values for age and height. Suppose the new child is 9 years old and is 55 inches in height. Simply plug these values into the equation as shown in *Exhibit 9-8* to predict the weight.

Again, similar to two variables, the underlying assumption is that the historical relationship between the predictors (the independent variables) and the predicted (dependent) variable will hold for any relationship.

Exhibit 9-8

Estimated Weight
Using the Multiple Linear Regression Equation

$$F = a + b_1X_1 + b_2X_2$$
$$= 8.3 + 7.1X_1 + .1X_2$$
$$= 8.3 + 7.1 \times 9 \ _{(years)} + .1 \times 55 \ _{(inches)}$$
$$= 77.7 \ _{(pounds)}$$

Pretty simple. But the best part is that the quantitative relationship of all sorts of observations can be related to each other using this technique. And, of course, the information should be matched to the prediction (i.e., one might be able to predict male or female child more accurately than 'child' if specific gender data were available. Let us now use multiple linear regression in a practical application relating to BCAs. We demonstrate with an expert system approach called *policy capturing.*

Policy Capturing

Policy capturing is a form of 'expert system.' In turn, expert systems are a special class of Artificial Intelligence (AI) systems. AI systems have been used for a variety of problems, such as speech recognition and understanding, image analysis, robotics, and consultation systems. They concentrate on developing rules to emulate an expert's knowledge about a subject area. As such, they are also called 'knowledge based systems.'

Expert systems have been around for over 40 years. NASA's DENDRAL, developed in the 1960s, is the most notable early expert system. DENDRAL was developed to remotely analyze the chemical composition of Martian soil—encoded with the knowledge of a chemist who specialized in organic chemistry. Such systems became more sophisticated in the 1970s, with rule based systems in models such as MYCIN (for diagnosis of infectious diseases), XCON (for assistance to the Digital Equipment Company in configuring their VAX computer systems), and PROSPECTOR (to aid in exploration of ore deposits).[127] Since then, many expert systems computer software routines have been developed and are available.

The fundamental notion is that the decision rules used by experts can be made explicit. Subjective rules are captured (by the analyst) as decisions are made. These decisions are then transformed into numerical form, such as those used in Likert-type scales commonly found in questionnaires. The numerical responses are then placed in a mathematical model that computes a composite value across the question responses to emulate how the 'human' expert would have answered the questions.

Policy Capturing and Linear Regression

One can create a simple policy-capturing model by computing the linear regression relationships among the several predictor factors (that the expert uses for decisions) and previous predictions by the expert using such cues. The model is used to infer the rules the expert 'appeared to use.' This process usually begins by having the analyst observe several-to-many examples of the expert's decisions. The expert is queried about what factors were used in each case, and a list of such factors is comprised over many cases, matched to the expert's decision for each case. After appropriate data gathering, a multiple linear regression equation is calculated using the list of predictors and decision outcomes.

To predict the expected outcome for a new case situation, the prediction values (i.e., X_1, X_2, X_3, etc.) are simply applied to the regression equation to calculate the expected expert's choice. It has been pointed out that this inference of actual rules is different from the more common expert system approaches. The latter generally attempt to survey domain knowledge to determine what rules were actually used, and then deduce what rules should be used.[128]

Surprisingly, simple policy-capturing methods have been found to generally make better decisions than the expert. [129] This has been confirmed by hundreds of additional studies.[130] Studies from psychology, education, personnel, marketing and finance have shown forecasts using policy capturing were more accurate that judgments made by experts using unaided judgment. One might speculate that this is because the expert often uses only a few of the factors for each case. However, over many cases, many different rules are used. The linear regression model can systematically use all of the appropriate factors (i.e., predictor variables) for each case, potentially making predictions more accurate.

Policy capturing is probably most appropriate for complex situations where normal decisions are unreliable, and valid expert judgments can be monitored and quantified. Development of these models becomes cost effective, especially when many judgments are needed.[131]

Developing a Policy-Capturing Model

Recall, during development of the 8-Day BCA example, that Jim had asked the information system expert for an opinion about the potential benefits of new PCs relative to the older ones. The expert's opinion was that about 75% of the downtime could be reduced with new PCs.

Suppose now that one wishes to capture the decision policy of this expert for other applications—rather than bother her with every case. An approach might be to observe the expert over a number similar situations, and annotate notes about what cues the expert uses over time. For the PC example, candidate factors might include the frequency of repairs of the existing machines, the estimate of reliability based on age of existing workstations, and the likelihood that the PC users would be willing and able to learn to use the newer PCs productively. Linear regression can be used to develop the relationships of such cues (i.e., the expert's 'policies') to the expert's predictions. This type of policy capturing is also called 'judgmental bootstrapping.'

The first step in building a policy-capturing model is to gather and transform the data into a form that the regression model can understand. One common way developed for the behavioral sciences, as alluded to earlier, is to use Likert scales.[xxxi] These are scales that have the respondent mark his/her answer along a continuum, of say from 1 (low) to 5 (high). To record the experts' opinions, you simple ask them to indicate their opinion about some situation, and what factors were considered in their decision. Over many cases, the observer tabulates a number of factors used by the expert for similar decisions.

It is important to get enough sets of observations to calculate meaningful statistical relationships. The observations hopefully include most of the likely predictor variables for the particular question, as well as the resulting decision (i.e., the dependent variable) made by the expert. One set of observations (i.e., a naive estimate) will be very suspect. Ten sets of observations are better and 30 observations even more so.

Illustration of a Policy Capturing Model

For example, management wishes to emulate decisions of the information system expert about likely produc-

---

[xxxi] To be really 'stuffy,' the author was taught in graduate school that Rensis Likert, the famous organizational scientist, pronounces his name "lick-ert," after the German pronunciation.

tivity improvements from new PCs in yet another office area. After a number of interviews and observations, the analyst deduces that the expert uses nine cues (predictor variables) more or less consistently. Taking the form of Likert type questions, they appear as shown in *Exhibit 9-9*.

Exhibit 9-9

Policy Capturing Predictors
Hypothetical 8-Day BCA savings estimate

Predictor	Questions:
$X_1 =$	**Are existing PC systems obsolete?** 1 = No, 2 = Some, 3 = Average, 4 = Much, 5 = Yes
$X_2 =$	**Are PCs essential to the core work process?** 1 = No, 2 = Some, 3 = Average, 4 = Much 5 = Yes
$X_3 =$	**Is there a pro-technical work environment?** 1 = No, 2 = Some, 3 = Average, 4 = Much 5 = Yes
$X_4 =$	**Is management PC computer literate?** 1 = No, 2 = Some, 3 = Average, 4 = Much 5 = Yes
$X_5 =$	**Would upgrades support office innovation goals?** 1 = No, 2 = Some, 3 = Average, 4 = Much 5 = Yes
$X_6 =$	**Are workers PC computer literate?** 1 = No, 2 = Some, 3 = Average, 4 = Much 5 = Yes
$X_7 =$	**Will training be provided for a new system?** 1 = Yes, 2 = Some, 3 = Average, 4 = Little, 5 = None
$X_8 =$	**Is current office productivity high?** 1 = No, 2 = Some, 3 = Average, 4 = Much 5 = Yes
$X_9 =$	**Is the work 'high tech'?** 1 = No, 2 = Some, 3 = Average, 4 = Much 5 = Yes

The analyst then develops a questionnaire using these predictor questions. As the expert evaluates new cases, a value is recorded for each of the questions, indicating the amount of influence each variable had. For example, a score of 1 = no expected improvement for the case under consideration; or 2 = little expected improvement, and so forth, might be recorded. The expert also records a 'final opinion' for each case based on subjective judgment (i.e.,1 = zero improvement; 2 = 25%, 3 = 50%, etc.). Hypothetical responses for predictor variables and for the overall ratings (i.e., the predicted or dependent variable) are shown in *Exhibit 9-10*.

Exhibit 9-10

Policy Capturing Model **Predictor Variable Responses** **(from the expert)**										

Case # **Predictors**	1	2	3	4	5	6	7	8	9	10
X_1) Existing PC system is obsolete?	1	1	5	4	5	3	4	3	3	4
X_2) PCs are essential to core work process?	5	5	2	4	2	5	3	4	5	5
X_3) Pro-technical work environment?	3	3	1	2	5	3	4	2	2	3
X_4) Management is PC computer literate?	4	3	3	3	5	3	4	3	4	4
X_5) Upgrades would support office innovation goals?	3	4	2	3	5	5	4	2	5	4
X_6) Workers are PC computer literate?	4	3	2	4	3	3	2	3	3	3
X_7) Likelihood that training for new system will be provided?	3	3	2	2	2	3	2	2	3	3
X_8) Current office productivity is high?	3	3	2	3	2	3	3	3	2	3
X_9) Work is 'high tech'?	1	3	1	5	5	5	2	3	4	3

Expert's Overall Prediction										

Expert's Estimates of Reduced Downtime $1 = 0\%, 2 = 25\%, 3 = 50\%, 4 = 75\%, 5 = 100\%$

Expert's Overall Prediction (each case)	3	3	2	4	5	4	4	3	4	5

Finally, the policy-capturing model is estimated using multiple linear regression software. The ten cases of predictor responses are loaded as *independent variables*, and the expert's overall prediction as the *dependent variable*. It takes the form of the equation in *Exhibit 9-11(a)*.

Exhibit 9-11 (a)

Policy Capturing
Multiple Linear Regression Equation

$$F = a + b_1X_1 + b_2X_2 + b_3X_3 + b_4X_4$$
$$+ b_5X_5 + b_6X_6 + b_7X_7 + b_8X_8 + b_9X_9 + e$$

Where: F = *the forecasted value*
  (i.e., the dependent variable)
  a = *the Y (intercept) value (when X = 0)*
  $X_1 .. X_9$ = *the predictor variables*
  $B_1 .. b_9$ = *the regression equation coefficients*
  (by which the $X_1 .. X_9$ values are multiplied)
  e = *error (from which standard error is calculated)*

Prediction Equation (from computer software calculations using data from Exhibit 9-10):

$$F = -2.64 + .66X_1 + .98X_2 + .65X_3 + .10X_4$$
$$+ .00X_5 + .16X_6 - .57X_7 - .39X_8 + .01X_9 + e$$

Using this regression equation, it is possible to predict, as would the expert, the expected savings for a similar office PC situation. Suppose, in the 8-Day BCA example, Jim had used this equation to estimate potential decreases in service calls. Jim would first subjectively determine the predictor values (i.e., $X_1 = 5$, $X_2 = 3$, and so on), as shown in *Exhibit 9-11 (b)*. Using these 'plugged in' values and calculating them, the equation predicts a 75% savings.

Exhibit 9-11 (b)

Policy Capturing Prediction

$F = -2.64 + .66X_1 + .98X_2 + .65X_3 + .10X_4$
$+ .00X_5 + .16X_6 - .57X_7 - .39X_8 + .01X_9 + e$

$F = -2.64 + .66(5) + .98(3) + .65(3) + .10(5)$
$+ .00(5) + .16(3) - .57(2) - .39(3) + .01(5)$

$F = -2.64 + 3.30 + 2.95 + 1.96 + .51$
$+ .00 + .48 - 1.13 - 1.17 + .03 = 4.29$

$F = 4$ *(rounded)*
(or 75% expected PC savings)

Where: **1 = 0%, 2 = 25%, 3 = 50%, 4 = 75%, 5 = 100%**

Forecasting

We now switch gears from prediction using general relationships to the more specific relationships of time related events and forecasting. All of the prediction models we have reviewed so far have been based on linear regression techniques. More specifically, we used time series regression to develop a model of historical events that could be used to forecast expected future events. We will now consider 'pure' time series forecasting.

True time series approaches simply attempt to capture patterns of the historical data over sequential observations, rather than attempting to relate them explicitly to some other variable (as did regression). Well-known approaches include moving averages, weighted moving averages and exponential smoothing.

Time series forecasting can have advantages over regression. For example, suppose from our historical data, we believe that the recent the pattern of events is more representative than events that occurred long ago. The time series regression method we used to fit the trend line and forecast the service call hours equally weighted all observations. This implies that we believed the data from the early months was of equal explanatory value to data from later months. A related problem is that the regression trend line is 'anchored' back near the center of the historical data, adding even more risk that future forecasts might be wrong (*see Exhibit 1-22*).

Time series approaches can adjust for such problems. For example, a moving average literally drops all older observations from the calculation, and moves the 'anchor' to the center of a much shorter series. Of course, the question of how much history should be shortened still looms. Another moving average technique includes all the observations, but more recent ones are weighted (e.g., such as multiplying the most recent value by 1.0, the second most recent value by 0.9, the third most recent value by 0.8, and so forth).

Both approaches can work, but require continual updates of many numbers. Fortunately, a third type of true time series, *exponential smoothing,* provides a computationally simple, data storage efficient method to accomplish similar effects—and has been proven to be sufficiently accurate (often more accurate than more sophisticated forecasting methods).[132] It provides an alternative time series forecasting method that has come into broad use for all sorts of forecasting analyses.

Exponential smoothing was introduced in the mid-1950s. It did not become widely popular, however, until the mid-1980s. By then, its accuracy had been proved comparable to more sophisticated forecasting methods, despite its simplicity. Further, the unfussy data requirements (only the last computed value is needed) contributed to its popularity. This allows for easy data storage and calculation for literally millions of forecasts on a continual basis.[133] The technique, in effect, simultaneously computes both a cumulative mean for 'all historical data' while it weights historical data, much like a moving average. But, it is a distinct process from either. Only two values, the 'smoothing parameter' (i.e., the weighting fraction) and last forecast number need to be maintained in computer storage, eliminating the tedious data storage and maintenance requirements. The general form of the equation is shown in *Exhibit 9-12.*

Exhibit 9-12

Simple Exponential Smoothing

$F_{(New)} = \alpha X$ *(current data observation)* $+ (1 - \alpha)F$ *(previous forecast)*

Where: F = the forecasted value
α = the smoothing parameter
X = the actual data

(α = the Greek letter alpha, is a fraction between 0 and 1, typically .1 or .2)

Exponential smoothing is similar to a moving average (i.e., the weights of past data decline exponentially), but it retains some fraction of 'all' past data similar to a weighted regression equation (though distant past values, for all practical purposes, are nil). To illustrate, we will review our PC service call data. *Exhibit 9-13* shows the calculation of forecasts of service call hours using simple exponential smoothing. The alpha (α) smoothing parameter is 0.1. Using R.G. Brown's formulation (1959), this calculates to an effective use of all 12 months of historical data, with earlier periods having increasingly less (exponentially weighted) influence on the forecast.[134]

Exhibit 9-13

Simple Exponential Smoothing Calculations

Month	Service Call Hours	Calculation (alpha = .1)	Fore-cast	Error	Errors Squared	Step 1 (Errors Squared)
1	22	assumed starting point	22.0	-1.8	3.2	
2	12.5	.1*22 + (1-.1) * (22) =	22.0	-9.5	90.3	
3	22.1	.1*12.5 + (1-.1) * (22) =	21.1	1.1	1.1	
4	31	.1*22.1 + (1-.1) * (21.1) =	21.2	9.8	96.9	
5	33.7	.1*31 + (1-.1) * (21.2) =	22.1	11.6	133.6	
6	27	.1*33.7 + (1-.1) * (22.1) =	23.3	3.7	13.7	
7	21	.1*27 + (1-.1) * (23.3) =	23.7	-2.7	7.1	
8	25	.1*21 + (1-.1) * (23.7) =	23.4	1.6	2.6	
9	22	.1*25 + (1-.1) * (23.4) =	23.6	-1.6	2.4	
10	21	.1*22 + (1-.1) * (23.6) =	23.4	-2.4	5.8	
11	15	.1*21 + (1-.1) * (23.4) =	23.2	-8.2	66.6	
12	33	.1*15 + (1-.1) * (23.2) =	22.3	10.7	113.5	
					536.9	Step 2 Sum of Squared Errors
					7.3	Step 3 Standard Error
13	(forecast)	.1*33 + (1-.1) * (22.3) =	23.4			

For exponentially weighted moving averages, the effective number of observations entering the forecast (n = 19) is estimated by:

$$n = \frac{2-\alpha}{\alpha} = \frac{2-.1}{.1} = 19$$

Actually, if more historical data were available, this weighting would have made use of up to 19 months of historical observations.

Compared with the previous calculation of the standard error (i.e., standard deviation) using the time series linear regression methods (i.e., 6.9 in *Exhibit 1-21*), the simple exponential smoothing standard error (i.e., 7.3) is slightly higher. Also note that the forecast for the next period (i.e., $M_{onth = 13}$) is 23.4, compared with 25 for the regression trend line (from *Exhibit 1-14*).

Both forecasts are close. Recall, however, that the regression trend also had an upward trend, increasing expected service call hours at a rate of about 10% per year, which was judged by the expert to be somewhat typical. To handle this problem, a number of adjustments have been developed to generalize exponential smoothing applications. Fundamental elaborations include Holt's (1952) 'double exponential smoothing' to adjust for trends, Winters' (1960) formulation to deal with seasonal data, and Gardner and McKenzie's (1985) 'damped trend' exponential smoothing (i.e., trends have generally been found to level off in the future).[135]

So, using the best of all these adjustments, we now calculate an exponential smoothing forecast, shown in *Exhibit 9-14*. The forecast model was developed using *AUTOCAST* which is a computerized expert forecasting system.[136] After the model tested for heuristics about trend, seasonality and damping, its actual forecast leveled out at an expected constant (no trend) 24 hours per month (versus 10% annually for the regression forecast). Note that the calculations of 95% confidence intervals, which the model calculated for 10 periods, are quite active, reflecting many of the dynamics considered by the expert system, despite the final 'flat' forecast.

The *AUTOCAST* software also calculated an estimated standard error of 6.8, very similar to the simple exponential model (i.e., 7.3) and the linear regression model (i.e., 6.9).

Exhibit 9-14

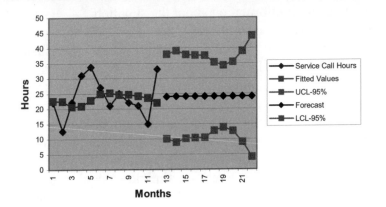

So, which of the three, or for that matter, any other forecasting method is best? There are many kinds of forecasting techniques, ranging from nearly totally judgmental (e.g., the Delphi technique), to totally mechanical, such as extrapolation (time series) and relational (regression) models. However, more sophisticated models (e.g., Box-Jenkins (ARIMA) and neural networks) have not generally performed better than simple models, such as those we have reviewed herein.[137]

In practice, if data are limited or difficult to come by, as is often the case, you must use what you have the best way you can. That is, learn as much about the situation as possible, and use common sense about which mechanical forecast seems appropriate. Scott Armstrong, a leading forecasting expert, advocates that combining forecasts from different methods, such as objective (e.g., time series) and subjective methods can often help improve prediction validity.[138] He also advises us, when using subjective methods, "to hire cheap experts to predict the future."[139] This recommendation is based on multiple studies, and should fortify your convictions that you too can forecast well, given enough information about the situation.[xxxii]

In our example case, the only 'hard data' readily available was the 12 months of service call hours history. Both mechanical forecasts, exponential smoothing and time series regression, produced similar standard errors and initial short-term forecasts. However, due to expert opinion about the 10% trend of increasing service calls, it seems prudent to use the regression prediction (with trend) rather than the exponential smoothing method (without trend). This additional subjective 'domain knowledge' is an example of using subjective predictions to supplement the mechanical calculations. Caution here, however. Much of the forecasting literature seems to advise against 'judgmental meddling' of pure forecast calculations without sufficient reason.

---

[123]Levin, p. 67.

[124] A. D. Aczel (1999). *Complete Business Statistic* (4th ed.). Boston: Irwin-McGraw-Hill, pp. 205–211.

[125] Ibid., p. 164.

[xxxii] Interestingly, over 100 studies on the value of experts have shown this finding. Few indicated that an expert's forecasts were significantly better than those of moderately well informed nonexperts about future events. Scott Armstrong does point out, however, that experts are often of great value for interpreting past and current situations.

[126] Ibid., p. 437.

[127] J. Liebowitz (Ed.). (1998). *The Handbook of Applied Expert Systems.* CRC Press: New York, pp. 164–165.

[128] J. S. Armstrong (2001). Judgmental bootstrapping: Inferring experts' rules for forecasting, in J. S. Armstrong (ed.), *Principles of Forecasting* (p. 173). Norwell, MA: Kluwer Academic Publishers.

[129] P. Meehl (1954). *Clinical versus Statistical Prediction.* Minneapolis: University of Minneapolis Press.

[130] S. G. Makridakis (1990). *Forecasting, Planning, and Strategy for the 21st Century.* New York: The Free Press, p. 34.

[131] J. S. Armstrong (2001). p. 171.

[132] S. Makridakis and S. C. Wheelwright (1989). *Forecasting Methods for Management* (5th ed.). John Wiley & Sons: New York, p. 24.

[133] Ibid.

[134] S. Armstrong (1985). *Long Range Forecasting: From Crystal Ball to Computer.* John Wiley & Sons, New York, p. 166.

[135] Makridakis and Wheelwright, pp. 24, 76–91.

[136] E. Gardner (1991). *Autocast II: Business Forecasting System.* Morristown NJ: Levenbach Associates.

[137] Armstrong (2001), p. 619; Makridakis and Wheelwright (1989), p. 25.

[138] S. Armstrong (1985), p.288.

[139] Ibid., pp. 91–96.

Art and science have their meeting point in method.
Baron Lytton (circa 1863)

CHAPTER TEN
Process Modeling

=================================**10**

Few things are harder to put up with than the annoyance of a good example.

Samuel Clemens (Mark Twain) (circa 1900)

Human processes are generally too complex to be captured by using statistical methods alone. More recently, with the advent of super fast computer technology and inexpensive information and communication processing, near-real process modeling of such activities has become both feasible and affordable.

Process models are developed to mimic or replicate real world human enterprises. At best, these models are still simplistic representations of real situations. The hope of analysts is that they can be made sufficiently accurate to reasonably represent the big picture. An important aspect of process modeling is the necessity to continually compare 'synthetic' depictions of processes with actual real world courses of action. This feedback allows for calibration of the underlying assumptions of the model to more accurately imitate existing or changed conditions.

Process models are developed by systematic identification of *entities*, *processes* and *activities* used to transform inputs into output events.

Entities

Key to clearly modeling a real world situation is identification of the basic object being processed—the *entity*. This could be the customer (who is being served), the 'widget' (that is being produced), and so on. The *entity* is produced or transformed by the processes and activities.

Processes

The sequences of multiple functional steps to produce outputs (i.e., desired entities) can be defined as *processes*. They can be conceptualized as actions to transform inputs into outputs using resources and operations. These steps are related in sequential or parallel ways, from initial introduction to final output.

When developing models, it is useful to recognize that the enterprise is usually comprised of several layers of processes (i.e., echelons). For example, a process model might be composed of three levels of processes, operational, intermediate and upper management. *Operational level processes* would provide direct conversion of inputs to outputs through sequences of functional steps. *Intermediate management processes* would not perform direct 'elbow grease' to a production process, but would provide coordination and control to help synchronize and direct operational processes. *Upper management processes* might represent functions for strategic planning, acquisition and organizing of needed resources.

A convenient approach when developing models is to conceptualize overall processes top down (so that all activities can be calibrated to the 'same sheet of music'). Then, from the big picture, processes are decomposed to subprocesses and constituent activities. Simulation techniques can then be applied to subprocesses, sequencing the individual activities from the bottom up (i.e., emulating problems as being solved by activities closest to the origins).[140] Simulation of process interactions and sequencing can provide insights for coordination, since significant organizational problems will often be found at the boundaries between processes.[141] Potential improvements can often be found by looking for disconnects either between horizontal process steps (i.e., such as local process managers not aware or sensitive to preceding or following process steps), or between vertical echelons such as micromanagement.

Activities

Just as functional steps can be defined as the basic components of processes, activities can be defined as the basic active elements of the functional steps. They provide the kinetic energy, to borrow a term from the physical sciences. They do the work of transforming the input entity into the desired output form—using resources and production protocols.

Recent literature in process reengineering distinguishes three kinds of activities: *value added*, *non–value added*, and *waste*. Activities involved directly in the performance of work are value added activities. Indirect activities such as management processes are operationally defined as non–value added for successful process operations. This is an unfortunate moniker (given by early process reengineering developers), since few would deny the value of good coordination and planning. Processes that do not contribute (but use resources) are waste activities. Typically, about 10% of all activities are value added, and most are non–value added.[142] Waste activities are generally low level (less than 2%) in healthy enterprises.

In assessing costs, resources from functional activities can be totally or partially dedicated to a function. For example, an administrative assistance activity that serves several offices (e.g., functional processes) can contribute part of their total resources (e.g., workers' available time and office resources) to each—say with 20% of capacity used in Office A, 15% in Office B, and so on. Their costs can be similarly apportioned when modeling the processes.

Modeling Processes

To develop an adequate process model, there are two fundamental considerations: description of the processes and their interrelationships. We will illustrate a structured approach by using the Integrated Definition (IDEF) model to describe processes. Then we will examine the possible ways to model their interrelationships using network theory and simulation techniques.

Processes and Activities

There are hundreds of activities in enterprise processes. Amazingly, however, there are relatively few main processes. Thomas Davenport, in his 1993 book, *Process Innovation: Reengineering Work Through Information Technology*, speculates that most companies have only about 10–20 key processes. Typical processes at the operational level can include product development, customer acquisition, customer requirements identification, manufacturing, integration of logistics, order management and post-sales servicing. Higher management processes might include performance monitoring, information systems management, asset management, human resource management, and planning and resource management.[143]

Since there are potentially hundreds or thousands of activities, along with associated production rules and resources, a systematic way for identifying and keeping track is needed. Fortunately, by the early 1980s such techniques were being developed and their use was made increasingly feasible by the rapid development of modern information systems. One of the most useful of such techniques is the IDEF approach.

Integrated Definition (IDEF)

IDEF modeling was an invention of its time—adapting integrated computer aided manufacturing software (ICAM) to help model existing processes. Early applications were developed to provide information engineers with a blueprint of organizational information processes to help engineer new, complex enterprise information systems.

The catalyst for this effort was spawned from the information revolution, beginning in the late 1940s-early 1950s. With the advent of cheap, accurate data processing by the 1970s and 1980s, organizations began modernizing by installing sophisticated computers and information systems. However, it soon became apparent that better understanding of organizational processes was needed for successful implementations of new information systems.

Tackling this problem, the United States Air Force commissioned studies during the 1970s to learn how to adapt existing techniques of Integrated Computer Aided Manufacturing (ICAM) to analyze human organizational processes.[xxxiii] From these studies, in turn, a series of techniques known as the IDEF (*I*CAM *DEF*inition) techniques were developed. These later became known as simply *I*ntegrated *DEF*inition models.

IDEF was eventually released as a generic process analysis approach by the Air Force, and selected, in 1991, as a Federal Information Processing Standard (FIPS) by the National Institute of Standards and Technology (NIST). Currently, IDEF0 and IDEF1X techniques are widely used in the government, industrial and commercial sectors, supporting modeling efforts for a wide range of enterprises and application domains.[144]

[xxxiii] ICAM software routines are an application of the more general Computer Aided Software Engineering (CASE) tools.

The main objective of IDEF, according to the 1993 NIST publication *Draft Federal Information Processing Standards (FIPS) Publication 183,* is:

> ...the construction of models comprising system functions (activities, actions, processes, operations), functional relationships, and data (information or objects) that support systems integration.[145]

The basic notions of IDEF are to: 1) describe current processes (i.e., 'as is' processes), and 2) systematically determine potential streamlining possibilities for more cost efficient 'to be' processes. With this knowledge, one can potentially design new information systems to support or enable innovative 'to be' scenarios (versus galvanizing less efficient 'as is' production scenarios).

IDEF techniques can be used to analyze the functions a system performs, and to record the mechanisms (means) by which these functions are accomplished.[146] They include:

1. *Function models* of activities or processes within an enterprise (which became known as IDEF0). The IDEF0 (Integration DEFinition language 0) is based on SADT™ (Structured Analysis and Design Technique™), developed by Douglas T. Ross and SofTech, Inc.

2. *Information models* to systematically collect information about the enterprise (which became IDEF1X).

3. *Dynamic models* to represent time-varying behavioral characteristics of the enterprise processes.

The IDEF Approach

In general, the IDEF approach seeks to identify activities, including required resources and controls, and then determine relationships of the activities to organizational processes. This is somewhat analogous to a chef who prepares a recipe using ingredients such as spices, vegetables, meats, and so on. Efficient operation of the enterprise processes depends on judicious inputs from the activities—not too little, nor too much of any given activity ingredient. Too few resources (e.g., processing stands for manufacture of widgets), or too much control (e.g., micromanagement), can create unnecessary inefficiencies (i.e., 'spoil the broth').

The result of applying IDEF0 to a system is development of a model that consists of a hierarchical series of diagrams, text, and glossary cross-referenced to each other. The two primary modeling components are *activity boxes* and directional *arrows* that indicated activity relationships. Perhaps an example can help explain.

An IDEF Example

This example IDEF study actually took place at a large budget defense supply center in the mid-1990s. The study was initiated in response to higher echelon instructions to develop plans for a 20% reduction of the workforce. In addition, the study was to consider how to absorb expected new tasks from other organizations (also being downsized). The enterprise duties consisted of worldwide wholesale procurement and distribution of energy products (e.g., jet fuels, diesel, gasoline, and so on) to U.S. defense forces. The agency consisted of about 600 personnel at the headquarters, and about 200 in field units who directly interfaced with 'retail' customers. The reengineering study was one of several major initiatives to help plan for the directed major organizational changes.[147]

The IDEF model was developed over 11 weeks, using off-station workshops, a private consultant facilitator, and a team of 17 mid-level managers from various technical and functional process areas. Team members represented functional activity interests of procurement, supply and transportation operations, quality, facilities management, information systems management, the budget, organizational management, and operations research. Workshops met for approximately a total of six weeks over the 11 weeks of total study time.

The team identified 167 activities, and developed seven key 'as is' processes to describe a significant proportion of enterprise operations. Four of these were then examined for potential reengineering initiatives—yielding fifty-eight Business Process Improvements (BPIs). Several BPIs showed potential for significant savings.

The results were enlightening. For example, it was shown that the existing administrative lead time between customer requests and completed acquisition of fuels could potentially be reduced by 11%. At that time, a 25% buffer of safety stocks was held for normal peacetime operations. This one BPI could be calculated to yield a potential reduction of over $10 million in inventory, with associated benefits of opportunity to invest that money elsewhere, as well as yielding reduced holding and ordering costs.[148] These opportunity cost savings alone, at the OMB Circular A-94 discount rate of 4.1% (see *Exhibit 8-4 (b)*), yields nearly ½ million dollars per year.

The information to develop the activities and processes was gathered from organizational accounting data, interviews and surveys. Over 95% of organizational employees were interviewed or completed structured questionnaires to identify what activities each did, and what percentage of their time was spent doing the activities. These data were then analyzed in the workshops using semi structured group discussions, brainstorming, and a special software called *Groupware* to allow anonymity when voting on sensitive issues. Also, invited functional experts outside the group gave presentations. Other organizational personnel outside of the team then validated that the derived processes seemed accurate, and where adjustments were needed. This permitted calibration of the modeled processes for the final model. Finally, an IDEF model was developed.

Developing the IDEF Model

The first step was to develop a series of input-output process boxes, starting from the most central activity (i.e., the activity that defines the basic purpose of the organization). Then process connections of activities, sub-activities and sub-sub activities were identified. Activity processes were specified using IDEF methodology as *in*puts, *c*onstraints, *o*utputs and *m*echanisms.

The *ICOM* acronym identifies these relationships. *Exhibit 10-1* illustrates the basic elements of the ICOM activity box. *I*nputs from outside, or preceding processes enter the left side of the activity box. *C*ontrols (e.g., business rules) and *M*echanisms (i.e., resources) enter from above and below, respectively. Arrows leaving a box on the right side indicate *O*utputs. Outputs are the objects produced by the activity process. Activity boxes and arrows represent the basic elements of the modeled enterprise process.[xxxiv]

[xxxiv] The term 'Activity Box,' as used here, is synonymous with the term 'Function Box' used in the 1993 NIST publication *Draft Federal Information Processing Standards (FIPS) Publication 183.*

Exhibit 10-1

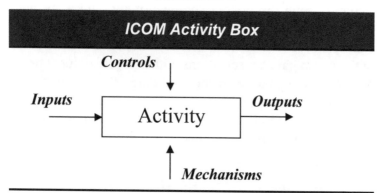

After the top-level activity process is defined, it becomes possible to decompose the overall process into the many activities that are required to perform the overall process. These activities are identified using what is called an 'activity node tree.' Identified subactivities are then joined to other activities by arrows to indicate their relationships (or partial relationships) to one another in the process. At this point, the basics are available to model the process using IDEF defined activities and relationships.

The Energy Product Organization's ICOM

We now return to our example IDEF model developed for the energy products organization. Using elementary IDEF steps, the team developed a top-level ICOM activity box, as shown in *Exhibit 10-2*. This activity box showed the overarching task of the organization: to provide energy products (from suppliers to customers). It illustrates the ICOM components, showing *I*nputs as customer orders and consumption data, and reports on supply availability. *C*ontrols included regulations and laws, industrial capacity, operating budgets, customer expectations about timing and quality requirements. *M*echanisms included resources such as people, equipment and facilities. *O*utputs were energy products and customer support.

Exhibit 10-2

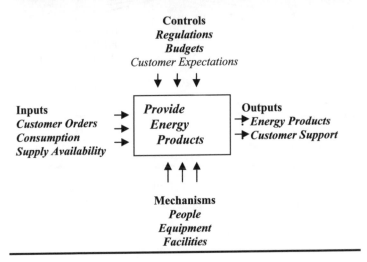

The next step was to decompose the top-level process view into subprocesses and relevant activities that contributed to the process. These were identified in an activity node tree, shown in *Exhibit 10-3*.

The numbering convention used for the model started at A0 for the top level (i.e., the A is read as Activity) with sub activities at the next level (i.e., the 'child' activities to A0, the 'parent') numbered A1, A2, A3, A4 and A5. The next level of child activities (to parents A1, A2, and so on) were numbered A11, A12; the following level—A111, A112, and so forth for additional levels by adding additional numbers.

Exhibit 10-3

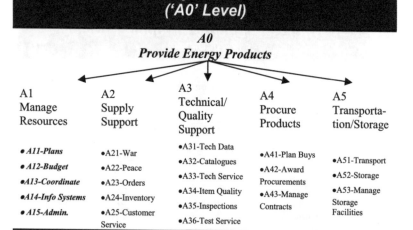

The IDEF process team then proceeded in this manner to identify lower (more detailed) levels of activity.

Process Flows

Using the hierarchy of activities and sub activities, the next step was to identify core processes—using team intuition and brainstorming, organizational charts, data from accounting, and so on. Seven basic processes were identified: bulk supply operations, daily delivery, procurement, facilities management, inventory distribution and storage, natural gas procurement, and requirements forecasting. An abbreviated form of one of the seven processes, supply support, is illustrated in *Exhibit 10-4* to show how indentured 'activity nodes' were used as ingredients to ascertain the overall process.

Exhibit 10-4

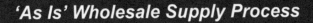

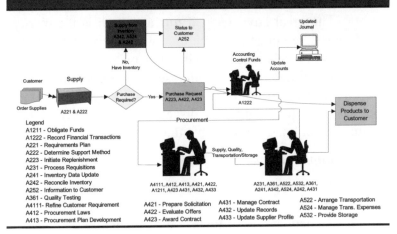

Legend
A1211 - Obligate Funds
A1222 - Record Financial Transactions
A221 - Requirements Plan
A222 - Determine Support Method
A223 - Initiate Replenishment
A231 - Process Requisitions
A241 - Inventory Data Update
A242 - Reconcile Inventory
A252 - Information to Customer
A361 - Quality Testing
A4111- Refine Customer Requirement
A412 - Procurement Laws
A413 - Procurement Plan Development

A421 - Prepare Solicitation
A422 - Evaluate Offers
A423 - Award Contract

A431 - Manage Contract
A432 - Update Records
A433 - Update Supplier Profile

A522 - Arrange Transportation
A524 - Manage Trans. Expenses
A532 - Provide Storage

Note that many of the activities from the node tree were used in the process, and that the activities came from whatever level of indenture required. Also, activities were partially used for different processes, as established by interviews with workers who performed them. For example, duties of an administrative assistant were spread out over many processes. The total time of use for any resource was controlled to avoid exceeding the total available time for a given activity. This is where queuing theory and simulation software were essential to ensure integrity of resource use.

This approach demonstrated the 'cookbook' concept—the manager (i.e., master chef) chooses the scope and intensity of the activities. First, total process output requirements had to be determined. Then resources necessary to provide proper performance of operations for the desired end results were provided. Finally, the sequencing of processes necessary for efficient throughput was arranged and calibrated. This included alignment of both sequential and parallel processes and subprocesses. The entire set of processes, from task inputs, through performance rules (controls) and resources (mechanisms), to outputs to the next activity or customer were considered.

The great advantage of this approach is the clarity made possible concerning the myriad of activity contributions and interrelationships. This 'big picture' view, along with detailed tracing of decomposed processes, allows enterprise experts to both visualize current processes, detect redundancies (or fragmented disconnects), and develop potential streamlined 'to be' substitute processes.

Improving 'as is' Processes

The reengineering team had identified the existing administrative lead time between customer requests and completed acquisition of fuels could potentially be reduced by 11%. This was accomplished by speculating about potential process flow improvements among the relevant major activities of supply, budget, quality, procurement, and inventory transportation/storage. Specific *business process improvements* (BPIs) were identified to make the 'to be' scenario viable. These included prospective process innovation actions such as streamlining purchase request process redundancies, automating 'data capture' for point of sale sales transactions, standardizing wholesale-retail business terminology, automating contract closeouts, improving forecasting techniques from near real-time data updates, and developing better customer and contractor consumption and production profiles.

Techniques to evaluate these potential 'to be' improvements involved a second major aspect of enterprise emulation—modeling of activities and processes. These techniques allowed evaluation of the 'arrows' that connected the various process functions. Keys to this type analysis include several major operations research disciplines. We shall examine four useful analysis approaches in the following chapters: network analysis, simulation/queuing (waiting line) theory, linear programming, and inventory theory. We begin with networks in Chapter 11.

---

[140] T. H. Davenport (1993). *Process Innovation, Reengineering Work Through Information Technology*, Boston: Harvard Business School Press, pp. 317.

[141] M. Hammer (1996). *Beyond Reengineering: How the Process Centered Organization is Changing Our Work and Lives*, New York: Harper Collins Publishers, Inc., p. 39.

[142] Ibid., pp. 33–34.

[143] Davenport, pp. 8–28.

[144] National Institute of Standards and Technology (1993). *Draft Federal Information Processing Standards Publication 183,* Director, Computer Systems Laboratory ATTN: FIPS IDEF0 Interpretation National Institute of Standards and Technology, Gaithersburg, MD 20899; available on the Internet at www.itl.nist.gov/fipspubs/idef02.doc.

[145] Ibid.

[146] Ibid.

[147] J. W. Brannock (2000). Challenges to process innovation at a large budget defense supply center, Paper # 2049. *Proceedings from 2000 International Management Conference* or *Society for Advancement of Management (SAM)*. 6300 Ocean Drive, FC 111, Corpus Christi, TX: SAM International Office, Texas A & M University.

[148] J. W. Brannock (1994). White Paper: DFSC Process Reengineering, working paper for evaluation of the IDEF Study Results, p. 6.

Methods of locomotion have improved greatly in recent years, but places to go remain about the same.
Don Herold (circa 1959)

CHAPTER ELEVEN
Network Analysis

==================================**11**

The means should be such as lead to the end; otherwise they are a wasted effort.

Jawaharlal Nehru (circa 1950)

Network techniques are essential tools for 'bringing alive' the basic elements of, say, an IDEF design (or of any other event-action process map). The core concept is that throughput object, an *entity*, is transformed from some beginning state to some end state by the process activities (i.e., nodes). The output entity is then transferred to the next activity node, represented by lines (called arcs) between activity nodes. The basic concept of nodes-arcs can be applied to all sorts of processes, such as manufacturing of products, flow of administrative documents, shipping of items from wholesale to retail outlets, receiving and selling items at retail stores, and so forth.

Entities can take at least two basic forms—*informational* and *physical*. Tracking the informational flow of documents is often the best way to understand the 'as is' and potential 'to be' states for business processes.[149] Physical entity processes are often more visible and intuitive to model. For example, some quite clever techniques have evolved to minimize physical distance and costs for distributing physical inventory. These network-modeling techniques explicitly assume that entities are processed using the prescribed processes and throughput times. These perfect conditions rarely exist, however, in real world processes. Therefore, in a later chapter, we will examine the consequences of uncertainty on process flows by using simulation methods.

Physical Networks

As entities pass through the activity nodes toward becoming outputs, a basic evaluation criterion is efficient throughput of the event-route network. For example, it serves no useful purpose for a delivery truck to take a longer route than necessary to deliver goods. Also, too much inventory can be unnecessarily costly. Storing *every item at every location*, for example, can cause inventory ordering and holding costs that exceed the opportunity benefits of having higher product availabilities. Often lower total costs are possible by enabling rapid distribution from centralized locations, or by lateral resupply from nearby locations. These are some of the opportunities that network techniques can help assess.

We will look at three general categories of network problems that are very useful when performing business case analysis: 1) *routing problems,* 2) *scheduling problems,* and 3) *assignment techniques.*

Routing Problems

Routing techniques can help determine the best ways to minimize costs, time or distance when distributing an entity to different network locations. Examples include determination of the least expensive way to send resources to all nodes in a network, the shortest distance to get to any one node from any other, or the quickest way to visit each node and return to home base.

Suppose, as a hypothetical situation, that the U.S. Defense Logistics Agency (DLA) desires to examine ways to streamline distribution of its eastern United States supply operations. DLA is a large supply chain management organization that manages 22 distribution depots, four million stock numbers, and 23 million transactions per year.[150]

Suppose that a study is required to determine likely savings if supplies are centralized from several storage locations to a central distribution center. Suppose further that the study scope is limited to nine existing East Coast depot locations. This is a reasonable number to allow for a follow on 'live pilot test,' should the economics of the 'paper study' prove sufficiently encouraging. Eventually, if the pilot is successful, streamlining initiatives could be expanded to the larger network of depots.

The analysts decide on a study approach to:

1) Determine the most efficient routings of items from a central depot to satellite depots.

2) Compare the net savings of the theoretically reduced centralized inventory with expected increased distribution costs due to more frequent deliveries from the central warehouses.

The study will need to establish the 'as is' (status quo) baseline (i.e., costs and operations of current processes), and of the potential 'to be' centralized distribution operations. The 'as is' model will be developed from interviews with subject matter experts (SMEs), cost records from accounting, and other sources. A structured information gathering approach, such as the IDEF technique, can be used to develop the 'as is' situation. The 'to be' scenarios can then be developed by evaluating potential new business rules for the central depot–satellite distribution process, and then by calculating optimal routings for the new distribution process. The benefits, costs and risks are then compared between the expected benefit/cost advantages of the two scenarios.

Assume management has designated Susquehanna, PA (near Harrisburg) as the potential central depot, to supply the eight remaining satellite depots, as shown in *Exhibit 11-1*.

Exhibit 11-1

Hypothetical Study
Eastern United States Defense Distribution Depots

Proposed Central Distribution Depot:

Susquehanna, PA

Proposed Satellite Distribution Depots:

Tobyhanna, PA
Columbus, OH
Richmond, VA
Cherry Point, NC
Anniston, AL
Warner Robins, GA
Albany, GA
Jacksonville, FL

We will now concentrate on the 'to be' network possibilities, assuming the 'as is' stage of the study has been completed, and has concluded that potential streamlining distribution opportunities exist.

The plan is to centralize inventories into one depot at Susquehanna, with transformation of remaining locations into 'satellite centers' with minimum inventory. The satellites primarily order and receive items. Interviews with SMEs have indicated that this will result in reduced overall inventory (see *Exhibit 14-20*), but will require assurance that management of distribution costs is both efficient and effective. More specifically, these requirements include:

1) For efficiency, there is a requirement for *continual distribution* (i.e., 'milk runs') of larger volume items from the central depot, using the *shortest overall distance*, with *vehicles returning home* for repeated reloading and distribution runs;

2) For effectiveness, a requirement exists for quick *lateral supply* among all centers. This involves determining the shortest distance between each pair of locations in the network to minimize transportation costs when 'sharing' demanded items during shortages.

3) For efficiency and effectiveness, 'fielding' *initial inventory items* involves determining minimum distances *one way* from the central depot to all satellites, without the return of vehicles requirement.

Fortunately there are network routing techniques that can help establish appropriate distribution routes to optimize each of these distribution performance requirements. These are illustrated in turn.

Requirement 1: Delivery vehicles must continually visit all depots and return home, using the minimal total distance.

This networking problem involves continual cycling of distribution vehicles from the central depot to satellites, with return to the central depot for repeated runs. It is the classic case for the network technique called the *traveling salesman problem*. It can be applied to all sorts of similar problems, such as routes for delivery trucks, traveling salesmen, or guards making rounds.

Using what is called a 'quick and dirty' algorithm, the 'traveling salesman' systematically progresses from one location to another. [151] At each new node, the shortest 'next' distance is chosen (from among the several paths). There are two key rules for this algorithm:

1) the optimal tour will never intersect itself, and

2) each location will be visited once, and only once.

This selection of new nodes continues until the traveler ends up back where the trip started. Then, by inspection, one goes back though the network (i.e., repeats the process) to see if any alternative connections would result in further reducing the total distance.[152] Let us look at a simple heuristic procedure that can be useful for solving smaller traveling salesman network problems.[153] Using the defense depots listed above, we first develop a network using a map as shown in *Exhibit 11-2(a)*.

The next step is to find the shortest route that connects all the locations and returns home at the end of the delivery run. Recall that the traveling salesman technique requires that the delivery vehicle visit each location once to drop off or pick up inventory, and then proceed to the next location. All locations must be visited on each delivery run, and can only be visited once per run. The delivery vehicle must complete this circuit by returning, in this example, to Susquehanna, PA, the starting point.

Exhibit 11-2 (a)

Optimal Traveling Salesman Route
(green lines)

The following illustrates the traveling salesman procedure:

1) On the first pass, the traveler leaves Susquehanna, PA, and proceeds to the nearest location, Tobyhanna, PA, 80 miles away.

2) The traveler then proceeds to the next nearest (not yet visited) location, Richmond, VA, 250 miles away.

3) From Richmond the traveler proceeds to Cherry Point, NC (180 miles).

And so forth—the traveler proceeds along the next shortest routes sequentially to Warner Robins, GA, Albany, GA, Jacksonville, FL, Anniston, AL, Columbus, OH, and finally back home to Susquehanna, PA. The green lines in *Exhibit 11-2(a)* illustrate the shortest route.

Exhibit 11-2(b) shows the actual steps for determining the shortest round trip route. It is illustrative to note that the 'first pass' proscribed a route leaving Cherry Point to Warner Robins, GA (420 miles), but on a second pass to search for shorter linkages, it becomes obvious upon inspection that branching first through Jacksonville (450 miles) results in a shorter overall path. The comparison sequences are: *1ˢᵗ pass*—Cherry Point, NC, to Warner Robins—420 miles, then to Albany, GA—120 miles, Jacksonville, FL—230 miles, and Anniston, AL—370 miles: a total of 1,040 miles.

However, upon inspection, a *2ⁿᵈ pass* path reveals the shorter path—from Cherry Point, NC, to Jacksonville—450 miles, followed by visits to Albany, GA—230 miles, Warner Robins, GA—120 miles, and Anniston, AL—120 miles was shorter. The 2ⁿᵈ pass computes to a total of 920 miles, and a net savings of 220 miles. This demonstrates the technique's recursive nature (and need for computerized algorithms for larger networks).

Exhibit 11-2(b)

Optimal Traveling Salesman Route Steps

First Pass	80 miles	Second Pass	80 miles
#1 Tobyhanna	250	#1 Tobyhanna	250
#2 Richmond	180	#2 Richmond	180
#3 Cherry Point	420	#3 Cherry Point	450
#4 Warner Robins	120	#4 Jacksonville	230
#5 Albany	230	#5 Albany	120
#6 Jacksonville	370 (1140)	#6 Warner Robins	120 (920)
#7 Anniston	470	#7 Anniston	470
#8 Columbus	_350_	#8 Columbus	_350_
#9 Home	_2470_	#9 Home	_2250_
Total Miles		Total Miles	

While simple to state, this heuristic approach is often quite difficult to solve. For very large problems, this procedure becomes exceedingly complex. To solve such large problems, Bell Laboratories developed a computer program that decomposes the problem into smaller portions, then reconnects subsolutions. The first step is to choose a random path (not necessarily free of intersecting branches), break the pattern into, say, three sections, and then connect the sections differently until shortest paths are determined.[154]

Also, another approach, *neural networks,* has been adapted to solve complex traveling salesman problems.[155] For very complex networks it involves what neural network analysts call 'massively recursive' cycling. That is, on the first pass, the shortest link for each successive node is connected. Then, on recursive passes, a (computerized) search for shorter paths is sought. All paths are reviewed until the shortest is found. Neural network techniques calculate 'weights' for each node-arc using either statistical probabilities or partial differential equations that are developed from previous passes through the network. These recursions are repeated until successive passes yield no improvements.

Requirement 2: Quick Lateral Resupply

This requirement is essentially to determine the shortest route from *any location* (i.e., main depot or satellite) to *any other location*. This is necessary since the business implies that any item shortage not satisfied by routine resupply can be 'borrowed' from any other location that has a 'spare.'

The *shortest route problem* approach can be used to determine these routes. This technique is notionally very simple. For each location, calculate the shortest individual distance from each of the other locations in the network. Then, determine the nearest location with available stock (say, from computerized central inventory records) to request the resupply action.

Calculations of shortest distances to Richmond were made as follows:

1) Find the closest depot to Richmond, and mark the number of miles (on a map).

2) Find the next closest depot, either adjacent or with *total combined miles* through (previously marked) intermediate locations.

3) Update distance of each new location with the distance to the last marked location mileage, plus the additional new mileage.

4) Continue until all locations have been marked.

Exhibit 11-3 illustrates these steps.

Exhibit 11-3

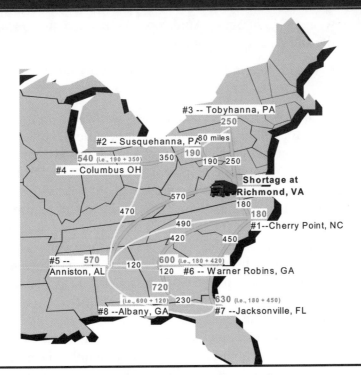

Hypothetical Lateral Resupply Routes

Rank Order of	#1 Cherry Point	180 miles
Closest Satellite	#2 Susquehanna	190
Depots from which	#3 Tobyhanna	250
to Resupply	#4 Columbus	540
Shortages to	#5 Anniston	570
Richmond	#6 Warner Robins	600
	#7 Jacksonville	630
	#8 Albany	720

For example, if Richmond should have an item shortage, the closest distribution satellite from which to borrow is Cherry Point. If Cherry Point cannot provide the item, the next closest potential supplier is Susquehanna, followed by Columbus, Anniston, Warner Robins, Jacksonville and Albany, in that order.

Requirement 3: Minimal Initial Provisioning Distances

Here we seek to *minimize the one-way transportation costs* for initial provisioning of a new item. However, unlike the traveling salesman problem, repeated runs are not needed. A one-time shipment to each location from a single source is all that is required, without a return of the delivery vehicle to home base. This problem can be useful for, say, outsourcing the deliveries of new or one-time deliveries by the least amount of miles to reduce commercial carrier costs. This networking technique is called the *minimal-spanning tree*. The green lines *Exhibit 11-4* illustrate the minimal one-way distances from Susquehanna to all other network locations.

The minimal-spanning tree is the simplest of the three routing algorithms. Here the goal is simply to connect the central location to all satellite locations using the minimum mileage while *spanning* the network. The lines connecting the central location to the satellites often look like a tree.

The procedure begins by selecting the origin node (Susquehanna—in this example). Then find the next nearest node and connect. Repeat, finding the next nearest (not yet connected) node from *any* connected node until all nodes are connected. This is known also as the *greedy algorithm*—at every step we are looking for the next minimum connection.

Exhibit 11-4

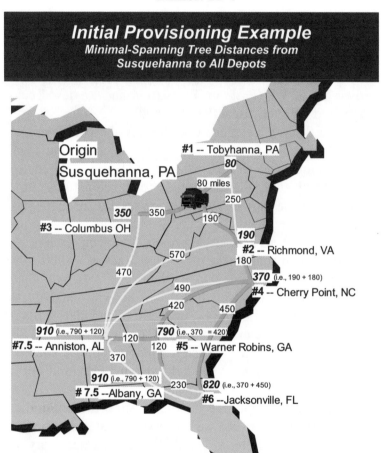

Initial Provisioning Example
Minimal-Spanning Tree Distances from
Susquehanna to All Depots

Shortest Total Distance (Minimal Route) to Provide Initial Supplies from Susquehanna to All Satellites		
#1 Tobyhanna	80 miles
#2 Richmond	190
#3 Columbus	350
#4 Cherry Point	370
#5 Warner Robins	790
#6 Jacksonville	820
#7.5 Anniston (tie)	910
#7.5 Albany (tie)	910

Scheduling Problems

Scheduling problems consider the best ways to sequence events and resources to minimize bottlenecks, prevent fragmented processes, and to identify critical steps that add unnecessary time or cost to projects. Perhaps the best known are PERT (Program Evaluation and Review Technique) and CPM (Critical Path Method).

PERT was developed in 1958 by the US Navy and Booz, Allen & Hamilton, a management consulting firm. The technique was needed to help track the hundreds of thousands of steps for the project to develop the Polaris submarine. It has since proven widely useful for managing other complex projects.

The Polaris submarine project was complex indeed, and involved management of 250 contractors, 9,000 subcontractors, and hundreds of thousands of individual tasks.[156] Major projects like this can become excessively expensive due to delays or lateness of smaller subsystems—such as material shortages or insufficient skills availability. Scheduling decision support routines such as PERT become essential to hold down costs and meet schedules.

PERT concepts are simple, despite the unfamiliar terminology. In fact, one author asserts that the concepts "…behind PERT were so simple that it was necessary to create a terminology…that would make it sound more exotic."[157]

To illustrate, we now review a simple case of a PERT application by returning to the 8-Day BCA example. Suppose that after the alternative to acquire new PCs has been chosen, the PC contractor has promised to deliver and set up the 18 PCs in one week (i.e., five 8-hour workdays). *Exhibit 11-5* illustrates the potential PC delivery network.

Exhibit 11-5

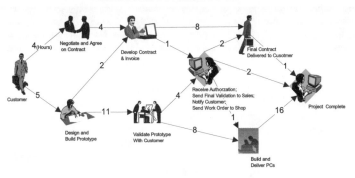

PERT Chart
PC Delivery Assembly and Delivery Flow

Contract to Provide 18 PCs

Major steps include two major paths that must be coordinated: the administrative path and the physical PC delivery path. Administratively, the contract and delivery schedule must be planned, coordinated, resourced, and finalized by customer receipt of the PCs. The physical schedule includes building the prototype PC, getting customer approval of the prototype, constructing the PCs, and physical delivery and set-up at the customer site.

The PERT technique permits the contractor to develop and coordinate all project steps. This is done in three steps: 1) compute the earliest time each node can be completed; 2) compute the latest time each node can be completed before the project is delayed; and 3) compute the slack time for each node.

1) *Compute the earliest time, T_E:* This is a forward pass through the network, com-

puting the earliest completion time for any single node.

Going from *left to right* on the project network chart, record the activity time (on top) of the succeeding node. *Exhibit 11-6 (a)* illustrates.

Exhibit 11-6 (a)

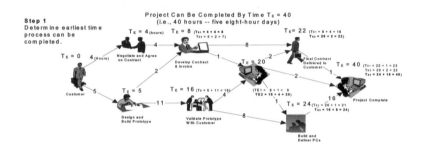

Forward Pass: Going from left to right	a)	*At first node: set* $T_E = 0$
	b)	*Add* T_E *to top of next node* (pick **largest total** *if multiple events feeding next event—all events must be included*)
	c)	*Continue to final node* (*final* T_E *is total project time*).

If several nodes lead in to a single node, record the *longest* activity time. Proceeding to the next connected node, record the cumulative value (i.e., the value on top of the last node plus the added activity time in-between). Again, if several nodes lead in, record the longest cumulative time. The final cumulative value of the final node is the earliest time the entire project can be completed.

> 2) ***Compute the latest time,*** T_L: This is a backward pass though the network, computing the latest time that any node

can be completed without being late for
the following nodes.

Going from *right to left*, subtract the activity time from the
end node and record (on bottom) of the preceding node as
shown in *Exhibit 11-6 (b)*:

Exhibit 11-6 (b)

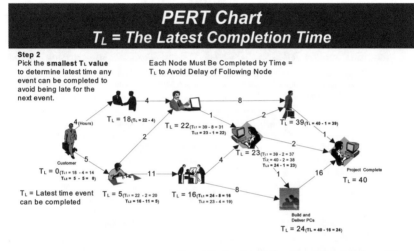

PERT Chart
T_L = *The Latest Completion Time*

Step 2
Pick the **smallest T_L value** to determine latest time any event can be completed to avoid being late for the next event.

Each Node Must Be Completed by Time = T_L to Avoid Delay of Following Node

$T_L = 18_{(T_L = 22 - 4)}$

$T_L = 22_{(T_{L1} = 39 - 8 = 31 \\ T_{L2} = 23 - 1 = 22)}$

$T_L = 39_{(T_L = 40 - 1 = 39)}$

$T_L = 23_{(T_{L1} = 39 - 2 = 37 \\ T_{L2} = 40 - 2 = 38 \\ T_{L3} = 24 - 1 = 23)}$

$T_L = 0_{(T_{L1} = 18 - 4 = 14 \\ T_{L2} = 5 - 5 = 0)}$

Customer

T_L = Latest time event can be completed

$T_L = 5_{(T_{L1} = 22 - 2 = 20 \\ T_{L2} = 16 - 11 = 5)}$

$T_L = 16_{(T_{L1} = 24 - 8 = 16 \\ T_{L2} = 23 - 4 = 19)}$

Project Complete
$T_L = 40$

Build and Deliver PCs
$T_L = 24_{(T_L = 40 - 16 = 24)}$

Backward Pass:
Going from right to left:

d) At last node: set T_L = Completion time (e.g., 40)
e) Subtract activity time of previous node(s) and record T_L to bottom of node (pick smalllest total if multiple events are preceding—all events must be included)
f) Continue to first node (T_L at the first node is the latest project starting time).

If multiple nodes precede, record the *shortest* activity time.
Receding backward to the next connected node, record the
cumulative value (i.e., the value on bottom of the last node
minus the activity time in-between). Again, if several nodes
lead in, record the shortest cumulative time. The final cumulative value of the final node is the earliest time the entire project can begin.

3) *Compute the Critical Path*: Compute the
slack time, *S*. This is the time available

to any activity to avoid slippage of the overall project.

The equation for slack time is $S = T_L - T_E.$ *Exhibit 11-6 (c)* illustrates. A positive S value indicates the activity can take extra time, perhaps to 'loan' the assets to a more critical function without impacting without impacting final project

Exhibit 11-6 (c)

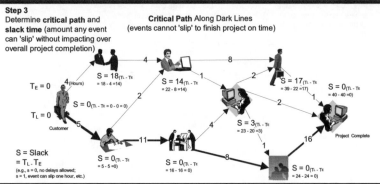

PERT Chart
S = Slack Time (=zero for critical path)

Step 3
Determine **critical path** and **slack time** (amount any event can 'slip' without impacting over overall project completion)

Critical Path Along Dark Lines
(events cannot 'slip' to finish project on time)

$S = Slack = T_L - T_E$ (i.e., $S = 0$, no delays allowed; $S = 1$, event can slip one hour, etc.)	g) At each node: calculate the Slack value (e.g., $T_L - T_E$)
The critical path connects events with lowest 'S' values—slippage along this path causes delay of total project completion.	h) Circle each node with '0' slack i) Connect zero slack nodes with longest paths. **This is the critical path.**

completion. With a negative S value, the next event will be started late. Connections of the 'zero slack' events with the *longest* paths indicate the critical path. A zero slack event must be completed on time if on the critical path, or else project completion will be late.

Soon after PERT was invented, analysts at Remington Rand and DuPont developed the Critical Path Method. The objective of both techniques is to identify the *critical path*. This is the path that contains events (i.e., nodes) that must be finished on time, or the total project completion will be delayed (and more costly). The two techniques are similar, but where PERT is more efficient in identifying scheduling problems, the Critical Path Method more easily computes 'crash time costs,' should a project need speeding up.[158]

Assignment Problems

Assignment techniques involve allocation of resources in a manner to take advantage of the 'selective competence' of resources. One person may be able to do one job faster than anyone else, yet be the only person capable of doing another job in a reasonable amount of time. In such cases, a cost effective process might involve a trade-off—the talented person doing the very difficult job, while a less well-trained person does the easier job.

Assignment techniques are basically tabular in nature and involve additions and subtractions of values within a matrix table while searching for maximum or minimum values (e.g., profits, cost, time, etc.). These techniques can be quite useful for many problems, such as allocating people or machines. They could also have been used for the traveling salesman and shortest route problems. However, those transportation type problems are more simply solved by using network flow techniques.

Problems involving over a dozen or so assignments are usually solved using a computerized algorithm. Solutions to larger problems may be neither simple nor intuitive. Fortunately, for many smaller problems, the manager can quickly, manually make optimal allocations 'on the back of an envelope.'

An example helps illustrate. Assume, from our 8-Day BCA scenario, that the supervisor in charge of assigning technicians for various jobs has four work orders. She also has four technicians available, as indicated in *Exhibit 11-7(a)*. How should she assign the technicians to minimize the total time all technicians require to complete these work orders?

Exhibit 11-7 (a)

Estimated Time to Do Each Job (in hours)					
		Technician			
		#1	**#2**	**#3**	**#4**
Job	**A**	8 *(hours)*	24	18	12
	B	12	28	4	24
	C	20	20	16	16
	D	20	28	24	8

Step 1

Determine the smallest amount of time any job will take if any technician can do the work. Then, subtract the smallest number from all other numbers. The resulting table is shown in *Exhibit 11-7 (b)*.

Exhibit 11-7 (b)

Step 1 Fastest time — any worker to do any job					
		Technician			
		#1	**#2**	**#3**	**#4**	**Time to Complete Each Job**
Job	**A**	**0** (i.e., 8 – 8)	16 (i.e., 24 – 8)	10 (etc.)	4	**8**
	B	8 (i.e., 12 – 4)	24 (etc.)	**0**	20	**4**
	C	4	4	**0**	**0**	**16**
	D	12	20	16	**0**	**8**

*Time to complete all jobs if anyone can do any job = **36 Hours***

Zeros indicate the fastest time the job can be done. From the table, we can see that Technicians #1, #3 and #4 are better suited for Jobs A, B and D, respectively. The non-zero number in each box can be read as the relative *additional* time it would take that technician to do the job. So, for Job A, it would take Technician #2 16 hours longer than the fastest (i.e., Technician #1); for Technician #2—ten hours longer, and for Technician #4—four hours longer. Technician #2, perhaps less trained, will generally require more time on any job. If technicians can be assigned to more than one job, Technician #3 might be assigned both Job B and Job C. Or, Technician #4 might be assigned to Job D and Job C.

Step 2

Determine the additional amount of time required if *all technicians* must be assigned to *one job each*. This essentially determines how many additional billable hours would be required if some jobs are done by slower workers.

This step involves subtracting the smallest number in each column from all that column's numbers in the table from Step 1. *Exhibit 11-7(c)* shows results.

Exhibit 11-7 (c)

		Step 2 *Fastest time — one worker, one job only*				
			Technician			
		#1	**#2**	**#3**	**#4**	*Time to Complete Each Job*
Job	**A**	0	12 (i.e., 16 – 4)	10	4	*8*
	B	8	20 (i.e., 24 – 4)	0	20	*4*
	C	4	0 (i.e., 4 – 4)	0	0	*16*
	D	12	16 (i.e., 20 – 4)	16	0	*8*
						40 Hours

That is, 36 + 4. Four hours are added as slower Technician #2 is assigned.

The smallest numbers in columns #1, #3, and #4 are zero, so there in no change (i.e., zero is subtracted from each number in these columns). The smallest number in column #2 is 4. The results of subtracting 4 from each column number are as shown. This essentially says that using Technician #2 on Job C will add 4 additional billable hours.

There are usually reasons why assignments should not be made to only the fastest technicians. By spreading the load, all jobs might be finished sooner in chronological time, even though some individual jobs are done by slower technicians (and cost more billable hours). This is because the faster workers would still have to do one job after another in sequence, versus all jobs being worked in parallel. Also, slower workers need the experience to eventually get faster.

Step 3

Make assignments. This involves assigning technicians to tasks using zero times from the table in step 2 to avoid adding any additional billable hour time. This is illustrated in *Exhibit 11-7 (d)*.

In summary, we have examined several useful problem solving algorithms to solve common logistics situations for distribution, scheduling and assignment of system resources. While these techniques are useful when problems can be meaningfully separated, many business situations are far too complex for subsequent understanding of system interrelatedness. This is where a totally different approach, simulation, becomes quite useful. Simulation is examined in greater detail in the next chapter.

Exhibit 11-7 (d)

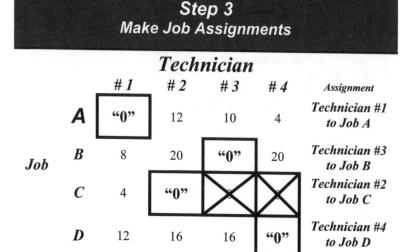

Step 3
Make Job Assignments

Technician

Job	#1	#2	#3	#4	Assignment
A	"0"	12	10	4	Technician #1 to Job A
B	8	20	"0"	20	Technician #3 to Job B
C	4	"0"	⊠	⊠	Technician #2 to Job C
D	12	16	16	"0"	Technician #4 to Job D

Step 3
a) Box the zero in row A.
b) *Box the zero in row B (and block the zero in row C).*
c) *Skip Row C until later (still has two unblocked zeros).*
d) *Box the zero in row D (and block the zero in the column above.*
e) *Box the final zero in Row C.*

Stop—all assignments have been made.

---

[149] Davenport (1993), p. 89.
[150] Information about DLA Defense Distribution Depots can be reviewed at http://www.ddc.dla.mil.
[151] R. Hesse and G. Woolsey (1980). *Applied Management Science: A Quick and Dirty Approach*. Chicago: Science Research Associates, Inc., pp. 102–105.
[152] Ibid.

[153] Ibid.

[154] Ibid.

[155] C. H. Dagli (Ed.) (1994), *Artificial Neural Networks for Intelligent Manufacturing*, London: Chapman & Hall, pp. 174–179; D. Garson (1998). *Neural Networks: An Introductory Guide for Social Scientists*. London: Sage Publications, pp 6–7.

[156] Ibid., p. 596.

[157] Hesse-Woolsey (1980), p. 109.

[158] R. I. Levin, D. S. Rubin, J. P. Stinson, and E. S. Gardner (1992). *Quantitative Approaches to Management* (8th ed.). New York: McGraw-Hill, Inc., pp. 608–618.

CHAPTER TWELVE
Simulation

=================================**12**
=================================

It is by imitation, far more than by precept, that we learn everything.
Edmund Burke (circa 1760)

So far we have analyzed network processes using techniques to optimize benefits or minimize costs implied by longer times, distances, critical paths, and so on. There are many problems in analyzing complex business cases that do not lend themselves to such ready formulation. They are either too 'fuzzy' to even pick a process model, or do not follow a neat enough sequence of steps to know, with enough clarity, which path leads to which other path.

Often, however, you can use simulation techniques to get close to an intuitively correct answer. Simulation techniques can model multiple events of a process—including sequential steps of a process and parallel steps of complementary processes which will 'join up' with main processes later. There are literally thousands of small calculations in most simulation models. Making use of a computer and special simulation software is usually essential.

Simulation generally involves two basic concepts, queuing (i.e., waiting line) theory and probability (i.e., stochastic) theory.

Queuing Theory

A 'queue' is the British word for a line. Waiting lines can be simulated to artificially game such situations as how long customers must wait at store checkouts, how many accidents might occur at a busy traffic center, potential backup of assemblies awaiting a machine process in a plant, and other similar events.

The basic notion of a queuing system is that entities arrive at some prescribed rate, say as inputs to a process to be serviced or worked on. Upon completion of the activity task at that stop, entities are then sent to the next step of the process. We visited the concept of 'activity' during the IDEF review — with the definition of an ICOM (i.e., Input-Control-Output-Mechanism) box (see *Exhibit 10-1*).

As an example of a process, suppose that orders arrive from customers at a rate of two (2) per day, and that it takes five (5) days to prepare, ship and transport an item to complete an order. Over time, if these rates were known to occur *with certainty*, and there was no restriction on processing (called the *infinite server* assumption), there would be a continual, *steady state* number of 10 (i.e., 2 * 5) items in the system, as illustrated in *Exhibit 12-1*.

Exhibit 12-1

Queuing System (Steady State Under Certainty)			
Period (Days)	Arrivals	Departures	Total in Queue
1	2	0	$2 = (1 * 2) - (1 * 0)$
2	2	0	$4 = (2 * 2) - (2 * 0)$
3	2	0	$6 = (3 * 2) - (3 * 0)$
4	2	0	$8 = (4 * 2) - (4 * 0)$
5	2	0	$10 = (5 * 2) - (5 * 0)$
6	2	2	$10 = (6 * 2) - (1 * 2)$
7	2	2	$10 = (7 * 2) - (2 * 2)$
Etc.	.	.	.

$$T_{\text{otal in Queue}} = (\# A_{\text{rrivals per period}} * \# P_{\text{eriods}}) - (\# D_{\text{epartures per period}} * \# P_{\text{eriods}})$$

Probability Theory

Most real world events, however, do not occur with certainty. Nor, generally, is there infinite server capacity. This is where probability theory enters the picture. Arguably, the most commonly used theoretical probability distribution in modeling arrivals to a process is the *Poisson distribution.*[xxxv] Say, for example, the average number of arrivals to a process is *one per unit of time* (e.g., one per minute). *Exhibit 12-2 (a)* illustrates the relative probability of zero, one, two, etc. arrivals during that period.

Exhibit 12-2 (a)

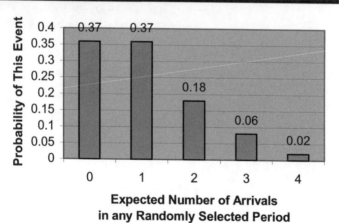

The probability of no (i.e., zero) arrivals, when the mean arrival rate is one per period, is 37%. The probability of

---

[xxxv] The Poisson distribution is named after the mathematician and physicist Simeon Poisson (1781-1840).

one arrival is also 37%. The probability of two arrivals is 18%, and so forth. The chances of four or more arrivals, when the mean arrival rate is one, are less than 2%.

Exhibit 12-2 (b) shows the calculations for determining the Poisson distribution (above), with an average of one arrival per period.

Exhibit 12-2 (b)

Calculation of Poisson Distribution Values (mean arrival rate = 1 per period)

The equation for the Poisson probabilities is:

$$P(x) = \frac{e^{-\lambda} \lambda^x}{x!}$$

Where:
$P(x)$ = *probability that the* X *value will occur.*
e = 2.71828
λ = *the mean arrivals (this is the Greek letter lambda, often used)*
x = *the number of arrivals for which you seek a probability of occurring.*
$x!$ = *the factorial*
(e.g., if $x = 3$, $x! = 3 \times 2 \times 1 = 6$).

Calculations: *P(0) = Probability of zero arrivals in the time period.*

$$P(0) = \frac{2.71828^{-1} 1^0}{0!} = \frac{.37 * 1}{1} = .37$$

$$P(1) = \frac{2.71828^{-1} 1^1}{1!} = \frac{.37 * 1}{1} = .37$$

$$P(2) = \frac{2.71828^{-1} 1^2}{2!} = \frac{.37 * 1}{2} = .18$$

$$P(3) = \frac{2.71828^{-1} 1^3}{3!} = \frac{.37 * 1}{6} = .06$$

$$P(4) = \frac{2.71828^{-1} 1^4}{4!} = \frac{.37 * 1}{24} = .02$$

Also, a different distribution, the 'exponential distribution,' is often used to predict the estimated time the entity remains in the process after arrival.

For a process that averages four arrivals per unit of time, the distribution is more spread out, as shown in *Exhibit 12-2 (c)*. For larger mean arrival rates, the distribution begins to look more like the normal curve.

Exhibit 12-2 (c)

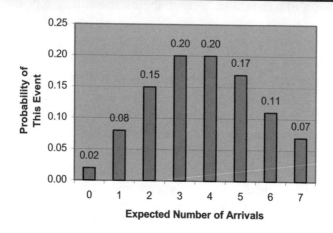

Let us now look at how the Poisson distribution can be used to model hypothetical arrivals of some entity to a process. Using an expected arrival rate of one entity per period of time (as seen in *Exhibit 12-2 (a)*), we will assign random numbers to imitate various arrivals at the same frequencies of the Poisson distribution.

To manually simulate arrivals where there is one arrival per period, one can use sequential two-digit numbers from a list of *random numbers*. Random numbers provide an unbiased estimate, and tables can be found in most statistics textbooks (or can be directly generated in some spreadsheet software). For example, numbers that fall within 00 to 36 can represent zero arrivals; within 37 to 73, one arrival; 74 to 91, two arrivals; 92 to 97, three arrivals; and 98 to 99, four or more arrivals. For more accurate estimates, simply repeat this process many times (with a computer) and average the results. Also, a warm-up period is advisable to reach steady state statistical values. The frequencies of your simulated arrivals will begin to look very much like the Poisson frequencies after many repeated trials.

To estimate the second factor, the mean time an entity is *in the system* (i.e., being processed), the *exponential distribution* is often used. Like the Poisson distribution, the exponential distribution becomes more spread out as the mean number of processed entities increases. It represents the probability that an entity still remains in the process, given one, two, three, or more periods of time.

Now, to estimate the number in the process for any random unit of time, it is simply a matter of multiplying the expected number of arrivals per period times the expected number of entities remaining in the process at any given period. This seems simple enough. However, when there are many nodes, related either sequentially or in parallel, a tremendous number of calculations are required. Add to this the need for many cycle iterations (to reach steady state averages) and the calculations quickly become very tedious. However, with the use of a quick computer and the development of super efficient computerized simulation languages, such calculations can be made relatively quickly and in a timely manner. These tools provide unprecedented capabilities to evaluate 'what if' scenarios that, not too long ago, could only be solved using analytical algorithms—and those solutions would often have been too simple to catch the true dynamics of the process.

Simulation Example

The data for our example were derived from published statistics by a large United States Department of Defense procurement organization. The Department of Defense purchases literally billions of dollars in petroleum products annually to fuel the Army, Navy, Air Force and various other organizations. In Fiscal Year 2002, for example, the central wholesale fuels acquisition center purchased 178 million barrels (at 42 gallons per barrel), at a cost of 4.8 billion dollars. During the same year, 135 million barrels were 'sold' to the Army, Navy, Air Force, and so on, from this central purchasing agency.[159]

Manual Calculations of Queues

With a few assumptions, it turns out for steady state processes that a number of interesting statistics can be calculated directly.

First, for the example petroleum purchases, let us transform the annual purchases and sales into monthly figures. Here we shall define 'sales' as 'arrivals' of customer orders, and 'completed purchases' in terms of average time for process customer orders.

Annual sales were 135 million barrels. From this, assume that customers are sufficiently distributed so that each month's requirement is similar. That is, the average demand, the *arrival rate*, is about *11 million barrels per month* (i.e., $135_{\text{million}} \div 12_{\text{months}}$).

Now to estimate departure rates. Purchases of 178 million barrels imply acquisition of about 15 million barrels per month (i.e., $178 \div 12_{\text{months}}$). Suppose an assumption can be made (say, from interviews with subject matter experts) that normal purchases average about one million barrels per acquisition. This implies that a purchase is completed about every two days (i.e., $30_{\text{days}} \div 15_{\text{purchase events}}$). The average time required to complete purchases (assuming the infinite server condition) is about 0.06667 months (i.e., 2 $_{days}$ ÷ 30 $_{days}$).

So, the implied *steady state number of orders in the process* per month (in millions of barrels) is *11 $_{arrivals}$ * .06667 $_{months}$* = *.773* million barrels of orders being constantly serviced. That is, the calculations indicate that there are orders for 773,000 barrels being processed at any given time, on a continuous basis.

Assumptions for Manual Calculation

Again, calculations depend on the assumption that the numbers of arrivals and departures are *known with certainty* (i.e., are deterministic) and evenly spread out over the period, with seasonality and trend not yet considered. Also, implicitly assumed, is that all incoming orders can be *handled at the same rate*, about two days (i.e., the infinite server assumption that entities are serviced and leave the queue as fast or faster than new ones arrive). Without the infinite server condition, a big backlog would occur as entities enter the process faster than they can be serviced. Other implicit assumptions are that the visiting population is sufficiently large to allow a random arrival rate, and that customers are treated first come, first served.

Simulated Calculations of Queues

Here, for model validity, we should expect that the simulated queues look similar to the manual calculations of the real world (empirical data) observations. Under the simulation, all the same statistical assumptions apply except for one—arrivals and departures are now modeled using probability distributions. Arrivals are still at 11 per month, and completed contracts (i.e., departures) take 2 days (*.06667 $_{months}$*). However, now the arrivals and departures are now considered averages, surrounded by *Poisson* and *exponential distributions* of events, respectively. The other assumptions, that all incoming orders can be handled at the same rate, that the visiting population is sufficiently large, and that customers are treated first come, first served are still in effect.

Using a computer, these rates were simulated for 100 iterations, and then averaged. After repeating the throughput calculations for 100 times, average simulated values do indeed approximate the manual (deterministic) values, providing a sense of model validity that the simulation is a fair representation of the real world values. *Exhibit 12-3 (a)* shows values from the two models under the infinite server assumption.

Exhibit 12-3 (a)

Comparison of Infinite Server Queues *Manual versus Simulated*		
Averages	**Manual (Deterministic) Calculation: Infinite Server**	**Simulation: (Stochastic) Infinite Server** *(100 Iterations Averaged)*
Average # awaiting service	*0*	*0*
Average # being serviced	*.733* *(733 million barrels)*	*.735*
Average orders in system	*.733*	*.735*
Average time awaiting service	*0*	
Average time in service	*= (.06667 months)* *= 2 days*	*2 days*
Average time in system	*2 days*	*2 days*

What If: No Infinite Server Assumption?

We shall now question the infinite server assumption. For example, assume that it is more reasonable to suspect that that there is only one organization (server), with a limited capacity to handle these large contracts. This is certainly reasonable for the wholesale petroleum example previously mentioned where each large contract consists of a maze of interrelated activities, each with limited functional resources for procurement, supply operations, quality assurance, legal, and so forth.

It so happens that theoretical *queuing equations* have been developed to directly calculate expected numbers of units in service for *limited numbers of servers.*[160] Taking the most extreme case for our example, *assume there is only one server* (versus an infinite server capacity). Calculations using the theoretical queuing equations for processing wholesale petroleum contracts are shown in the last column of *Exhibit 12-3 (b).*

Simulation of the 'One Server' Scenario

Here again, for model validity, we should expect the *queuing equation values* to look similar to the real world (empirical data) observations. We have already shown that simulations do indeed mimic real world processes, given enough averaged iterations to reach steady state conditions. Given this, we assume that by changing the simulation conditions to reduce infinite server capacity down to one server, the simulated queues will fairly represent a more 'burdened' throughput process. We test this by again simulating *arrivals* per unit of time *using a Poisson distribution* and *service times* using an *exponential distribution.* However, since there will be delays for induction of new entities into service (anytime the preceding entity has not departed), we will now compute two additional values: the *average number* of new orders (entities) that spend time in a queue for service (when the server is backed up and busy, and an the *average time* entities must wait in this queue. The middle column of *Exhibit 12-3 (b)* shows simulation values after 100 iterations.

Exhibit 12-3 (b)

Restricted Single Server Queues		
Simulated versus Manual		
Averages	**Simulation: (Stochastic)** (100 Iterations Averaged)	**Queuing Equations: (Deterministic) Single Server**
Average # awaiting service		$N_q = \dfrac{\lambda^2}{\mu(\mu-\lambda)}$
Nq = Average # in queue		$N_q = \dfrac{11^2}{15(15-11)}$
	= 2.03	= 2.01
Average # being serviced		
Np = Average # in process	= 0.740	—
Average orders in system		$N_s = \dfrac{\lambda}{\mu-\lambda}$
Ns = (Nq + Np)	(2.03 + 0.74) = 2.77	$N_s = \dfrac{11}{15-11} = 2.75$
Average time awaiting service		$T_q = \dfrac{\lambda}{\mu(\mu-\lambda)}$
Tq		$T_q = \dfrac{11}{15(15-11)}$ (= 0.183 month)
	= 5.86 days	= 5.49 days
Average time in service		—
Tp		
	=1.02 days	
Average time in system Ts = (Tq + Tp)		$T_s = \dfrac{1}{\mu-\lambda}$ $T_s = \dfrac{1}{15-11}$ (= 0.25 months)
	(5.86 + 1.02) =6.88 days	= 7.50 days

λ = average number of arrivals (Greek letter lambda)
μ = average time between arrivals (Greek letter mu)

Comparison of calculations between the analytical queuing equations and the simulation method shows that the results are very close. Theoretically, they would be equal with sufficient iterations of the simulation process.

The Erlang queuing equations are more direct, though not as flexible. Simulation offers agility to game 'what if' situations, and to combine overall results from related sequential and parallel servicing processes. For example, in simulation, one can build in 'balking' (e.g., the customer goes to another line) when the waiting line becomes too long. Also, simulation allows direct measurement of the effects of different arrival and departure distributions when data patterns indicate such a need.

Note the significant difference in the delays of input queues (awaiting service) between the infinite server and the single server scenarios. The single server 'bogs down' the throughput as new arrivals cannot get into service due to previous arrivals still in work Analysis of such waiting lines can provide informed estimates of needed process capacity improvements.

Summary

Simulation, waiting lines and queuing are important tools to 'game' complex processes and their interrelationships. The answers from simulation will generally provide pretty close approximations, though not as precise as analytical equations. For example, even after 100 iterations the simulation was still slightly different in the example above. Another popular analytical approach, one that provides 'optimal' and 'precise' answers to resource utilization, is *linear programming*, reviewed in the next chapter.

---

[159] *Defense Fuel Supply Center Fact Book, Fiscal Year 2002*. Ft. Belvoir, VA, Defense Energy Support Center, Defense Logistics Agency, www.desc.dla.mil, pp. 18 and 52.

[160] R. I. Levin, et al., pp. 720–721.

CHAPTER THIRTEEN
Linear Programming

==**13**

The highest form of efficiency is that which can utilize existing material to the best advantage.
Jawaharlal Nehru (circa 1950)

The simplex method is the basic technique that was originally used in *linear programming*. The technique was 'invented' by American mathematician George Dantzig, then a planning expert for the U.S. Air Force, in 1947.[161] In practice, linear programming has become one of the most used quantitative aids for business analysis.[162] Numerous applications can be found in finance, marketing, production scheduling, human relations management planning, distribution, ingredient blending, petroleum product production, and other enterprises.

Linear programming (LP) is a very efficient way for dealing with a finite number of possible allocations of resources (i.e., constraints) while maximizing some benefit or minimizing some cost (i.e., objective function). It is a step-by-step procedure that assumes that the constraint-objective function relationships are linear (i.e., additive) as resources are allocated toward final process solutions.

The oil companies in the United States were the first to start using linear programs in the late 1940s with the advent of the first large capacity computers. Their management of petroleum products serves as a good example for the power of this technique. Such problems involve thousands of constraints and decision variables. Linear programming techniques allow computation of optimal decisions about how much crude oil to pump from thousands of wells around the world, how to allocate tankers for transport to refineries, and how much gasoline, kerosene, jet fuel, and so on, to be 'cracked' from crude for delivery to customers.[xxxvi]

Arguably, 99% of all LP problem solutions require use of a computer.[163] Manual solutions are generally found only in simple (two-variable) classroom illustrations. Having said that, we shall first look at trivial classroom type problem to get a flavor for the allocation process, then revisit our traveling salesman and assignment problems—this time using linear programming.

Graphical Linear Programming Example

Let us revisit contractor who will provide the PCs identified in the 8-Day BCA section. The contractor's task is to determine the expected costs of new PCs in order to offer a competitive price. This involves estimating costs of operations, plus a reasonable profit.

Suppose accounting records are available for sales for the two main models of PCs that the vendor sells: the Deluxe and Standard configurations. From experience, the contractor prices the Deluxe Model at $1,500, and the Standard Model at $1,000. Based on historical costs of technicians' labor, inventory of components, and overhead for continual update of test equipment, past profits have averaged $300 per unit for Deluxe Models, and $200 per unit for Standard Models.

[xxxvi] While the simplex method is still widely used, a new method has been developed for extremely large linear programming problems was developed by Narendra Karmarkar of AT&T Bell Laboratories in the late 1980s for problems that are impractical for simplex solution.

Records also indicate the average resources used to produce the two types of PC models. Inventory investment is maintained at $42,000 by policy (historically, enough for an average week's production plus safety levels for commonly used components). There are twelve technicians (12 * 40 hours = 480 hours), and six test stands (6 * 40 hours = 240 hours, during normal work shifts). Expected resource requirements and profits are summarized in *Exhibit 13-1*.

Exhibit 13-1

Profits and Resources to Produce PCs			
Resources	*Deluxe Model*	*Standard Model*	*Available Resources*
Profit (per unit)	$300	$200	
Resources (used per unit)			
Inventory	$600	$525	$42,000
Labor Hours	6	5 2/3	480 hours
Test Stand Hours	4 4/5	2	240 hours

The data are now in place to develop the linear programming model. It consists of the 'objective function' (i.e., values we want to maximize or minimize) and 'constraint functions,' which specify the limits of resources used. We will use the simplex method, which systematically solves simultaneous linear equations. This method requires that all variables be of positive value (i.e., the non-negativity constraint—X_1, $X_2 \geq 0$). The linear programming model is illustrated in *Exhibit 13-2*.

Exhibit 13-2

LP Model to Produce PCs

Profits

Maximize: $\$300 * X_1$ + $\$200 * X_2$

(deluxe units) (standard units)

Subject to:	Inputs		Total Resources
Inventory	$\$600 * X_1$ (each deluxe unit produced)	+ $\$525 * X_2$ (each standard unit produced)	≤ $42,000
Labor	$6_{hours} * X_1$ (each deluxe unit produced)	+ $5.67_{hours} * X_2$ (each standard unit produced)	≤ 480 hours
Test Stands	$4.8_{hours} * X_1$ (each deluxe unit produced)	+ $2_{hours} * X_2$ (each standard unit produced)	≤ 240 hours

Where:

$X_1, X_2 \geq 0$

≤ is the symbol to indicate that total inputs must be less than or equal to the available resources on the right hand side (correspondingly, ≥ indicates values greater or equal).

The graphical solution is shown in *Exhibit 13-3*. A feasible solution requires that none of the constraints be exceeded. The area surrounded by Points A, B, C, D and E represent the feasible region. Because only linear equations and inequalities are used, the optimal solution will always occur at a corner point of the feasible region, where two constraints intersect. To find the optimal solution, simply pick the corner point that either maximizes or minimizes

Exhibit 13-3

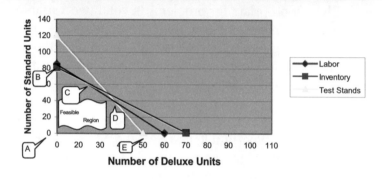

Graphical Linear Programming Solution

Point	Basic Constraints	Equations	Production Units	Profit
A		Deluxe Units (DU) = 0 Standard Units (SU) = 0		$ 0
B	Inventory	Inventory Constraint $600 * DU + $525 * SU = $42,000 600 (0) + 525 * SU = 42,000 SU = 42,000 ÷ 525 = 80	DU (deluxe units) = 0 SU (standard units) = 80 (solutions by standard algebra)	80 (standard units) * $200 = $16,000
C	Inventory and Labor	Inventory $600 * DU + $525 * SU = $42,000 Labor 8 hours * DU + 5.67 hours * SU = 480	DU (deluxe units) = 17 SU (standard units) = 60	17 * $300 + 60 * $200 = $17,100
D	Labor and Test Stands	Labor 8 hours * DU + 5.67 hours * SU = 480 Test Stands 4.8 hours * DU + 2 hours * SU = 240	DU (deluxe units) = 35 SU (standard units) = 34	35 * $300 + 34 * $200 = $17,300
E	Test Stands	Deluxe Units (DU) = 0 Standard Units (SU) = 0	DU (deluxe units) = 50 SU (standard units) = 0	50 (deluxe units) * $300 = $15,000

the objective function, depending on the goal of the problem. For our example, Point D, at a value of $17,300, maximizes the profits for the objective function.

The graphical solution above, while intuitive, is generally inappropriate for problems beyond two variables. However, the underlying solution by simultaneous linear equations, using the simplex method, remains valid for more complex problems, and is computationally easy for a computer. The actual mechanics of the simplex method are found in most quantitative texts and are not reviewed here. However, there are a number of computerized programs that solve these type problems (e.g., the Microsoft Excel Spreadsheet 'Solver' program, found under 'Tools').

We shall now revisit two practical problems, transshipment (previously solved using the shortest route networks technique) and the assignment of workers (previously solved using tables). These can also be solved using linear programming.

Shortest Routes using Linear Programming

Recall that we previously solved a lateral resupply (i.e., transshipment) problem by finding the shortest routes between several potential source depots and the Richmond Depot (see *Exhibit 11-3*). The idea was that if Richmond was short some needed item, the information system could be queried to select the nearest location with a spare to make the loan to Richmond. Now, suppose there are several 'needy' locations, as well as several supplying locations. This is a typical problem in industry, say, when several factories produce items for several customers, and seek to minimize overall shipping miles.

For our example, we shall now use linear programming to simplify the problem. Our hypothetical scenario is that severe weather has disrupted electrical service in many of the inland states, and the Defense depot system must seek to distribute available spare portable generators from eastern depots to help with the crisis. The table in *Exhibit 13-4* illustrates the locations with spare generators and those with additional requirements.

Exhibit 13-4

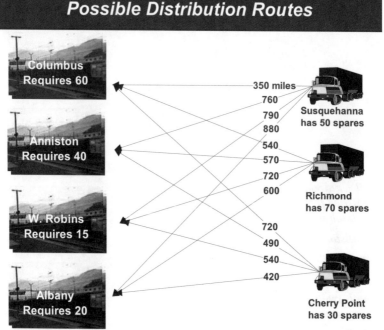

Possible Distribution Routes

Columbus Requires 60

Anniston Requires 40

W. Robins Requires 15

Albany Requires 20

350 miles
760
790
880
540
570
720
600
720
490
540
420

Susquehanna has 50 spares

Richmond has 70 spares

Cherry Point has 30 spares

Question: Which routes to use and how many should be shipped on each?

We now compute the least miles required to transship enough generators to satisfy the requirements by using linear programming and a computer. The linear programming model is shown in *Exhibit 13-5*.

Exhibit 13-5

Linear Programming Model
Transshipment of Generators from
Three Source Locations to Four Destinations

Minimize miles	*To:*	Columbus	Anniston	Warner Robins	Albany
From:	Susque-hanna	$350\,X_{11}$	$+\,760\,X_{12}$	$+\,880\,X_{13}$	$+\,790\,X_{14}$
	Richmond	$540\,X_{21}$	$+\,570\,X_{22}$	$+\,720\,X_{23}$	$+\,600\,X_{24}$
	Cherry Point	$720\,X_{31}$	$+\,490\,X_{32}$	$+\,540\,X_{33}$	$+\,420\,X_{34}$

Subject to:

All requirements satisfied for:

Columbus	X_{11}	$+\,X_{21}$	$+\,X_{31}$	$=60$
Anniston	X_{12}	$+\,X_{22}$	$+\,X_{32}$	$=40$
Warner Robins	X_{13}	$+\,X_{23}$	$+\,X_{23}$	$=15$
Albany	X_{14}	$+\,X_{24}$	$+\,X_{24}$	$=20$

And Available Spares not exceeded from:

Susquehanna	X_{11}	$+\,X_{12}$	$+\,X_{13}$	$+\,X_{14}$	≤ 50
Richmond	X_{21}	$+\,X_{22}$	$+\,X_{23}$	$+\,X_{24}$	≤ 70
Cherry Point	X_{31}	$+\,X_{32}$	$+\,X_{33}$	$+\,X_{34}$	≤ 30

$X_1, X_2 \ge \boldsymbol{0}$

The resulting calculation to deliver all required generators while not exceeding available spares from any source location is shown in *Exhibit 13-6*.

Exhibit 13-6

Solution to Transshipment Problem

Minimize Miles	*To*	Columbus	Anniston	Warner Robins	Albany
From	Susquehanna	50			
	Richmond	10	40		5
	Cherry Point			15	15

Tobyhanna, PA

Susquehanna
Ships 50 Units

Columbus OH   50   10 to
Receives 60 Units   Columbus
(10 from Richmond)

Richmond, VA
Ships 55 Units

40

5 to Albany

Cherry Point, NC
Ships 30 Units

15 to WR
15 to Albany

Anniston, AL
Receives 40 Units

Warner Robins, GA
Receives 15 Units

Albany, GA-Receives 20 Units(5 from Richmond)
Jacksonville, FL

Assignments Using Linear Programming

We now revisit the assignment problem, previously solved using a tabular method (see *Exhibit 11-7*). The initial assignment problem table is recreated below, shown in *Exhibit 13-7.*

Exhibit 13-7

Assignments Estimated Time to Do Work (in hours)				
Technician	# 1	# 2	# 3	# 4
A	8	24	18	12
B	12	28	4	24
C	20	20	16	16
D	20	28	24	8

Job (hours) labels the rows A, B, C, D.

Recall that the manual tabular method required several tableau steps. The simplex method of linear programming also requires several such steps, but the advantage is that with relatively inexpensive computer software the problem can be solved very rapidly. Also, these routines provide much useful information, such as how much slack (i.e., unused resource) is available for surplus resources, and sensitivity calculations to assess how much costs, profit or resources can change before the optimal solution becomes invalid.

From the tabular solution, we saw the optimal assignment of technicians was Technician 1 to Job A, Technician 2 to Job C, Technician 3 to Job B, and Technician 4 to Job D (see *Exhibit 11-7 (d)*). Using linear programming, the solution to the problem is the same.

First, we set up the initial linear programming model in Exhibit *13-8 (a)*.

Exhibit 13-8 (a)

Linear Programming Model for Assignment of Technicians				
Minimize Job Times **Technician**	**#1**	**#2**	**#3**	**#4**
Time to Complete **Job A**	$8X_{11}$	$+24X_{12}$	$+18X_{13}$	$+12X_{14}$
Job B	$12X_{21}$	$+28X_{22}$	$+4X_{23}$	$+24X_{24}$
Job C	$20X_{31}$	$+20X_{32}$	$+16X_{33}$	$+16X_{34}$
Job D	$20X_{41}$	$+28X_{42}$	$+24X_{43}$	$+8X_{44}$

Subject to:
Only one technician assigned per job:

Technician #1	X_{11}	$+X_{21}$	$+X_{31}$	$+X_{41}$	$=1$
#2	X_{12}	$+X_{22}$	$+X_{32}$	$+X_{42}$	$=1$
#3	X_{13}	$+X_{23}$	$+X_{33}$	$+X_{43}$	$=1$
#4	X_{14}	$+X_{24}$	$+X_{34}$	$+X_{44}$	$=1$

Time spent on a job does not exceed normal completion time:

Job A	X_{11}	$+X_{12}$	$+X_{13}$	$+X_{14}$	≤ 1
Job B	X_{21}	$+X_{22}$	$+X_{23}$	$+X_{24}$	≤ 1
Job C	X_{31}	$+X_{32}$	$+X_{33}$	$+X_{34}$	≤ 1
Job D	X_{41}	$+X_{42}$	$+X_{43}$	$+X_{44}$	≤ 1

Then the model solution is calculated, as shown in *Exhibit 13-8 (b)*.

Exhibit 13-8 (b)

Linear Programming Solution For Optimal Assignments

Technician	*# 1*	*# 2*	*# 3*	*# 4*
Job				
A	8 (hours)			
B			4	
C		20		
D				8

The linear program calculates the cost (in hours spent), where the tabular method implied these values as extra hours that could be eliminated. The point is, many problems can be solved using different methods—the easiest method is often preferred.

Summary

So far, we have had a cursory overview of several of the most useful methods to help quantify business costs and benefits. Statistical analysis, process modeling, network analysis, simulation and linear programming can all provide excellent measurement tools for analysis of business situations. One of the biggest cost areas for business, and one of the most complex, is inventory management. Inventory models borrow from all of the technical areas mentioned so far, and comprise one of the most promising subjects for potential 'to be' improvements for many business cases. Inventory is reviewed in detail in Chapter 14.

---

[161] J. J. O'Connor and E. F. Robertson (1996). George Dantzig, University of Saint Andrews, Scotland, http://www-history.mcs.st-andrews.ac.uk/history/References/Dantzig_George.html.

[162] Levine (1992), p. 397.

[163] Hesse-Woolsey (1980), p. 197.

CHAPTER FOURTEEN

Inventory

================================== **14**

During the 1940s 50% of production costs were labor—efficiency focused on labor; by the 1990s materials were 60%, labor around 15%—efficiency focus shifted to material planning.

Carol A. Ptak (circa 2000)

The cost of inventory and material flow is now believed to exceed the cost of labor in many manufacturing and materials handling companies. Efficient use of human skills resources (labor) is still very important as well, and was covered in the section under business process modeling. Here we shall concentrate on material inventory.

The typical cost of material in a manufacturing company can average 60 to 70% of the total cost of goods sold.[164] So it behooves the smart business enterprise to be aware of effective inventory control concepts and techniques.

Optimal Inventory Costs

We will look at two basic approaches for determining best potential 'to be' inventory management processes: inventory models for generally less expensive consumable items, and models for expensive recoverable (i.e., reparable) items.

Consumable Item Management

The *Economic Order Quantity (EOQ)* is perhaps the oldest and best-known inventory model for managing consumable items. It is used in many public and private sector applications. Ford Harrison of Bell Telephone Laboratories is generally credited with its development in 1915, though it is often referred to as the 'Wilson EOQ' or simply the 'Wilson Q,' based R. H. Wilson's 1934 *Harvard Business Review* article, "A Scientific Routine for Inventory Control." Wilson also worked for Bell Labs.[165]

EOQ models are used to estimate the lowest total costs between 'cost to order' and 'cost to hold.' This is the point where ordering cost equals holding cost.

For illustration, we revisit our hypothetical PC vendor from the 8-Day BCA scenario, and examine the inventory management scenario for components used to assemble PCs. Lets assume that the vendor's records indicate that value of inventory consumption to fill orders for PCs has averaged around $42,000 per week or $2,184,000 annually (i.e., $42,000 x 52 weeks). Reordering costs (C_O) have averaged about $1,500 per order. These expenses cover such activities as research on latest PC components and software, labor costs of technicians and buyers, and inventory receiving, management and accounting. Costs to hold these items for a year (C_H) have averaged 20%, and include interest on revolving credit, storage and theft protection, insurance, taxes, pilferage and obsolescence.

As can be seen in *Exhibit 14-1*, the combined cost of ordering and holding inventory has been manually calculated to be lowest at about 12 orders per year (i.e., the EOQ). This estimate was calculated by successive combinations of $C_O + C_H$, for progressively smaller (and more frequent) orders. For example, if *only one order was placed per year*, the C_O would be $1.5 thousand, and the C_H would be $281.4 thousand. This is calculated by first assuming that the average inventory is $1,092 thousand (i.e., $2,184 thousand $\div$ 2).

Exhibit 14-1

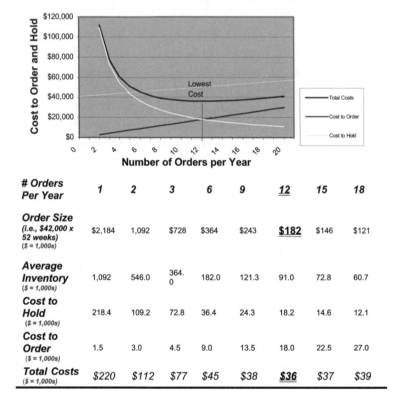

Total Cost Curve
Total costs lowest when ordering
Economic Order Quantity (EOQ)
= $182,000 twelve times a year

# Orders Per Year	1	2	3	6	9	12	15	18
Order Size (i.e., $42,000 x 52 weeks) ($ = 1,000s)	$2,184	1,092	$728	$364	$243	$182	$146	$121
Average Inventory ($ = 1,000s)	1,092	546.0	364.0	182.0	121.3	91.0	72.8	60.7
Cost to Hold ($ = 1,000s)	218.4	109.2	72.8	36.4	24.3	18.2	14.6	12.1
Cost to Order ($ = 1,000s)	1.5	3.0	4.5	9.0	13.5	18.0	22.5	27.0
Total Costs ($ = 1,000s)	$220	$112	$77	$45	$38	$36	$37	$39

C_H is then calculated to be $218.4 thousand (i.e., $1,092 * .20$). $C_O + C_H$ (i.e., $1.5 + 218.4 = 219.9$ ($\approx$ $220 thousand). The orders per year are then increased, and respective increases in C_O and decreases in C_H tallied, as shown in *Exhibit 14-1*.

As seen in the example, the combined total of $C_O + C_H$ is smallest at 12 orders per year at $36 thousand. This calculates to an average order size of $182 thousand (i.e., $2,184 ÷ 12$). Costs to order (C_O) generally increase the more times orders are made, and required order size decreases as more frequent orders are placed. Cost to order normally consists of expenses incurred for such elements as salaries of employees for purchasing, data entry, receiving, accounts payable, etc.

Cost to hold (C_H), also known as carrying cost, is often expressed as a percentage (say 20–30%) of the average annual value of items held, and may be available from your business accounting records if the company uses EOQ accounting policies. As shown in the example, average inventory is usually calculated as ½ of the amount of inventory bought during a period. The implicit assumption here is that items are used at a relatively constant rate—starting at 100%, then winnowing down to zero just before replenishment. *On average*, about ½ the stock is tied up awaiting consumption. C_H can consist of a number of expenses, including storage, record keeping, opportunity cost of tied up capital, space, insurance, pilferage, and taxes attributed to storage.

It so happens that these key statistics can also be calculated directly, which is more convenient for automated inventory management systems. Using EOQ equations, the optimal (exact) values of EOQ calculate to just less than 12 reorders per year at $181,000 inventory per order, as shown in *Exhibit 14-2*. Because of the robustness (i.e., flatness) of the total cost curve near the optimal solution, one can often 'eyeball' a nearly optimal answer, as shown in the tabular exhibit above.

Exhibit 14-2

EOQ Direct Calculations

Equation

1	**Total Costs (TC)**	= Cost to Order (C_O) + Cost to Hold (C_H)	= Number of Orders * Cost per Order + Average Inventory * Holding Cost per Unit	$= \dfrac{D}{Q} Co + \dfrac{1}{2} Q C_H$
2	**Optimal EOQ (Q^*)**		1st derivative of equation 1 using differential calculus	$Q^* = \sqrt{\dfrac{2DCo}{C_H}}$
		EOQ Example	Order size $181,000 (this differs from the tabular solution of $182,000 and reveals that the optimal reorder point is 12.066 orders per year— about two days less than a month)	$Q^* = \sqrt{\dfrac{2(2,184)(1.5)}{.20}} = 181$
3	**Total Cost of System TC (Q^*)**		Derived for Q^*	$TC(Q^*) = \sqrt{2DCoC_H}$
		TC (Q^*) Example	Total Cost of $36,000 to Order and Hold Inventory	$TC(Q^*) = \sqrt{2(2,184)(1.5)(.2)} = \$36$

Where: D = *Annual Demand*
Q = *Quantity Ordered (each order)*
Q^* = *Optimal Economic Order Quantity (EOQ)*
CO = *Cost to Order (each order)*
CH = *Cost to Hold (typically a percentage of value of inventory)*
$TC(Q^*)$ = *Total Cost of System for Optimal EOQ*

Inventory Reorder Points and Quantities

Exhibit 14-3 depicts graphically the well-known 'saw tooth' graph of inventory system reorder behavior.

Exhibit 14-3

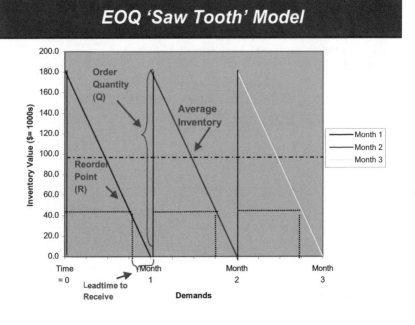

The implicit assumptions are that we have perfect knowledge about consumption during a given period of time, that the optimal reorder quantity is the Wilson Q, and that the reorder is made at the exact lead time required to ensure replenishment stocks will arrive at the instant just after the last of the existing stocks are consumed. The beginning of the month begins fully resupplied, followed by a systematic draw down of inventory, finally reaching zero stocks just before the new replenishment inventory arrives.

It turns out that total costs are relatively stable (i.e., the curve is flat) near the optimal EOQ in the total cost curve, as was seen in *Exhibit 14-1*. This gives some flexibility if the demand rates are too noisy, or the holding and ordering costs are rough estimates. However, where customer service is highly important, it is necessary to take into account the irregularities of stock consumption. For example, what if inventory consumption is variable (i.e., stochastic), more like the illustration in *Exhibit 14-4*?

Exhibit 14-4

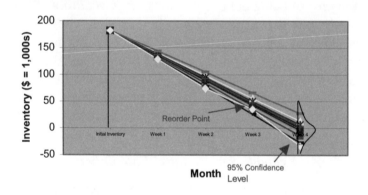

Service Level

In *Exhibit 14-4* we observe inventory consumption over several months (periods), layered on top of each other. Even if it is assumed that there is enough flexibility to increase or decrease orders to match beginning month inventories, end of month inventories will often vary (i.e., run short or high) of customer demands.

To compensate, inventory systems can add a *safety stock* to compensate for the potential backorders. This, of course, adds cost. The hope is that the added costs of safety stock exceed the lost opportunity costs (i.e., revenues, disrupted production, and good will) that occur when stock runs out. Lost opportunity costs, however, are often difficult if not impossible to calculate, especially in manufacturing situations. Therefore, many companies do not attempt to determine costs of being out of stock. Rather, they adopt what is called a *service level* policy. The service level is defined as the amount of stock required to avoid backorders *during reorder lead time*.[166] A safety stock is developed based on the historical variation of sales to assure, say, a 95% confidence of no inventory shortages before the reordered EOQ replenishment arrives.

This policy shifts the inventory evaluation criterion from *cost* of being out of stock to some *probability* of being out of stock that managers feel they can live with. A reorder point is calculated that includes both the mean consumption during procurement lead time, plus the safety stock. When inventories fall to this point, the EOQ is ordered. Upon arrival of the EOQ, a new cycle of inventory consumptions begins, and inventories are drawn down until the reorder point is again reached.

An Example Service Level Calculation

For our example problem, the order lead time is given as one week. This computes to an inventory value of $45,250 (i.e., ¼ of $181,000 monthly demand). Next, we wish to compute required safety stocks to ensure a 95% confidence of no backorders during lead time demand. For this calculation, establish a standard error from observed variations of end-cycle stocks over many cycles.

Exhibit 14-5 illustrates *service level* calculations for assurance at the 95% confidence level. The end-of-cycle variations indicate that stock used during lead time varies around the $45,250 with a standard error of ± $19,500. A safety stock is calculated to assure against the worst case (i.e., running short of stock) to assure 95% confidence. Using statistics, this is $32,175 (i.e., 1.65 * 19.500). The service level policy, then, will be to reorder the EOQ level whenever the existing inventory drops to the combined level of mean consumption ($45,250) plus safety level ($32,175), or $77,425.

Exhibit 14-5

Service Level at 95% Assurance ($ = 1,000s)				
Mean value of inventory consumption during lead time =			$ 45	
Standard Error of Ending Inventory (10-month history)				
Month	Available Stock	Desired Stock	Errors	Errors Squared	Step 1 Errors Squared
1	-6.7	0	-6.7	44.9	
2	13.4	0	13.4	179.6	
3	0.0	0	0.0	0.0	
4	26.8	0	26.8	718.2	
5	-13.4	0	-13.4	179.6	
6	-3.4	0	-3.4	11.6	
7	6.7	0	6.7	44.9	
8	3.4	0	3.4	11.6	
9	-26.8	0	-26.8	718.2	
10	-33.5	0	-33.5	1122.2	
				3030.8	Step 2 Sum of Squared Errors
				$19.5	Step 3* Standard Error

* Standard Error = $\sqrt{3080.8/8}$ (i.e., 10 – 2 degrees of freedom).

Calculation of Service Level (95% = 1.65 standard errors)

$45 _lead-time demand_ + $(1.65 * \$19.5)$ _safety stock_ ≈ $77 _reorder point_

Exhibit 14-6 graphically displays the normal probability distribution for 95% service level policy. These
calculations implicitly assume that the mean and standard
error are normally distributed.

Exhibit 14-6

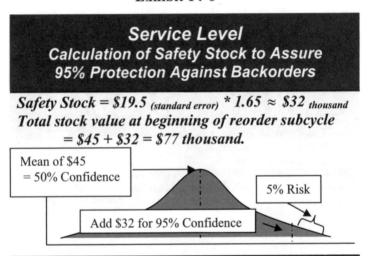

Service Level
Calculation of Safety Stock to Assure
95% Protection Against Backorders

Safety Stock = $19.5 (standard error) * 1.65 ≈ $32 thousand
Total stock value at beginning of reorder subcycle
= $45 + $32 = $77 thousand.

Mean of $45
= 50% Confidence

5% Risk

Add $32 for 95% Confidence

Business Case Analysis Considerations

Fill Rates

Many business inventory systems use *fill rate* as a
primary performance criterion. Fill rates are defined as the
probability of having a backorder anytime during consumption of the 'total EOQ consumption cycle.' Service levels,
reviewed above, refer to protection against stock-outs and
backorders during procurement lead time.

An important distinction can be made between *service levels* and *fill rates*. The service level policy of 95%
applies to the reorder period only. The probability of being
able to supply a request during the entire EOQ inventory
cycle is much better than 95%, since there is much more

stock during the first part of the cycle (after replenishment of the entire EOQ). [167] Demands during the one-week reorder subcycle are protected at 95%. However, for the entire four-week Wilson Q cycle (i.e., the total $181,000 cycle inventory), the first three weeks are hardly in jeopardy. [xxxvii] It may be important, during business case analysis studies, to ensure that fill rates are not being improperly used, when service levels may be more appropriate indicators of supply management performance. For example, when the total EOQ draw down cycle is much longer than the order lead time cycle, the fill rate may be very high—yet the service level subcycle may be constantly running too many backorders. Real process improvements may be possible by implementing an appropriate service level policy.

Lack of Historical Data

Often, for large enterprises managing thousands of reparable items, there is little historical data about an item, such as mean demand rates during procurement lead time, variation of these demands, and so on. For such situations, a rule of thumb was adopted by the U.S. Air Force, which manages millions of items in its standard base supply system. A sort of pseudo safety level is estimated using a proxy standard error that is calculated as $\sqrt{3Q}$, where Q is the average quantity demanded for the reorder lead time period. Using this estimate of the standard error, the total resupply pipeline requirement is calculated as shown in *Exhibit 14-6.* [168]

[xxxvii] Actual calculation of the increased total cycle *fill rate* confidence can be calculated. Using 'Unit Normal Loss Integrals' (from a statistical table) a value of .02064 is related to 1.65 standard errors. Multiplying .02064 * 19.5 (i.e., the standard error) = .40248. This is the proportion of risk related to the entire EOQ of 181. 1 - .40248 ÷ 181 = .99777, a very high confidence, indeed, for the entire EOQ cycle.

Recoverable Item Management

Perhaps the biggest distinction for inventory system analysis is between consumable items and recoverable items. An entirely different inventory management approach has evolved for recoverable items.

The consumable item EOQ calculations above are based on two basic categories, costs to order and costs to hold. Generally, the large majority of items in most inventory systems are small, relatively inexpensive bits and pieces. These items are good candidates for EOQ and consumable item management policies. However, inventories typically consist of a mixture of items, where some are more economical to repair than to consume. It can make good economic sense to evaluate the more expensive recoverables on a one-for-one basis.

A few examples of recoverable items include engines, radar units, telephone switching boxes, computer servers, and ship diesel engines. Such items are often expensive subcomponents of higher systems. They generally qualify as recoverable items when it has been determined that they are more economical to repair than to discard during maintenance activities. Further, these higher assemblies are often 'parent units' for multiple 'child' subcomponents, some of which are also recoverable items, and others which are consumables (e.g., nuts, bolts, fasteners, etc.). Such inventory distinctions can be made to progressively deeper item indentures, the highest end item to the lowest sub-indentures of individual items.

Due to the joint relationships among indentures, inventory management of recoverable items subject to corrective and/or preventive maintenance can be substantially more complex than management of items queued for standard manufacturing processes. Recoverables require a special kind of inventory management—one that considers highly variable resupply delays, item-by-item, versus the relatively fixed requirement lead times often assumed for consumable items.

Special recoverable item inventory management methods have been developed for management of these important items. The techniques explicitly calculate items in all stages of resupply, including repair and transportation.

Recoverable items are generally resupplied from multiple channels with variable lead times. These can include repair lead times for minor and major maintenance processes, and procurement lead time for replacement of condemned items. For example, in the 1980s the Air Force (for whom most of the following techniques were developed) was speculatively believed to have repaired approximately 9 out of 10 recoverable items. Substantial savings were possible, since costs of repair/refurbishment was approximately $1/6^{th}$ the cost of purchasing new items.

Of the nine processed into maintenance, five were recycled through minor repair at local (base level) and four were sent to depot level repair.[169] The remaining 10 percent were condemnations, and replacements were purchased new.

The management of recoverable items requires the supervision of a 'pool' of recoverable 'carcasses' in the resupply pipeline (to assure some minimal level of total system performance). It also implies the need for development of methods to control costs of limited financial resources to ensure the biggest bang for the buck. While their collective *dollar value is high* (often over ½ the total enterprise inventory value), recoverable items generally represent a *small percentage of the total number* of inventory items (often less than 10 percent).[170] Typically, an item can be managed as a recoverable when it is expensive enough to warrant cost of individual unit data collection and item management, and when it is more economical to fix than to replace. For example, the U.S. Air Force had a rule of thumb that if jet engine casing components could be refurbished for less than 60% of the cost of new casings, they were recovered—otherwise they were replaced with new ones.[171]

Recoverable Item Models

The underlying assumption for recoverables is that cost of downtime for a lower assembly is less than cost of downtime for its higher assembly. 'Spares' become feasible because downtime of the higher assembly is minimized. 'Remove and replace' actions return the higher assembly to serviceable condition more quickly, while its less costly subcomponents experience downtime.

The concept is really a simplification of the previous EOQ models—except now, instead of the pool of items purchased as an economic quantity of 'new items' that sit on the shelf until demanded, a pool of used items are moving though a repair process. The objective is to produce one refurbished item just in time to meet a new demand caused by the generation of an additional reparable carcass.[172]

To help understand this concept, we will review the principles of recoverable item management using *S-1, S inventory techniques*. These formed the basis for inventory models developed by the Rand Corporation for the U.S. Air Force in the 1960s-1970s.

The Conventional S-1, S Model

The notion is that total requirements for a specific item can be determined by adding the requirements of its respective serviceable and resupply pipeline segments. The required number of serviceable items is precisely the number needed for end item applications. When one item in the pool of serviceable items becomes reparable, the pool of S installed items becomes S-1. Theoretically, an immediate replacement is 'just becoming serviceable' from the repair processes. The newly serviceable item replaces the reparable, and the newly reparable item enters the repair pipeline process—theoretically balancing both the serviceable and reparable pools in the swap.

For example, consider a fleet of 60 aircraft where each aircraft must have its radar set calibrated every month. Assume it takes five days to do a calibration. This process will generate 720 radar set calibrations per year from the 60 aircraft—two sets arriving for calibration each day. This calculates to 10 sets continually in calibration (i.e., $10 = 2 \times 5$), similar to the steady state queuing example in *Exhibit 12-1*.

If there are no additional radar sets, the operational ready rate of the aircraft fleet is 83% (i.e., with 10 sets in repair, only $50 \div 60 = 83\%$ of the aircraft have operable radar sets). Suppose we purchase 10 additional radar sets. The total pool now consists of 70 units: 60 installed in aircraft plus 10 in the resupply pipeline. The steady state number of sets in repair is still 10, but the aircraft ready rate improves to 100% (i.e., 60 aircraft continually have good sets).

When buying additional assets to fill the repair pipeline, the system is not actually buying spares, but, rather, resupplying pipeline fillers. Theoretically, there is no such thing as a spare under the deterministic concept—no spares are sitting idly on a shelf awaiting issue. All items are in continual use—either as installed components or reparable undergoing repair. The assumption is that an item becomes available (i.e., serviceable) at the exact moment a new demand occurs.

The simplest S-1, S recoverable inventory models consider only the cycle delay time required to minimize the downtime of the higher assembly. The focus is on the expected delays of subcomponents due to reparable (recoverable) activities. In real world reparable processes, resupply times are inconsistent. Arrivals for repair are variable, and there are different mean times from various sources of replacement (e.g., from local shops, depots or new purchases of condemnations). The respective resupply times from the various sources are usually averages, with associated variances that, if known, can allow calculation of standard errors. This permits development of stochastic (probabilistic) models of the inventory resupply processes that hopefully predict more realistic inventory requirements.

An example of the Conventional Model

Let us first consider the possibility of different delay times due to different sources of resupply. Using the example of aircraft radar sets above, we calculated that two units are generated for calibration per day, and each requires a five-day repair cycle time. Suppose, however, that actual repair observations indicate that about only one-half of the units can be processed though local resupply, and the other one-half requires comprehensive maintenance at a centralized depot facility. The local repair echelon now requires a continual number of five units in resupply (2 per day $*$ 5 days to repair $*$ $.5$ proportion repaired locally $= 5$).

The other ½ of recoverable carcasses require depot level repair. Suppose the average resupply time from the depot echelon is assumed to be 30 days. Using the steady state queuing equation (e.g., *Exhibit 12-1)*, the requirement computes to 30 units continually in resupply due to the depot (i.e., 2 per day $*$ 30 days to repair $*$ $.5$ proportion repaired at depot $= 30$). In practice, some units are repaired and some condemned and purchased new. In the case, the 'thirty days' for depot resupply would be the weighted average from all higher echelon activities. By combining local and depot requirements, the total quantity (Q) of recoverable carcasses to prevent 'holes' in aircraft increases to 35 (i.e., 5 $_{repaired\ locally}$ + 30 $_{resupplied\ from\ depot}$ = 35). *Exhibit 14-7* illustrates.

Exhibit 14-7

Required Reparable Carcasses
Radar Sets: Two Resupply Echelons (Local and Depot)

*Local Resupply Pipeline: 2 $_{DDR}$ * .5 $_{PLR}$ * 5 $_{RCT}$* = 5
*Depot Resupply Pipeline: 2 $_{DDR}$ * .5 $_{PLR}$ * 30 $_{RCT}$* = <u>30</u>
Total Pipeline Requirement = Q = <u>35</u>

Where: **Daily Demand Rate (DDR) * Probability of Local Repair (PLR) * Repair Cycle Time (RCT) = Pipeline Requirement**

In this example it makes sense to acquire 35 extra units to become carcasses in the resupply processes to enable sufficient numbers of serviceable items to prevent radar set 'holes' in operational aircraft. This illustrates why there are theoretically no spares sitting on the shelf. This is actually a basic form of 'just-in-time' inventory.

Since the demand and resupply factors are averages, individual resupply actions will vary around them. In this example, the total number required for resupply, Q, is actually a weighted average of the two resupply echelons, local and depot. This average can be statistically interpreted to mean that there will be sufficient items (or more) becoming available on time about half the time. Suppose we now wish to increase the chances that the variable resupplies met some acceptable performance goal, such as a 95% confidence level. If it can be assumed that the 35 units in resupply are normally distributed, and historical data are available to compute standard error, then resupply quantities sufficient for the 95% confidence can be estimated as shown in *Exhibit 14-8* (i.e., the mean + 1.65 * standard error).[xxxviii]

Exhibit 14-8

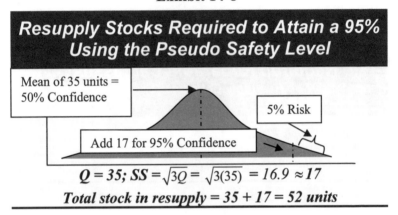

Resupply Stocks Required to Attain a 95% Using the Pseudo Safety Level

Mean of 35 units = 50% Confidence

5% Risk

Add 17 for 95% Confidence

$Q = 35; SS = \sqrt{3Q} = \sqrt{3(35)} = 16.9 \approx 17$

Total stock in resupply = 35 + 17 = 52 units

A positive feature of the Air Force's proxy measure for the standard error was that the calculated size of the safety stock proportionately diminishes relative to the average quantity Q in the resupply pipeline. However, in practice this model was found to be conservative—that is, service level calculations tended to stock too many items to achieve the target fill rates. Further, it did not consider costs across multiple items. It could handle only one item at a time. To provide more useful estimates to handle these issues, the Rand Corporation developed a new inventory model, the *Base Stockage Model,* to consider the benefit/cost ratios for comparison of multiple items.[173]

[xxxviii] A proxy of the standard error is calculated as $\sqrt{3Q} = \sqrt{3*35} = 10$. The safety factor to add to Q to attain a 95% confidence level = (1.65 * 10) = 16.5 ≈ 17 (rounded off).

Rand's Base Stockage Model

The U.S. Air Force think tank for inventory, the Rand Corporation, developed this model in the early 1960s to allow explicit consideration of costs and backorders among multiple items. The basic improvement to the conventional model was the ability to develop shopping lists that allow item-by-item comparisons of benefit/cost ratios. Benefits are calculated by a refinement of the Poisson distribution application that allows specific calculation of each item's expected backorders.

This differed from previous models that calculated a confidence level that specific demands would be satisfied. Instead, the performance measure shifted to minimizing partial (marginal) backorders among multiple items over time. The marginal improvement in reduced backorders was then weighted by the benefit-to-cost ratio allowing development of a shopping list of ranked items from highest to lowest bang for the buck. The allocation begins by adding the item with highest benefit-to-cost ratio, then the next highest, and so forth. The process repeats with remaining items until all required spares have been identified, or until a budget limit has been met.

To calculate expected backorders, Rand developers used Palm's Theorem.[174] This theorem states that if arrivals (for repair) are Poisson distributed, the number of units tied up in the resupply queue take on a similar Poisson distribution shape.[175] For example, let's compare the expected backorder reduction for three different items, with required resupply quantities Q of two (2), four (4), and five (5), respectively.

A recursive form of the expected backorder calculation is shown in *Exhibits 14-9 (a)*, *(b)*, *(c)* and *(d)*. First, the familiar queue of expected items in the resupply pipeline is calculated. This is where daily demands multiplied by expected delays = quantity Q expected to be in some form of repair, calibration or inspection.

Exhibit 14-9 (a)

Calculation of Average Quantity Q
Expected in the Resupply Pipeline

Item	1	2	3
Daily Demand Rate	.4	.4	.4
Probability of Local Repair	1.0	.8	.7
Repair Cycle Time	5	5	5
Depot Resupply Time	30	30	30
Unit Cost	$500	$300	$100
Q = Number in Resupply	2	4	5

Where:
- $Q_{Item\ 1} = (.4 * 1.0 * 5) + (.4 * 0.0 * 30) = 2$
- $Q_{Item\ 2} = (.4 * .8 * 5) + (.4 * .2 * 30) = 4$
- $Q_{Item\ 3} = (.4 * .7 * 5) + (.4 * .3 * 30) = 5$

Exhibit 14-9 (a) illustrates the quantity Q expected to be in resupply due to all delays. Now, if there are no serviceable spares to replace these reparables, the average number of backorders will equal the number of holes created as items become unserviceable. That is, for 2 in resupply/repair status, there will be two holes or ***expected backorders (EBOs)***. For 4, there will be four EBOs, and so forth.

This is shown in Exhibit *14-9 (b)* for the 'Spares = '0' line.' The average Q is then converted into expected partial Qs in resupply using the Poisson equation and Palm's theorem assumptions, as shown. As spares are added, there is a corresponding reduction in expected backorders.

Exhibit 14-9 (b)

Expected Backorders (EBOs) (Given the average demand rate Q and available spares S)			

Item	*1*	*2*	*3*	
Expected Backorders	***EBOs***	***EBOs***	***EBOs***	***Spare s = S***
Sample Calculations for Item 1 (Q = 2)	Q =2.00 (EBO = Q with zero spares)	Q =4.00 (EBO = Q with zero spares)	Q =5.00 (EBO = Q with zero spares)	0
EBO = 2 – 1 + .135 =	1.135	3.018	4.007	1
EBO = 1.135 – 1 + .135 + .271 =	.541	2.110	3.047	2
EBO = .541 – 1 + .135 + .271 + .271 =	.218	1.348	2.172	3
EBO = .281 – 1 + .135 + .271 + .271 + .180 =	.075	.781	1.437	4
EBO = .075 – 1 + .135 + .271 + .271 + .180 + .075 =	.022	.410	.877	5
EBO = .022 – 1 + .135 + .271 + .271 + .180 + .075 + .022 =	.006	.195	.493	6

Where:

$$EBO = (EBO_{previous} - 1) + \sum_{xi=0}^{si} p(x_i | Q)$$

(read as: EBOs minus 1 plus the sum of probabilities that fractional EBOs (x) will occur, given that Q = the expected pipeline quantity at steady state)

Sample Poisson probabilities for arrivals (x)= 1, 2,...etc., when Q = 2:
- *Probability of one arrival = .135 (i.e.,*

  $$p(x = 1) = \frac{e^{-Q} * Q^x}{x!} = \frac{2.718^{-2} * 2^1}{1!} = \frac{.135 * 1}{1} = .135$$

- *Q Probability of two arrivals = .271 (i.e.,*

  $$p(x = 1) = \frac{e^{-Q} * Q^x}{x!} = \frac{2.718^{-2} * 2^2}{2!} = \frac{.135 * 4}{2 * 1} = .271, etc.....$$

- *Probabilities for x = 3, 4, 5,...etc., and Q = 4, 5,...etc. can be calculated or found in tables of most statistical textbooks.*

Calculations for reduced partial EBOs, given the addition of spares, are shown in the follow-on lines in Exhibit *14-9 (b)*. Also shown in the first column of the table are the actual calculations for EBO reductions for Q = 2. While these calculations are tedious by manual methods, they are done in lightning speed by computer.

Finally, the expected partial EBOs are arrayed in a shopping list using a marginal benefit-to-cost ratio approach. *Exhibit 14-9 (c)* illustrates.

Exhibit 14-9 (c)

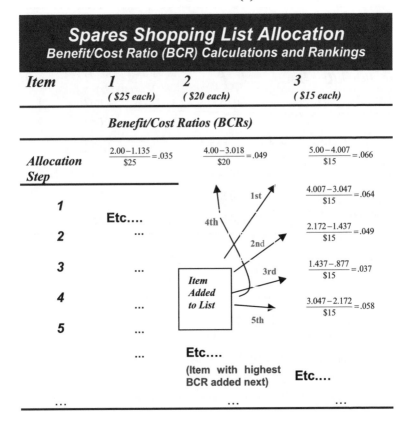

Item	1 ($25 each)	2 ($20 each)	3 ($15 each)

Benefit/Cost Ratios (BCRs)

Allocation Step	1	2	3
	$\frac{2.00-1.135}{\$25}=.035$	$\frac{4.00-3.018}{\$20}=.049$	$\frac{5.00-4.007}{\$15}=.066$
1	Etc....	1st	$\frac{4.007-3.047}{\$15}=.064$
2	...	4th	$\frac{2.172-1.437}{\$15}=.049$
3	...	2nd	$\frac{1.437-.877}{\$15}=.037$
4	...	Item Added to List 3rd	$\frac{3.047-2.172}{\$15}=.058$
5	...	5th	
	...	Etc.... (Item with highest BCR added next)	Etc....
	...	...	...

Spares with higher benefit/cost ratios are added in descending order. This marginal allocation process prioritizes purchases based on the highest benefit/cost ratios (i.e., biggest bang for the buck). The allocations continue to be added to the shopping list until either all partial backorders have been satisfied or some budget constraint has been met. *Exhibit 14-9 (d)* shows the shopping list for a budget of $2,800.

Exhibit 14-9 (d)

Budget Allocation					
Highest Benefit/Cost Ratios Determine Selection					
Item	*1* ($25 each)	*2* ($20 each)	*3* ($15 each)	**Budget**	
Allocation Step	**Number of Spares Purchased**			**Total Costs**	**Total EBOs**
1	0	0	1	$15	10.007
2	0	0	2	$45	9.047
3	0	0	3	$90	8.172
4	0	1	0	$110	7.190
5	0	0	4	$170	6.455
6	0	2	0	$210	5.547
7	0	3	0	$270	4.785
8	0	0	5	$345	4.225
9	1	0	0	$370	3.360
10	0	4	0	$450	2.793
11	0	0	6	$540	2.409
12	2	0	0	$590	1.815
Etc....	...	...	...	...	...
	...	...	...	...	...
26	7	0	0	$2,410	0.035
27	0	9	0	$2,590	0.001
Totals	<u>8</u>	<u>9</u>	<u>11</u>	<u>**$2,790**</u>	<u>0.000</u>

Budget limit of $2,800 cannot be exceeded —calculations end.

Purchases are cut off after the 27th allocation. Adding any additional item (from these three) will exceed the budget. Since the chances of EBOs are nearly eliminated, the 27th allocation would provide high assurance of mission readiness.

A useful property of this technique is that the resulting calculations form a convex curve that allows convenient computerized comparisons among items. Though beyond the scope of this book, it can be shown that the marginal approach is really the equivalent of the LaGrange multiplier technique often used in computerized systems to constrain inventory costs to a prescribed level.[176]

Follow-on Reparable Inventory Models

The *base stockage model* provided the conceptual 'backbone' for future Air Force recoverable inventory models. It improved the conventional fill rate and service level approaches by allowing cost-marginal comparisons among multiple items. However, it was never fully implemented by the Air Force due to the near-term development of improved models, notably the *METRIC* model in the mid-1960s, and the *MOD-METRIC* and *Aircraft Availability* models in the early 1970s.[xxxix]

METRIC extended marginal EBO calculations to allow explicit consideration of multiple locations, and multiple echelons (i.e., tradeoffs between local and depot delays). MOD-METRIC refined METRIC to allow for the calculation of indentured subcomponent requirements. Explicit calculations could be made to account for influences of 'child' SRUs (shop-replaceable units) required for higher 'parent' LRUs (line replaceable units). Finally, the Aircraft Availability Model encompassed the qualities of METRIC and MOD-METRIC, and basically added a 'higher indenture,' at *fleet level*, to ensure a balance among different types of aircraft (or other major end items). A

[xxxix] METRIC: Multi-Echelon Technique for Recoverable Item Control; MOD-METRIC: Modified METRIC.

high-level overview of salient qualities of these models follows.

METRIC: Multi-Items, Locations, and Echelons

This technique, developed for the Air Force by C. Sherbrooke at the Rand Corporation in 1966, extends the base stockage model to consider high cost, low demand items using the S-1, S policy (i.e., where items are not batched for repair or resupply).[177] Recall that the base stockage model minimizes backorders among multiple items subject to budget constraints *at the customer level*. The METRIC model allows calculation of additional expected delays *from higher echelons* such as the depot or from manufacturers for replacement of condemnations. It then sequentially allocates a given depot item to bases based on the highest marginal reduction of backorders among the various customer locations. After this allocation, benefit-to-cost ratios are computed similar to the base stockage model technique, and items are sequentially added to the shopping list at each customer location until the budget constraint is met. *Exhibit 14-10* illustrates:

Exhibit 14-10

METRIC Model
(Multiple-Echelon Technique for Recoverable Item Control)
Simple Resupply Case: Radar Sets
Two Echelons: Local and Depot Repair

*Daily Demand Rate (DDR) * Probability of Local Repair (PLR)*
+ Order and Ship Time (OST) + Depot Delay Time (DDT)
= Pipeline Requirement Quantity Q
*Local Resupply Pipeline: 2 $_{DDR}$ * .5 $_{PLR}$ * 5 $_{RCT}$ = 5*
*Depot Resupply Pipeline: 2 $_{DDR}$ * .5 $_{PLR}$ * (5 $_{OST}$ + 25 $_{DDT}$) = 30*
new term

Total Pipeline Requirement = Q   = 35
Note: Previous resupply time (see Exhibit 14-7) included only a single repair cycle time from depot. Here, the depot RCT is expanded to include two elements, and OST and DDT.

METRIC enabled use of the marginal approach to estimate optimal stocks of a given item among *multiple locations*. This is done by first computing an expected depot delay time (DDT). These depot backorders are not important in themselves, but only for their contribution to backorders at the operating location (due to added delays). These calculations involve an elaboration of the Base Stockage Model to explicitly calculate optimal allocation of centralized depot serviceable outputs, similar to previous methods for one location at a time, as was shown in *Exhibit 14-9 (b)*.[xl] *Exhibit 14-11* illustrates the relationship of expected backorders to a given budget constraint by using METRIC calculations.

Exhibit 14-11

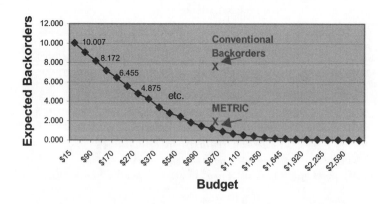

Expected METRIC Backorders for Different Budget Constraints

[xl] Depot Q = (all arrivals from base) * the expected delays (for retrograde and repair times).

In practice, the Air Force found some undesirable traits using the METRIC model. It tended to select cheap items first, increasing risk that more complex, expensive components might not make the cut at budget limits. Often these more complex components are also longer lead time than expected—causing potentially serious end item shortages. Also, METRIC tended to stock too many items, in practice, at depots. This having been said, METRIC will still tend to improve customer level backorders above the conventional model due to the constrained optimization calculation routines.

MOD-METRIC: Multi-Items, Locations, Echelons and Indentures

The METRIC model calculates additional expected customer location backorders due to delays from higher echelons such as the depot or from manufacturers. Similarly, the MOD(ified)-METRIC model calculates additional expected customer item backorders due to *delays from lower indentured items*. In other words, MOD-METRIC encompasses the basic features of METRIC (i.e., multi-item, multi-echelon, multi-location), and adds the influence of missing subcomponents in recoverable items processes.

This approach generally assumes that the assemblies removed from the end item (called Line Replaceable Units (LRUs) are less expensive than the end item. Therefore, it is efficient to incur to pursue a remove and replace maintenance activity, incurring most of the downtime on the cheaper assemblies.

In similar fashion, sub-sub assemblies (called Shop Replaceable Units (SRUs) are assumed to be cheaper to maintain than their parent LRUs. Efficient inventory policy minimizes end item downtime with respect to LRUs, and LRU downtime with respect to SRUs. A logical extension is that longer downtimes, such as delays for depot repairs, are concentrated on less expensive SRUs. *Exhibit 14-12* illustrates.

Exhibit 14-12

MOD-METRIC Model
Simple Resupply Case: Radar Sets
Two Echelons: Local and Depot Repair

Daily Demand Rate (DDR)
- *Probability of Local Repair (PLR) { (Repair Cycle Time (RCT) + SRU Delay Time (SDT)}* ◄new term
- *+ {Order and Ship Time (OST) + (Depot Delay Time (DDT)}*

  = Pipeline Requirement Quantity Q

Local Resupply Pipeline: $2_{DDR} * .5_{PLR} * (1_{RCT} + 4_{SDT})$ *= 5*
Depot Resupply Pipeline: $2_{DDR} * .5_{PLR} * (5_{OST} + 25_{DDT})$ *= 30*
Total Pipeline Requirement = Q *= 35*

Note: Here, both the local and depot RCT are expanded: local includes repairs and SRU delays, depot includes OST and DDT.

LRUs are removed and replaced on end items (such as aircraft on the flight line); then SRUs are removed and replaced from LRUs in resident back-shops for local repair or shipment to depot repair.

Under the MOD-METRIC model, insufficient re-supplies of SRUs induce delays to remove and replace actions for LRUs, thus generating backorder holes at the LRU-to-end item indenture level. The end result is the calculation of optimal mix between LRUs and SRUs for a given budget constraint.[178] The model tends to allocate proportionately more funds for LRUs, helping mitigate METRIC's problem of allocating funds to too many of the less costly SRUs.

Availability Models

By minimizing customer location levels of backorders in previous models, it was implicitly assumed that all items contribute equally to availability of end items. Also, it was assumed if an item fails, serviceable items in resupply allow nearly instantaneous replacement, making the end item immediately available. This may lead to inadequate resupply calculations for different fleets of end items.

Repair of major end items can vary greatly in the lead times required to get replacement parts for fleets such as military or commercial ground vehicles, ships and aircraft. Lowest costs may not be the appropriate criterion, especially for high priority missions and tasks. Very expensive supply support missions may be more essential than inexpensive ones. Availability models were developed to help balance operational priorities among several missions based on mission essentiality *and* 'least cost' requirements.

Again, we will review the high level assumptions of availability models developed for the U.S. military. Availability models begin with the expected backorders produced by METRIC type calculations and budgets, and then attempt to rebalance budget allocations based on target availability rates. Availability models were developed in the 1970s. Two of the more prominent were the Aircraft Availability Model developed for the Air Force[179] and the SESAME model developed for the U.S. Army.[180]

Availability Model Illustration

Assume, for example, that analysts wish to assess the availability of a certain fleet of end items, say aircraft, given the inventory posture. Suppose the resupply system supports a single location, single echelon, single indenture and multi-item (similar to METRIC) process. For simplicity, assume there are only three items that are resupplied to support 24 aircraft. For a budget cutoff of $590, the allocations are for 2, 4 and 6 spares, respectively, as shown in *Exhibit 14-13* (adapted from *Exhibit 14-9 (d)*).

Exhibit 14-13

Budget Allocation
Highest Benefit/Cost Ratios Determine Selection

Item	*1* ($25 each)	*2* ($20 each)	*3* ($15 each)	*Budget*	
Allocation Step	*Cumulative Number of Spares (green = added item)*			*Total Costs*	*Total EBOs*
1	0	0	1	$15	10.007
2	0	0	2	$45	9.047
3	0	0	3	$90	8.172
4	0	1	3	$110	7.190
5	0	1	4	$170	6.455
6	0	2	4	$210	5.547
7	0	3	4	$270	4.785
8	0	3	5	$345	4.225
9	1	3	5	$370	3.360
10	1	4	5	$450	2.793
11	1	4	6	$540	2.409
12	2	4	6	$590	1.815
Allocations at Budget Cutoff	<u>2</u>	<u>4</u>	<u>6</u>		

From the table in *Exhibit 14-9 (b)*, we see that this computes to expected backorders (EBOs) of .541 for item 1, .781 for item 2, and .493 for item 3.

Availability Calculations

Expected fleet availabilities can now be computed using availability formulae as shown in *Exhibit 14-14*.

Exhibit 14-14

Expected Fleet Availabilities
Given the Funded Level for
Expected Backorders (EBOs)

Item	*1*	*2*	*3*	
Expected Backorders (EBOs)	**EBOs**	**EBOs**	**EBOs**	**Spares = S**
Sample Calculations for Item 1 (Q = 2)	Q =2.00 (EBO = Q with zero spares)	Q =4.00 (EBO = Q with zero spares)	Q =5.00 (EBO = Q with zero spares)	0
Funded EBO level =	.541			2
		.781		4
			.493	6

Where:
   EBO = Q – S, given the Poisson Probability of Q

Expected Availabilities for three items with EBOs = .541, .781 and .493, respectively in a Fleet (F=24 aircraft, one of item per aircraft):

- *Fleet Availability for item 1* $= p(A) = 1 - \dfrac{EBO}{F} = 1 - \dfrac{.541}{24} = 1 - .022 = .978$

   That is, there are 24 aircraft, therefore 24 potential holes for failed 'part 1' items. The proportion of end item locations that have expected EBOs = EBO/F. This is the expected nonavailability proportion. Therefore, the proportion assumed to be available = 1 – EBO/F.

- *Fleet Availability for item 2* $= p(A) = 1 - \dfrac{EBO}{F} = 1 - \dfrac{.781}{24} = 1 - .032 = .968$

- *Fleet Availability for item 3* $= p(A) = 1 - \dfrac{EBO}{F} = 1 - \dfrac{.493}{24} = 1 - .020 = .980$

   - *Availability for all aircraft, considering (only) parts 1, 2, and 3*
     $$= p(A) = \prod_{i=1}^{n} (1 - \frac{EBO}{F}) = .978 * .968 * .980 = .928$$

(i.e., the probability of fleet availability equals the product of the individual item availabilities).

Where:
   Π (Greek letter Pi) = Multiplication of Elements

We see that the respective expected availabilities of aircraft due to funded item replacements yield an expected fleet availability of 92.8%, even without funding all expected EBOs (i.e., holes). This is a useful statistic. It allows

managers to examine the budget allocations at the highest
indenture level, the end item fleet level, to compare with
the relative availability 'health' of other types of end item
fleets. If, say, a policy exists to have all types of aircraft
funded toward a minimum of 80% availability, this technique can help balance funds across different benefit/cost
scenarios to ensure some minimum performance, despite
budgeting constraints. If components for this fleet were
funded less, say to a fleet availability of 80% (down from
92.8%), funds could be shifted to other fleets that have not
met the minimum availability targets.

The equation in *Exhibit 14-15* illustrates the
technique:

Exhibit 14-15

Transformation of Availability Products into Separable, Additive Terms

$$p(A) = \sum_{i=1}^{n} \ln\left(1 - \frac{EBO}{F}\right)$$

where:
$\ln$ = 2.718281828, the value of the natural (Napier) logarithm (a constant).

Example:

Availability for all aircraft, considering (only) parts 1 ,2, and 3

$$= p(A) = \sum_{i=1}^{n} \ln\left(1 - \frac{EBO}{F}\right) = \ln(.978) + \ln(.968) + \ln(.980) = \ln(.928)$$

$$= p(A) = \sum_{i=1}^{n} \ln\left(1 - \frac{EBO}{F}\right) = (-.022) + (-.032) + (-.020) = (-.075)$$

Transforming back to original units, $e^{-.075} = .928$
where: $e = 2.718$

The probability of fleet availability equals the sum of the individual item availabilities.

Since part-by-part availabilities are multiplied and
therefore nonlinear, the individual item influences are

therefore not separable as were METRIC type calculations. However, the actual model calculations were made additive by use of natural logarithms. This procedure allows transformation of the nonlinear model into a linear model with separable, additive probabilities.

One final adjustment is required. When applied, the availability calculations can also consider additional probabilities for situations where *quantity per application (QPA)* may be more than one per end item. The equation for this is shown in *Exhibit 14-16*.

Exhibit 14-16

Availability Equation
Multiple Quantities Per Application (QPAs)

$$p(A) = \prod_{i=1}^{n} (1 - \frac{EBO}{F*QPA})^{QPA}$$

It was found, however, that where there were large numbers of items in reasonable investments in stocks, the QPA calculations had minimal effect on optimal allocations to reduce backorders.[181]

Perhaps the biggest benefit of availability models is the visibility afforded to managers at the fleet level. For example, assume two fleets of aircraft are both under the enterprise level budget. Fleet X is state of the art, with relatively complex, expensive components. Fleet Y is unglamorous—but also performs essential missions. If fleet X is provided a disproportionate overall budget allocation, leaving fleet Y 'high and dry,' policy decisions can be made to, say, lower the acceptable availability of the winner (fleet X) to help bring up the availability to the loser (fleet Y) to some acceptable performance level. This may be better for the overall process, even though it technically distorts the optimal allocation scheme at the parts level.

Availability Inventory Models in Perspective

In practice, U.S. Air Force experience has indicated that generally both availability and METRIC models arrive at nearly the same results. At very low budgets, there are differences, and availability models were found to not necessarily improve requirements allocations.[182]

Further, the Air Force has found the availability model to be conservative (much like METRIC) due to real world maintenance practices that cannibalize (swap) parts among existing aircraft, borrowing from end items that are already down for other reasons. Additionally, computations provide less reliable estimates when the fleet size is small.

Finally, METRIC type availability models develop budget allocation schemes based on available budgets. When the money runs out, the 'lucky' components get funded—the remainder must await another allocation cycle (or real world workarounds, such as cannibalizations from other end items).

This approach may seem counterintuitive to field-operating units. These ultimate customers are likely to be more focused on day-to-day performance than budget allocations (from higher echelons). From their perspective, a realistic assessment of availability is backwards from budgeter's view—they want to know how many components will be available to assure fleet *readiness*.

Readiness Models: Dyna-METRIC

Approaching inventory management from the readiness perspective is different from the METRIC focus. Planners using METRIC related models are focused on how to best allocate the budget funds, given *how much* money is in the budget. Readiness planners are more likely to want to know *what* components are needed for a required state of availability—then budget for them.

Rand analysts began to reexamine earlier assumptions that resupply processes can be modeled using Palm's Theorem (see *Exhibit 14-9*). These models were developed under 'stationary' assumptions. That is, the mean demand and resupply rates were implicitly assumed to persist indefinitely. Also, the resupply system was assumed to act as an infinite server, and not bog down.

However, dynamics that change 'business as usual' inventory requirements can occur for many reasons. Examples might include demands for heater replacement elements during winter or need for additional automobile tire stocks just before vacation seasons. Also, capacity constraints can delay recycle times, such as backlog for computer repairs due to test equipment malfunctions, increased waiting time due to lack of trained workers, and so forth, violating the infinite server assumption.

To address readiness concerns for the U.S. Air Force, Rand analysts began developing 'dynamic' inventory readiness models in the late 1970s. By the mid-1980s they had developed a family of readiness assessment models under the general model name of Dyna-METRIC in the mid-1980s. The modeling focus was to compute inventory requirements required to meet readiness objectives (versus minimizing backorders subject to prescribed budget constraints). This involved adjusting previous steady state METRIC models to consider surges to normal operations.

The impact of surge requirements can be significant, as illustrated in *Exhibit 14-17,* adapted from a 1980 Rand document.[183]

Exhibit 14-17

Steady State versus Dynamic Stock Requirements (80% Confidence Level)

Steady State: Constant Arrivals and Resupply Time

	Arrivals	Resupply Time	Quantity in Resupply	Required Stock Levels
Normal	.8 per day	5 days	= 4 + safety stock	= 7
Surge	1 per day	5 days	= 5 + safety stock	= 8 (peak value)

Dynamic (1): Surge Arrivals (surge to 3, then decline to a 30-day average of 1.0 per day). Constant Mean Repair Time = 5

Day 1	3.0	5	6.2	9
Day 2	2.7	5	8.1	11
Day 3	2.5	5	9.8 (etc.)	12
...	...	...	...	...
Day 5	2.0	5	12.4	14 (peak value)
...	...	...	...	...

Day 1 Calculations: $6.2 = 4.0$ (from stead state) $+ 3$ (new surge arrivals) $- .8$ (repaired)
Day 2 Calculations: $8.1 = 6.2$ (from day 1) $+ 2.7$ (new surge arrivals) $- .8$ (repaired)

Dynamic (2): Surge Arrivals (surge to 3, then decline to a 30-day average of 1.0 per day). Random Repair Time around mean = 5 (from exponential distribution)

Day 1	3.0	5	6.0	9
Day 2	2.7	5	7.4	11
Day 3	2.5	5	8.3 (etc.)	12 (peak value)
...	...	...	...	...
Day 5	2.0	5	9.0	12
...	...	...	...	...

Note the dramatic increase of required stocks for surge: up from 8 to 14 for Dynamic (1), and 8 to 12 for Dynamic (2).

Exhibit 14-18 graphically displays the different inventory requirements for the three models: steady state, Dynamic (1)—i.e., dynamic demands with deterministic resupply times, and Dynamic (2)—i.e., dynamic demands with stochastic resupply times.

Exhibit 14-18

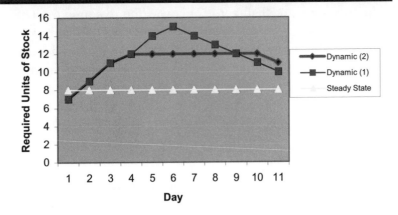

Where increased activity is modeled as:
  Steady State = Q + Safety Stock
(Daily Arrivals = 1 per day; Constant mean repair time = 5 days: Q + SS = 8 units).
  Dynamic (1) = Q + Safety Stock (fixed mean recovery time)
(Daily Arrivals =Surge to 3, then exponential decline resulting in a 30-day average of 1.0 per day; Repair time is a constant mean of 5 days).
  Dynamic (2) = Q + Safety Stock (distributed recovery time)
(Daily Arrivals =Surge to 3, then exponential decline resulting in a 30-day average of 1.0 per day; Repair time is a distributed variable with a mean of 5 days and a variance > 0).

The basic calculation adjustment was to adapt Palm's Theorem to allow consideration of nonstationary processes. In 1976, Rand analysts had postulated that the classical form of Palm's Theorem could be generalized to include dynamic (non–steady state) processes.[184] In 1980, the Rand Corporation published the first mathematical 'proof.'[185] As can be seen, both dynamic models calculate greater peak values (i.e., would require more pipeline carcasses) than the steady state model. Further Dynamic (1) model, using only the mean resupply delay time, computes a larger peak requirement than the Dynamic (2) model, which 'convolutes' the distributions between arrival and repair functions where repair events have a variance around the mean greater than zero. This was the dynamic the U.S. Air Force selected for readiness assessment. Though computationally more demanding, the Dynamic (2) model may be more representative of many scenarios—and increasingly more affordable to use in the modern information age of computers. Since dynamic models tend to calculate a need for more peak spares, managers must still decide how much risk they are willing to take relative surge demand periods.[186]

Accuracy of Recoverable Inventory Models

In many ways, it becomes apparent that these are not broad based logistic models. Really, any source of delay can hamper end item availability—lack of tools or technicians, test stands, fuel, and so on. The particular focus is that the right mixes of LRUs, SRUs and consumables are available for each end item (e.g. aircraft, diesel engine, etc.), given item costs, demand and resupply behaviors.[187]

These, as all models, are simplifications of reality—attempts to represent and summarize enough of the real world variables to make sense as a tool to help estimate requirements. With millions of items, some recoverable, some consumable, some end items proper, there are many potential problems with the accuracy of these 'item level'

calculations that are combined to estimate total funds allocations, or total fleet availabilities.

Further, there are a number of inherent limiting assumptions, even if the millions of data factors are somewhat accurate. The backorder models do not account for the
possibilities of item cannibalization (borrowing parts
merely shifts holes around), or for potential lateral resupply
from other locations. If real world processes permit item
cannibalization and lateral resupply, inventory requirements will tend to be overstated. The other extreme, assuming full cannibalization or lateral resupply might tend to
understate need for inventory. Another concern is that the
infinite server assumption can tend to understate resupply
times as items become tied up in repair or distribution
nodes due to limited capacity. To their credit, The Rand
Corporation introduced a 'Monte Carlo' simulation version
of the dynamic model (i.e., Dyna-METRIC, Version 6) in
1993 to adapt for some of these problems.[188]

Another problem is that there may be inappropriate
mixing of model assumptions. There are two kinds of computations. *Requirements computations* seek to attain the
highest end item availabilities, subject to expected 'out-
year' budget constraints. *Assessment models* reverse this,
and seek target availabilities based on performance requirements. Budget requirements (often established years
in the past) might be quite different when executed on recently developed availability targets. The implicit assumption is that dollar totals for tactical inventory acquisitions
will be close enough, and that strategically planned budgets
will be sufficient, even if different items are eventually acquired. This introduces an inherent flaw between method-
ologies. Item-by-item computations may be reasonably accurate for near-term operations and significantly off for
strategic requirements. To handle the strategic horizon, the
U.S. Air Force utilizes a different approach for estimating

out-year budget requirements: macro inventory budget models. The next section gives insights into how these models work, and how they differ from item-by-item (micro) models.

Macro Inventory Budget Models

The first macro inventory requirements model, POSSEM, was introduced in 1983 and used by the U.S. Air Force to forecast recoverable item spares requirements for the 2–7 year budget-POM forecasting horizon. The ALERT model replaced it in 1984. [xli]

The ALERT model takes a totally different perspective from item-by-item METRIC backorder type models by sidestepping the near-term assumptions of item level inventory computations. Instead, linear regression equations are developed between historical budget forecasts and the actual budget costs that were then incurred. ALERT is considered an inventory requirements model—but the focus is on long-term (i.e., multi-year) budget-POM forecasts, not individual items.

Obviously, much can happen between assessing near-term needs and long-term strategic remedies. In a forecasting sense, six months is considered a long-term forecast horizon. A primary impetus for developing ALERT was when significant budget variances occurred during the 1980 and 1982 timeframe. Budget projections (from earlier years) were so understated when the 'payable bills showed up' that the U.S. Air Force placed high priority on developing better budget projections. As quoted from the *Air Force Journal of Logistics* (Spring, 1987):

[xli] POSSEM (Peacetime Operating Stocks Spares Estimation Model); ALERT (Air Logistics Early Requirements Technique), POM (Program Objective Memorandum—the strategic plan budget for the five years immediately following the federal government's next year's budget in the PPBS (Plans and Programs Budgeting System)).

In 1980, defense logistics budgets were cut in half. In 1982, requirements processes were simultaneously shocked by cumulative double-digit inflation; 'catch up' from 1980 budget cuts; induction of some of the most extensive weapon system modifications in history; and a host of imponderables ranging from national policy and economic recession to methodological changes in computational models.[189]

The result was a rapid spike in the Air Force recoverable item budget requirement. The projected budget (calculated in 1980) ballooned from about $2.1 billion to $3.3 billion dollars when the bills showed up in 1982, a 60%, surge. As U.S. Senator Everett Dirksen once observed, "millions and millions—after a while you're talking real money."

Necessity being the mother of invention, the United States Air Force Comptroller introduced POSSEM in January 1983. The Air Force Materiel Command (formerly the Air Force Logistics Command) replaced the first model with a refinement model, ALERT, in 1984.

Macro Model Features

POSSEM and ALERT are both multiple linear regression models. POSSEM simply measured the historical relationships of two external variables, fleet age and fleet value, to past budget costs. The notion was that older fleets, or more costly ones, tend to be more expensive to maintain and can serve as predictors for expected component costs. ALERT uses the same variables, but augments the equations with the actual computed requirements from METRIC type models. ALERT also considers time periods such as each chronological year as a predictor variable.

Using the ALERT model, U.S. Air Force analysts make separate calculations for aggregate budget requirements for several major recoverable item categories (e.g., dollar support requirements for items for B52, A10, C130, F16, and other aircraft fleets). A 'step-wise' linear regression model is used to eliminate 'weaker' predictor variables. Also, to account for known budget peaks, not expected to continue, a dummy variable is added as a 'switch' to discount historical events that are improbable for future occurrence.

As an example, the ALERT model estimate for the F16 aircraft fleet recoverable item budget estimate for Fiscal Year (FY) 1985 was calculated as $135.4 million, as shown in *Exhibit 14-18.*

Exhibit 14-18

	ALERT Forecast Example F-16 Spare Recoverables Budget Requirement (FY 85)$ = millions		
	Predictor Variables		
Actual Budget	*Computed Requirement (METRIC Model Item Level)*	*Year (19xx)*	*Dummy*
$ 5.9	*$19.7*	*78*	*0*
26.2	*24.9*	*79*	*0*
39.2	*44.4*	*80*	*0*
75.7	*56.3*	*81*	*1*
59.7	*27.9*	*82*	*0*
61.5	*22.9*	*83*	*0*
???	*53.4*	*84*	*0*
	Prediction Equation *(from linear regression computer program)*		

$$F = a + b_1x_1 + b_2x_2 + b_3x_3$$
$$F_{85} = -714.7 + .6\,(53.4) + 9.2\,(84) + 17.8\,(0) = \boldsymbol{\$90.1}$$

Seven years of historical data, from FY 1978 – FY 1983, were used to predict the expected budget for FY 1984.[190] Data were aggregated to annual figures. After applying a computerized step-wise linear program algorithm, three variables, the METRIC calculation, the year, and the dummy were considered statistically adequate as predictors for the budget forecast calculation.

To complete the forecasting process for the overall budget, similar calculations are made for each major budget category (i.e., each aircraft fleet in the Air Force case). This is essentially a decomposition of the macro-forecast into many individual forecasts. While the reliability of individual forecasts fluctuates significantly from year to year, the aggregation of all forecasts tends to provide relatively stable and accurate total budget estimates.

The forecasting literature generally supports this approach. Forecasts concern the future—'not yet happened' events. They are at best educated guesses about what could happen, given a scenario. Where there are ample historical data or subject matter experts are available, forecasting methods can help (i.e., regression analysis, time-series, and judgmental techniques).

Recent research about appropriate forecasting techniques has provided excellent insight into when or when not to use certain techniques.[191] Generally, it has been found that simple models usually perform as well as sophisticated models. Decomposition of complex problems into constituent subprocesses can often help by providing an intuitive feel for the forecasts. Recombining multiple forecasts has been shown to reduce errors, perhaps canceling high and low 'misses.' Also, interestingly, when human judgment is needed, estimates by experts are often no more accurate than those of average citizens with relevant information about the situation.[192]

Forecasting is basically an educated guess about expected future events—like a golf shot, hopefully close, though rarely expected to 'hole out.' Your best estimates are most likely going to miss. Forecast errors tend to increase further into the future. Also, forecasts of decomposed subprocesses, regardless of their intuitive appeal, tend to be less accurate that aggregated, combined forecasts.[193] These forecasting caveats have been categorized as the three rules of forecasting, shown in *Exhibit 14-19*.[194]

Exhibit 14-19

Three Rules of Forecasting

- *Forecasts are always wrong*
- *Forecasts are more wrong farther in the future*
- *Forecasts are more wrong in more detail*

These rules help us to understand why the U.S. Air Force macro forecast model might tend generally to be more accurate (though far less detailed) than item-by-item predictions for the multi-year forecast horizon.

Micro versus Macro: Which Is Best?

It depends on the purpose of the forecast, and the forecast time horizon. Micro models are superior for tactical inventory decisions (i.e., actual item purchases). Their primary virtue is they are programmatic (i.e., requirements can be calculated to specific utilization plans).

However, (item-by-item backorder) micro model inaccuracies can be significant in the multi-year horizon, especially during dynamic economic or technology periods. Macro models can be superior for this long-range forecast horizon. However, even when the aggregate forecasts are more accurate, near-term micro model adaptations will still likely be needed for allocation decisions. In summary, for near-term allocation and operations requirements, use micro models; for out-year budget projections, use macro models.

Location Models: The Square Root Law

The *square root law* states that the total stock in a future number of locations can be approximated by multiplying the total amount of inventory at the existing locations by the square root of the number of future facilities, divided by the number of existing facilities. This result has been verified by numerous reviews.[195]

The square root law can be useful for determining potential inventory impacts due to centralization or decentralization initiatives, such as consolidating or expanding distribution locations. This approach was not covered in the previous distribution networking or inventory sections, and can be extremely valuable for studies concerning streamlining, expanding or reducing stock locations.

The square root law was first introduced by D. H. Maister (1976) in the *International Journal of Physical Distribution*.[196] The following are excerpts from this seminal work:

> The formulation of the square root law [applies]...If inventories of a single product (or stock keeping unit) are originally maintained in a number (n) of field locations...but are then consolidated into one central inventory...then the ratio:

$$\frac{decentralized\ inventory}{centralized\ inventory} = \sqrt{n}$$

> It should be noted that previous writers asserted that the result is applicable only to *safety stocks*, and not to *working* or *cycle* stocks...this restriction need not be universal...if inventory levels are controlled by some form of Economic Order Quantity (EOQ) based on the Wilson Lot Size Formula, then the result applies to cycle stocks.[197]

The square root law is based on several assumptions. It is assumed that there is minimum 'sharing' of inventory across stocking locations, and that there is little correlation of sales between stocking locations. Also, it is assumed that lead times to customers and customer service levels remain relatively constant regardless of the number of stocking locations.[198]

For example, in a real world study, records showed significant actual inventory reductions were achieved through consolidation of 23 supply points into eight central locations. Actual inventory reductions were 54%. Reductions implied by the square root law calculate to 41%.[199] Actual savings were higher that theoretical savings in this example. *Exhibit 14-20* illustrates how computations are made:

Exhibit 14-20

Square Root Law

$$F_{\text{(future inventory)}} = I_{\text{(existing inventory)}} * \sqrt{\frac{n_2}{n_1}}$$

where: n_1 = existing locations; n_2 = future locations
Example
$n_1 = 23$ existing locations; $n_2 = 8$ future locations

$$F = I * \sqrt{\frac{n_2}{n_1}} = I * \sqrt{\frac{8}{23}} = I * .59 = 59\% \text{ of future inventory}$$

Direct calculation of savings:

$$= 1 - \sqrt{\frac{n_2}{n_1}} = 1 - \sqrt{\frac{8}{23}} = 1 - .59 = 41\%$$

Summary of Inventory Techniques

Inventory is a major cost area for most business enterprises. Fortunately, much has been learned about effective supply policy. We have merely covered the tip of the iceberg with this review. Most of the commercial literature deals with consumable item management, especially economic lot sizes and economic order quantities. However, many of the recoverable item management techniques developed for the U.S. military could provide valuable insights into existing business practices and help evaluate business case analysis alternatives.

Macro inventory approaches such as the ALERT model can be useful for estimating out-year budget requirements at the corporate enterprise level. Location analysis, using the square root law, can help quantify strategic potential inventory benefit/cost expectations for major process reengineering programs such as expansion, centralization, and outsourcing of inventory management functions.

Overview of Techniques

This concludes the review of many of the most useful techniques for comprehensive business case analysis. Topics included economic, statistical, process modeling, network analysis, simulation, linear programming, and inventory management analysis. These techniques build upon the conceptual base presented in Part II.

The concepts section implied that comprehensive business case analysis must consider impacts of process innovations on both the social (human) and technical (mechanical) processes. Techniques help quantify many of the sociotechnical considerations.

Finally, in Part IV, Procedures, we show the actual procedures for composing and presenting a successful business case analysis.

---

[164] C. Ptak (2000). *ERP: Tools, Techniques and Applications for Integrating the Supply Chain.* Washington D.C.: St. Lucie Press, pp. 9–10.
[165] R. H. Wilson (1934). A scientific routine for stock control. *Harvard Business Review*, 13 (1), 116–128.

[166] R. Levin, D. Rubin, J. Stinson, and E. Gardner, Jr. (1992). *Quantitative Approaches to Management* (8th ed.). New York, McGraw-Hill, Inc., pp. 331–333.
[167] J. M. Masters (1983, 3 Jan – 18 Mar). Inventory management. *Air Force Institute of Technology Course LM 6.28.*
[168] Ibid. Origin of this rule of thumb estimate of a standard error is unknown, perhaps the result of a previous study.
[169] Ibid.
[170] Author's experience due to multiple recoverable item analysis cases.
[171] Ibid.
[172] Masters (1983).
[173] Ibid.
[174] C. Palm (1938). Analysis of the Erlang traffic formula for busy-signal arrangements. *Ericsson Technics*, No. 5, pp. 38–58; cited from H. S. Campbell and T. L. Jones, A systems approach to base stockage: its development and test. Paper prepared for 29th National Meeting of the Operations Research Society of America, Santa Monica, CA, May 19, 1966.
[175] W. Feller (1968). *An Introduction to Probability Theory and Its Applications, Vol. I* (3rd ed.). New York: Wiley, pp. 460–462.
[176] R. Hillestad (July, 1982). *Dyna-METRIC: Dynamic Multi-Echelon Technique for Recoverable Item Control: R-2785-AF.* The Rand Corporation, Santa Monica, CA.
[177] C. C. Sherbrooke (1968). METRIC: multi-echelon technique for recoverable item control.
[178] J. Muckstadt (1973). A model for a multi-item, multi-echelon, multi-indenture system. *Management Science* 20 (4), 472–481.
[179] T. O'Malley (1983). *The Aircraft Availability Model: Conceptual Framework and Mathematics: AF201Report.* Logistics Management Institute, Bethesda, MD.
[180] U.S. Army Inventory Research Office (1980). Mathematics for SESAME model. Department of Army Technical Report TR 80-2. Philadelphia, PA.
[181] Masters (1983).
[182] Ibid.
[183] J. Muckstadt (1980, November). *Comparative Adequacy of Steady-state Versus Dynamic Models for Calculating Stockage Requirements: R-2636-AF.* The Rand Corporation, Santa Monica, CA.
[184] G. Crawford (1981). *Palm's Theorem for Nonstationary Processes: R-2750-RC.* The Rand Corporation, Santa Monica, CA, p. 2.

[185] R. Hillestad and M. Carrillo (1980, May). *Models and Techniques for Recoverable Item Stockage when Demand and the Repair Process are Nonstationary—Part I: Performance Measurement: N-1482-AF.* The Rand Corporation, Santa Monica, CA.

[186] Crawford (1981), p. 26.

[187] Masters (1983).

[188] K. Issacson and P. Boren I (1993). *Dyna-METRIC Version 6: R-2636-AF.* The Rand Corporation, Santa Monica, CA

[189] J. Brannock (1987, Spring). POSSEM-ALERT: The search for a requirements forecasting system. *Air Force Journal of Logistics*, XI (2), 31.

[190] Author's notes while working on the model.

[191] J. S. Armstrong (Ed.) (2001). *Principles of Forecasting: A Handbook for Researchers and Practitioners.* Boston: Kluwer Academic Publishers.

[192] J. S. Armstrong (1985). *Long-Range Forecasting: from Crystal Ball to Computer* (2nd ed). New York: John Wiley & Sons, pp. 91–92.

[193] Armstrong (2001), p. 265.

[194] C. Ptak (2000). *ERP: Tools, Techniques and Applications for Integrating the Supply Chain.* Washington D.C.: St. Lucie Press, p. 47.

[195] W. Zinn, M. Levy, and D. Bowersox (1989). Measuring the effect of inventory centralization/decentralization on aggregate safety stock: the square root law revisited. *Journal of Business Logistics,* 10 (1), 1–14; P. Evers (1996). The impact of transshipments of safety stock requirements. *Journal of Business Logistics* 17 (1), 107–133; P. Evers and F. Beier (1998). Operational aspects of inventory consolidations decision making. *Journal of Business Logistics* 19 (1), 173–187.

[196] D. H. Maister (1976). Centralisation of inventories and the square root law. *International Journal of Physical Distribution and Materials Management* 6 (3).

[197] Ibid., p. 124.

[198] J. Coyle, E. Bardi, and C. Langley, Jr. (2003). *The Management of Business Logistics: A Supply Chain Perspective* (7th ed.). Mason, OH: South-Western, pp. 258–260.

[198] Armstrong (2001), p. 265.

[198] Crawford (1981), pp. 32–36.

[199] Author's notes from European consultation study (2001).

IV

PROCEDURES

Why, When and Where to Begin, and What to Do

Method is like packing things in a box; a good packer will get in half as much again as a bad one.
Richard Cecil (circa 1800)

CHAPTER FIFTEEN

Business Case Analysis
Purpose and Events

==================================== **15**

*One's success in business today turns upon the possibility
of getting people to believe one has something they want.*
Gerald Stanley Lee (circa 1935)

Why perform business case analysis?

All organizations must learn to adapt—to select
projects that take advantage of developing opportunities, or
to improve processes that need calibration or restructuring.
A Business Case Analysis (BCA) can provide both the ra-
tionale and justification for such choices.

There will always be more deserving initiatives than
your organization will be able to fund. A good BCA can
help identify the best alternatives in clear, unambiguous
terms. With these skills, you can become recognized as a
'go to' decision maker to help management ensure the right
projects are identified, evaluated and funded.

When should a BCA be performed?

We all perform mini-BCAs every day—when we
shop for groceries, decide on replacing tires for our automobiles, or determine what vacation to take. In these personal situations, we routinely seek out the necessary information to help make such decisions. We generally recognize our permissible budget and can determine, first hand,
our priorities.

Where to Begin?

One of the most promising places to begin is to compare existing organizational capabilities with desired goals. Such thoughts are often clearly articulated in the organization's strategic plans. Otherwise, the analyst must try to size up the situation through interviews with key experts, and quantification of company financial and operations data. A key area to look is where performance indicators show that continual business results have begun to erode. This can expose the potential needs for calibration or reengineering of processes. BCAs can be primary tools for describing and measuring such problems and for evaluating potential new initiatives for their solutions.

Many near-term projects often come from daily or weekly staff meetings, based on recent activities, reports and problems. Selection of solutions is typically a subjective process, influenced strongly by perceived available resources and timing, and by the judgment of the day-to-day managers. For routine, one-of-a-kind problems, these decisions are probably reasonably adequate. But for bigger problems, information for making decisions for support and timing are often beyond day-to-day routines. These can include projects such as how to develop and implement new management information systems, how to reorganize for more efficient operations, or how to convince headquarters of need for new equipment or personnel.

Many of the obvious problems are well known at the operating level, but, because of scarce funds, are a hard sell to higher echelons that 1) do not really understand the details, and 2) have many competing demands from lower echelons for financial support from limited budgets. Also, needed changes can emanate from the 'strategic vision' of headquarters, with little awareness of the need at operational levels. Either way, the BCA provides the methodology to help choose best alternatives and inform significant 'others' of the why, how and wherefore.

In larger organizations, it is not uncommon for the requirement for a BCA to be assigned *after* a higher-level decision has been made to develop a project. As the action officer assigned to conduct the BCA, you may not have been in the staff meetings or office conferences that spawned the project requirement. Such projects may have face validity, but still need the analytic evaluation to inform management of the risks and potential paybacks. Valuable sources of information about potential benefits and costs may be available from those initial meetings or their attendees.

Financing the Study

It often falls upon the BCA action officer to not only conduct the study, but to help the sponsor justify resources and funding for it. The BCA can be an excellent investment, but this benefit may need explaining to potential funding sources. The BCA's value lies in providing information to help explain the nature of potentially high gain projects, and in avoiding excessively risky ventures.

The amount spent on the actual BCA study is frequently dwarfed by the potential benefits/costs of the project. In a recent large study on which the author participated, projected a five-year cost avoidance in excess of $100 million was projected if major processes reengineered. The cost of this BCA study was less than 0.4% (i.e., .004 = $400,000) of expected benefits. While the study was still costly, it provided information to justify streamlining a complex supply chain management process across a multinational business concern with potential savings of millions of dollars. The potential payback of the best alternative was $250 for each $1 invested in the BCA study.

Making a Case to Fund Your BCA

An old adage is that "prior information is 99% of brilliance." Knowing that there are available study funds, or that management already sees a problem but requires better information, can go a long way toward knowing what level of effort can be supported by the business case study. Local levels often will not have funds for new, innovative programs. In such cases, a strong *study plan* can help explain the study need and scope to gain support from needed sponsors.

Where Do Study Funds Come From?

Larger enterprise operations often do have technical resources and budgets for strategic improvement initiatives. Also, keep alert that funds may become available at the end of the fiscal year for application against needed but previously delayed programs. It is not uncommon for such funds to "show up" due to normal business tempo dynamics. Many of the original out-year budget requirements may have changed or become obsolete since their original acceptance as strategic initiatives.

Also, there may be higher level requirements that have evolved at upper management level, such as a change in the strategic orientation of business processes and technology. In such cases, the call for a business case analysis may come down from higher echelons. A sophisticated BCA can often make the difference between support or nonsupport of larger new initiatives.

The rivalry for funding major projects can be quite keen. This is where a strong case for the need of a BCA study can be made. Sometimes this involves 'educating' management by developing a strong, comprehensive *statement of work* for the study. The statement of work is a major section of both a *task order* and *study plan*. It can be included in either a *draft task order* (for management to review), or for a *draft study plan* (often unsolicited) to provide essential information for potential sponsors.

The Golden Rule

When competing for BCA study funds, follow the *Golden Rule: "Them what's got the gold, makes the rules."* Take time to learn why the proposed project that will be examined is important. Try to get the big picture of how and where this project fits into bigger strategic programs. Then adapt the words of the statement of work in the draft task order (or study plan if there is no preceding task order) toward these 'higher' goals. If you can communicate the need and potential study benefits in a clear, understandable and creditable way, chances for funding will improve. Also, by successfully competing for the study funds, those managers who buy in will have a vested interest in the business case analysis findings.

Six Critical Steps

Six major steps are involved in performing professional business case analysis. They include the following:

1) **Task Order**—the study sponsor's description of what the BCA is to analyze;

2) **Study Plan**—the proposed analysis approach that will be used in the BCA;

3) **Kickoff Meeting**—to calibrate differences between the task order and study plan;

4) **The Study**—performance of the actual BCA study;

5) **Draft Final Report**—preliminary report of BCA findings to clear up misunderstandings;

6) **Final Report and Briefing**—to incorporate final comments and missing information; and brief the sponsor about study assumptions, findings and recommended alternative solutions.

The Task Order

The *task order* is perhaps the most important document of the study effort other than the actual BCA report itself. It sets the direction and scope of the study. It is analogous to aiming a cannon at a distant target. Even if the aim is a little off, the target may be completely missed. It specifies the problem background, objectives, scope and expected deliverables.

There are typically several sections in the task order, including a *statement of work*, a *schedule* of study events, an expected *level of effort*, expected study *deliverables* and the *sponsoring activity*. It is the primary document to clearly identify what the customer (of the study) requires.

The statement of work is the nucleus of the task order. It generally consists of a narrative of the problem background, a specific statement of the problem, and the expected scope of the study effort. The scope subsection helps frame study expected level of effort. Study deliverables can include both informal and formal information meetings, as well as funding levels for required analytical hours, travel and other resources.

Exhibit 15-1 shows an abbreviated example of a written task order for the 8-Day BCA, with typical sections.

Exhibit 15-1

Task Order
(Abbreviated Example)

Task Order
Business Case Analysis
For Upgrading Office PCs

I. STATEMENT OF WORK
BACKGROUND:
The contracting division depends on automated information to perform eighty percent of its functions. The major worker level asset is the PC workstation. Existing PCs are over three years old, and have begun experiencing costly delays due to downtime....

PROBLEM STATEMENT:
A business case analysis is required to determine the relative benefits and costs for the following alternatives:
 1) Maintain Status Quo
 2) Upgrade Existing PCs
 3) Purchase New PCs
 4) Lease New PCs...

SCOPE:
The study will include an evaluation of productivity and acquisition costs for the four alternatives. This will include research on existing PC technology and prices ....

II. SCHEDULE
Date	*Milestone*
dd/mm/yy	*Survey Status Quo*
dd/mm/yy	*Research state of the art PCs and prices*
dd/mm/yy	*...*

III. LEVEL OF EFFORT *(budgeted resources)*
IV. DELIVERABLES (e.g., study plan, in-process reviews (IPRs, reports, and so on)
V. SPONSORING ACTIVITY

The task order should be a written document, especially for more comprehensive BCA studies. It is a good idea to request a written task order (or help the sponsor prepare one)—even if all work will be done locally, in-house.

In the author's experience, while this step is one of the most important, it is also the most overlooked or ignored. Lack of a written task order can result in costly misunderstandings between the analyst(s) and the sponsor. This can cause credibility problems for acceptance of the final report. An additional value for a written task order is it might facilitate buy-in of other decision makers, either for helping clarify the problem or for funding the effort. Remember *The Golden Rule*.

The Study Plan

The *study plan* rivals the task order in importance. It outlines how the analyst for the BCA intends to accomplish the study. Where the task order specifies what the customer needs, the study plan specifies what the analyst will (can) deliver. The study plan is a product of the analyst, and reflects specific knowledge about what is technically possible for the study to accomplish. If the differences in perspective between the sponsor and analyst are too large, they should be dealt with before the study effort begins.

There may be good reasons why the analysis proposed in the study plan might be different from that specified in the task order. These can include too little time or too limited a scope to perform the work. In such cases, the study plan might propose a more general, less detailed analysis that is achievable. Also, the given levels of funding or resource allocations (such as the number of available analyst hours or allowable travel funds) may only allow a lower level of effort. The study plan helps identify these problems for reconciliation prior to study initiation.

Exhibit 15-2 shows a hypothetical example of a written study plan, with typical sections.

Exhibit 15-2

Study Plan
(Abbreviated Example)

Study Plan
Business Case Analysis
For Upgrading Office PCs

I. STATEMENT OF WORK
   BACKGROUND:
The contracting division depends on automated information to perform eighty percent of its functions. The major worker level asset is the PC workstation. Existing PCs are over three years old, and have begun experiencing costly delays due to downtime....

   PROBLEM STATEMENT:
A business case analysis is required to determine the relative benefits and costs for the following alternatives:
   1) Maintain Status Quo
   2) Upgrade Existing PCs
   3) Purchase New PCs
   4) Lease New PCs...

   SCOPE:
The study will include an evaluation of productivity and acquisition costs for the four alternatives. This will include research on existing PC technology and prices ....

II. STUDY APPROACH
   ANALYTICAL TECHNIQUE:
The study will quantify total ownership costs (i.e., costs of acquisition, purchase price and cost of use) among the alternatives. Quantitative estimates of benefits will also be made for each alternative. Classical economic analysis and statistical forecasting methods will be used to compare the existing (status quo) and alternative benefit cost ratios....

III. SCHEDULE *(similar to task order)*
IV. LEVEL OF EFFORT *(identify resources, not to exceed to task order budget)*
 V. DELIVERABLES *(similar to task order)*
 VI. SPONSORING ACTIVITY *(same as task order)*

Normally, especially for larger studies, the analyst should be given time to develop a *draft study plan* ahead of time, typically around two weeks. After the analyst's review of the task order and preliminary review of the business situation, the draft study plan can be prepared and sent as a 'read-ahead' to the sponsor. This is where the *kickoff meeting* comes in.

The Kickoff Meeting

The *kickoff meeting* facilitates understanding and reconciliation of any in confusion between the task order and study plan. This meeting can be thought of as the last step in a dialectic process. The sponsor proposes via the task order what analysis is needed (the thesis). The analyst, via the study plan, evaluates the best efforts that can be achieved, given such considerations as the scope, the specified level of effort, and so on (the antithesis). The two parties then work to agree on a final, mutually acceptable course of action at the kickoff meeting (the synthesis).

The meeting serves as a forum where the sponsor, analyst, and other interested parties can be brought together for a discussion of the proposed study. It is often a good idea to send a read-ahead draft study plan to the sponsor about a week before the kickoff meeting. Appropriate, notes can accompany the draft study plan to indicate significant differences, if any, from the original task order.

At the meeting, specifics of the proposed study effort are discussed. This can include an overview of BCA objective by either the sponsor or analyst. Needed adjustments to the study plan are then addressed and reconciled. Final changes for the BCA are agreed upon, and the draft study plan is adjusted appropriately. These final adjustments act as the final agreement between the sponsor and analyst—the 'psychological contract' of what is expected from the business case analysis study. The final (amended) study plan is then completed and forwarded to the sponsor in about one week. This version of the study plan represents the sponsor-analyst contract.

The BCA Report

Development of the BCA report is the ultimate goal of the BCA effort. After specifying the study objectives and scope in the task order and study plan, the actual study begins. Information gathering will involve a 'data call,' interviews, site visits, and interim briefings.

Plan 12 Weeks for Larger BCA Studies

In the author's experience, the BCA study should take about 12 weeks for larger studies. Too much shorter puts undue pressure on analysts to write the report and get the answer before adequate data, site visits, interviews and surveys can be gathered and deciphered. This invites 'hasty conclusions' and 'glittering generalities.' There can be too much dependence on analogous 'best practices' and previous studies that may not be relevant. If the study takes too much longer than 12 weeks, it can lead to information overload, second guessing, boredom, and the potential for 'paralysis by analysis.'[xlii]

Study Format

A successful format for the BCA *final report* should include easily identifiable parts. Successful formats used by the author have included five major sections. The first section (1–5 pages) is the *executive summary*, which provides a quick overview of what the study was all about, with general conclusions and recommendations. The second section explains the *background and problem* (2–10 pages). The third section presents the *actual problem* exposé and *evaluation* of the possible solutions (the business case— 15–30 pages). The fourth section presents the *economic*

[xlii] The author has encountered 'continuing' studies that have lasted for years in both in-house and level of effort contracts. While these may be suitable for maintenance of a database that feeds a continual assessment model, they tend to become 'bureaucratized' into a set way of considering assumptions, and not suitable for 'new discovery' efforts such as a BCA.

analysis that evaluates the benefit-to-cost ratios and qualitative aspects among alternatives (15–40 pages). And the fifth section presents a *summary and conclusions* (1–10 pages).

Exhibit 15-3 illustrates a sample BCA report format.

Exhibit 15-3

Business Case Analysis Report
(Abbreviated Example)

Business Case Analysis
For Upgrading Office PCs

I. EXECUTIVE SUMMARY
This study evaluated the requirements for enhancing worker productivity through upgrading of information management systems. More specifically, it addressed....

II. BACKGROUND AND PROBLEM STATEMENT:
The contracting division depends on automated information to perform eighty percent of its functions. The major worker level asset is the PC workstation. Existing PCs are over three years old, and have begun experiencing costly delays....

III. BUSINESS CASE ANALYSIS
Scenario: Previous policies have dictated the need for continual improvement and upgrade of productive capabilities. An important aspect of this is the systematic upgrade of PCs to keep pace with the rapid growth of information technology....
The Business Case
The continual increase in PC maintenance and service call costs, as well as....
The study evaluated productivity and acquisition costs for four alternatives:
1) Maintain Status Quo
2) Upgrade Existing PCs
3) Purchase New PCs
4) Lease New PCs...
Pros and Cons

Alternative 1, Maintain Status Quo
Pros: Status quo advantages include minimum disruption of existing operations due to training and familiarization with new technology....
Cons: There are two major disadvantages to the status quo alternative: increasing costs of upkeep and decreasing productivity of the workers. Costs of maintenance....
Alternative 2, Upgrade Existing PCs....

IV. ECONOMIC ANALYSIS
Descriptive Statistics
The overall operation consists of 18 workers with a combined 'loaded' salary base of $....The PC maintenance and service call costs have averaged $....
Comparison of Alternative Costs
The economic analysis compares Alternatives 1, 3 and 4. Alternative 2 was eliminated as unfeasible. The 'total cost of ownership' was used to differentiate the benefit/cost ratios....Alternative 1 (status quo) was substantially more costly over a three-year expected economic life of new PCs, as shown in Exhibit....

V. SUMMARY AND CONCLUSIONS

1) The Executive Summary—comprised of around one to five pages—is most effective if presented in the front part of the report (though it is developed last, of necessity, in the actual study effort). It helps to begin your report with a clear, precise overview of why the study was necessary, and what the conclusions suggest as a course of action. Managers who will ultimately make the 'go/no go' decisions about the BCA proposals are often extremely busy, and a good *executive summary* will entice more thorough reviews. If you 'connect' in the executive summary section, chances are greatly improved that those most interested will then read the body of the BCA report in more detail.

Imagine yourself, for example, browsing in a bookstore or library. According to a *Wall Street Journal* article, the average book browser will spend less than eight seconds looking at the front cover and less than 15 seconds reading the back cover. Extend this notion to a comprehensive BCA, which can range between 100 and 250 pages with technical content and appendices, and the chances of the right people reading it and understanding the finer points of analysis become 'iffy,' to say the least.

2) The Background and Problem Statement describes what the study is about and why it was needed. Key elements in this section include the study purpose and objectives, as well as the study scope and level of analysis. Finally, a*lternatives* (of potential *to be* scenarios) to the existing situation can be introduced. These alternatives were likely to have been discussed and agreed to during the Task Order–Study Plan–Kickoff Meeting processes.

3) The Business Case is the backbone section of the BCA report. This is where potential alternatives are evaluated, and arguments for or against the alternatives are fully developed. This typically begins by developing a scenario that expands the Problem Statement by defining in detail just what the current situation is and why change is needed. This is where the '99% perspiration' will lead, hopefully, to the '1% inspiration' of a doable change to the *status quo* operations.

To be competitive, potential benefits of new alternative should, at the very least, be at least as good as those of the status quo (i.e., the 'do nothing' alternative). There can be one or several alternatives in addition to status quo, depending on the study. It is often instructive to provide an overview of the pros and cons for all of the alternatives to help develop intuitive, qualitative comparisons. The alternatives offering the most potential are then quantitatively compared in the *economic analysis section*.

4) The Economic Analysis develops costs and benefits to enable quantitative comparisons of the alternatives. There is typically no need to quantitatively compare alternatives that were shown to be qualitatively infeasible during the previous *business case* development. Alternatives that remain are statistically examined using quantitative approaches such as 'present value analysis,' and benefit/cost ratios allow quantitative comparisons.

5) The Conclusions Section sums up the business case analysis report. It allows the analyst to suggest informed conclusions about which, if any, of the new alternatives are recommended to replace status quo operations. This is also the section where the analyst can provide insights on how to proceed with a recommended solution, if appropriate.

There is much room for give and take between the analyst and client if a read-ahead draft final BCA report is sent before the final briefing and report are completed.

Draft Final Report

A *draft final report* should be sent to the client about 10 working days before the final briefing and report, to give the sponsor time to review and prepare questions. Then a scheduled *final briefing* should be arranged. If multiple organizational echelons are involved, a series of briefings may be required.

Draft Final Briefing

The *final briefing* is typically scheduled after allowing a reasonable time for the sponsor to review the draft final report, typically about a week to ten days. Often, this briefing incorporates recommended adjustments after the analyst and sponsor have informally discussed the findings and recommendations.

This briefing can be a most critical step to the sponsor, since it offers opportunities to invite other important organizational members who have responsibilities in the BCA study area. It is a crucial step to help foster understanding and buy-in from the sponsor and other interested decision makers. It permits the analyst to explain an overview of the *business case*, the pros and cons of the *alternatives*, the metrics used in the *economic analysis*. It also can serve to bring out implicit assumptions (and possible mistakes) that bear on study conclusions. After the meeting, needed changes and suggestions agreed to at this meeting will be incorporated into the *final report*. It is often a good idea to also update the briefing itself so that it is available to the sponsor for follow-on briefings, as appropriate.

Final Briefing and Report

The *final report* incorporates final agreed changes and calibrations form the final briefing session. It should be forwarded to the sponsor after amending as necessary to include agreed changes from the final briefing. This is typically in about a week or ten days after the final briefing. There should be sufficient copies of the final report for all key stakeholders, as specified in the tasking documents.

Summary

We have just reviewed the why, when, where and how of performing a Business Case Analysis.

Key Points:

➤ A business case analysis is typically recommended for important projects to both qualitatively and quantitatively evaluate and compare benefits and costs of potential changes that might improve current business situations.

➤ To initiate a business case analysis, a good *task order* will help explain what the study sponsor hopes to accomplish, and to clarify scope and level of effort permissible for the study.

➤ The *study plan* repeats the *task order* objectives from the analyst's perspective, and develops realistic approaches to accomplish the study.

➤ The *kickoff meeting* informs the sponsor and others interested in the study about the problem and study approach. Differences between the *task order* and *study plan* are reconciled, enabling agreement on expected study efforts and scope.

➤ The actual BCA study timing should be scheduled for about 12 weeks' duration.

➤ Key sections of the BCA *final report* include:

> ➤ The *Executive Summary*—to achieve buy-in from stakeholders for acceptance and funding of recommended actions.
>
> ➤ The *Background and Problem Statement* to clearly identify the study focus and scope, and define the *alternatives*.
>
> ➤ The *Business Case,* which fully develops the alternatives and qualitatively evaluates those that make good business sense.
>
> ➤ The *Economic Analysis,* to quantitatively compare the benefits and costs for selection of the best alternative.
>
> ➤ *Conclusions* to summarize study results and recommend the best course of action.

Anyone can perform a BCA using the techniques outlined in this book. For larger projects, such as evaluating upgrades of large computer-based management information systems, or assessing multi-location, multiple echelon reorganizations, use of professional analysts may be more appropriate.

Professional help is often available through existing organizational level of effort contracts or in-house analysis groups. The approaches and techniques described herein can provide valuable guidelines for developing and monitoring these type studies.

Exhibit 15-4 summarizes the six critical steps of the overall BCA process.

EXHIBIT 15-4

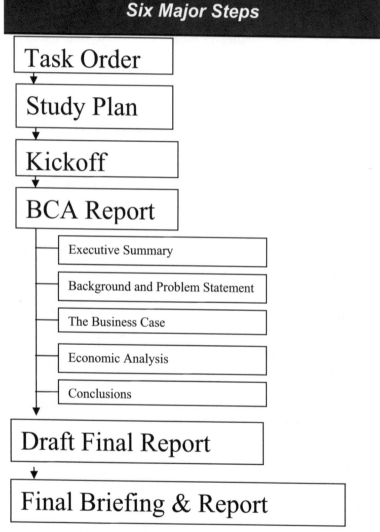

Business Case Analysis:
Six Major Steps

Task Order

Study Plan

Kickoff

BCA Report

Executive Summary

Background and Problem Statement

The Business Case

Economic Analysis

Conclusions

Draft Final Report

Final Briefing & Report

CHAPTER SIXTEEN

Business Case Analysis
Example of Final Briefing

16

Speeches cannot be made long enough for the speakers, nor short enough for the hearers.
James Perry (circa 1810)

The *final briefing* is often the key to 'bring to life' details of the study. The analyst normally presents the briefing during a meeting with the sponsor and other important organizational members. It should be built as an overview of the *draft final report,* and sent as a read-ahead about a week before. During the briefing, the attendees are allowed to question the information and logic of findings and recommend study improvements. This is key for achieving buy-in from the sponsor and important decision makers. Examples of briefing charts for the 8-Day BCA (from Chapter 1) follow:

Slide 1

Narrative: "This study was tasked to evaluate the possibility of replacing our aging workstations."

Business Case Analysis
Acquisition of Workstations

Slide 2

"As shown, the study timeframe was only a week —to correspond with year-end budget obligations."

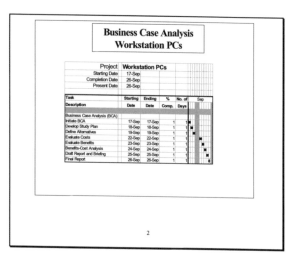

Business Case Analysis
Workstation PCs

Project	Workstation PCs				
Starting Date	17-Sep				
Completion Date	26-Sep				
Present Date	26-Sep				

Task	Starting	Ending	%	No. of	Sep
Description	Date	Date	Comp.	Days	
Business Case Analysis (BCA)					
Initiate BCA	17-Sep	17-Sep	1	1	
Develop Study Plan	18-Sep	18-Sep	1	1	
Define Alternatives	19-Sep	19-Sep	1	1	
Evaluate Costs	22-Sep	22-Sep	1	1	
Evaluate Benefits	23-Sep	23-Sep	1	1	
Benefits-Cost Analysis	24-Sep	24-Sep	1	1	
Draft Report and Briefing	25-Sep	25-Sep	1	1	
Final Report	26-Sep	26-Sep	1	1	

2

Slide 3

"The basic problem is aging PCs, resulting in lost worker productivity and expensive maintenance and repairs."

Problem Statement

• A need exists to replace desktop computers in the contracts management office.

    • Existing computers lack storage and speed capacity to support the new software required for many of the daily work situations.

    • Workstations are frequently 'down,' causing costly work delays and maintenance costs.

3

Slide 4

"First, let us review some constraints. Time to complete the BCA was eight days, including today and final changes by tomorrow. Information sources are as shown."

Assumptions

- Adequate Information can be gathered to assess benefits and costs, given:

  •Study time frame—8 days

  •Information from four areas:

  •Users of Current PC
  •Office of Information Technology
  •Operations Research Office
  •Financial Management Office

4

Slide 5

"The basic steps of the BCA were as shown."

Study Approach

Business Case Analysis

- **Define Problem.**

- **Develop Alternatives.**

- **Evaluate Alternatives.**

- **Conclusions.**

5

Slide 6

"As I stated during the introduction, the basic problem is aging PCs, resulting in costs due to lost productive time and repair expenses."

Define Problem

- Workstation PCs have excessive downtime

  - Nearly five years old

  - Excess costs of maintenance and repair

  - Excess disruption of work—loss of productive work hours

6

Slide 7

"The following alternatives were considered."

Develop Alternatives

- Four Alternatives considered
  - Alternative

    - 1: Status Quo (no change)

    - 2: Update existing PCs

    - 3: Buy new workstations

    - 4: Lease-to own

7

Slide 8

*"The second
alternative,
upgrading
components of
the older PCs,
was dismissed
early on the
advice of
information
technology
SMEs."*

Evaluate Alternatives

- Alternative 2 (Upgrade Existing PCs) was considered infeasible and eliminated from further economic analysis

  - Subject Matter Experts (SMEs) from the Office of Information Technology advised against upgrades

  - SMEs indicated that unacceptable reliability problems result in upgrades due to incompatibility of new components in aging workstations

- The following alternatives were economically evaluated
  - Alternative — Status Quo
  - Alternative 2 — Buy New
  - Alternative 3 — Lease-to-Own

8

Slide 9

*"So, the decision
involved either
keeping the older
PCs or replacing
them with
new ones.
Requirements
for new PCs were
developed from
interviews with
users, technicians
and promotional
materials. The
requirements are
as shown."*

**New Workstation
Requirements**

- State of the Art — $1,500 each

- Features
  - **Industry Standard GHz Processor**
  - **Industry Standard GB Memory**
  - **Industry Standard GB Hard Drive**
  - **Industry Standard Flat Screen Monitor**
  - **All-in-One Color Printer, Scanner, Copier, Fax**
  - **DVD & CD RW Drives**
  - **Industry Standard Operating System**
  - **Industry Standard Modem**
  - **Wireless Networking Card**
  - **Industry Standard Graphics**
  - **Industry Standard Office Suite**
  - **6 USB Ports**

9

Slide 10

"Next, to develop criteria to help choose an alternative, costs and benefits were evaluated. Historical 'Total Costs of Ownership' were developed first."

Costs

- Alternative Compared for Total Cost of Ownership
  - Purchase Price
  - Cost of Procurement
  - Cost of Ownership

10

Slide 11

"Under TCO, acquisition costs of the purchase price plus administrative procurement costs are considered. Purchase price was determined to be $1,500 per PC for 18 units."

Cost (continued)

- **Purchase Price**
  - Alternative 1: $0

  - Alternative 2: $27,000
    - $1,500 each x 18 workstations

  - Alternative 3: $25,950
    - Present Value of Three Installment Payments over 24 months
      - OMB Circular A-94 Discount Rate 4.1%

11

Slide 12

"Procurement costs were 7.6% standard costs the Financial Management Office assesses, plus 2.5% added receiving costs that were not part of the procurement factor."

Cost (continued)

- Procurement Costs
  - Alternative 1: $0
  - Alternative 2: $2,727
    - $10.1% x $27,000
      - 7.6% to Develop Purchase Order (Financial Management Office)
      - 2.5% estimated for receipt/handling
  - Alternative 3: $2,727
    - Total 'face value' of Procurement
      - PV of future payments not a consideration under Financial Management accounting procedures

12

Slide 13

"Costs of Use, the third major cost category, was derived from two sources: costs for technicians' service calls and lost worker productive hours. SMEs estimated new PCs would reduce these 75%."

Cost (continued)

- Costs of Use (12 months)
  - Alternative 1 (*status quo*): $18,488
    - $12,553 reimbursements for PC repair technician hours
      - 285.3 Service Call Hours x $44.00 Reimbursable Rate
    - $ 5,935 estimated lost productive worker hours
      - 60% of Workstation Downtime x $34.67 Average Labor Rate
  - Alternative 3 (*buy*): $4,622
    - 30% x $27,000
      - Estimate 70% savings of downtime costs
  - Alternative 3 (*lease-to-own*): $4,622
    - Estimate 75% savings of downtime costs

Slide 14

*"All three costs comprise the **estimated total ownership costs**. Historical Status Quo costs of $55,464 substantially exceed new PC costs after acquisition costs are recouped."*

- Total Ownership Cost
  - Base Year Figures
    - *Status quo* figures represent cost of downtime during past 12 months
    - *New PCs* costs represent estimated values for past 12 months had new PCs been in place

		Total Ownership Cost (Historical Average—Exhibit 1-8)		
		Alternative 1: Status Quo	Alternative 3: Buy New PCs	Alternative 4: Least-to-Own
			(estimated 75% reduction in service calls)	
Base Year	Cost of Acquisition	$0	$2,727	$2,272
	Purchase Price	$0	$27,000	$25,950
	Cost of Use	$66,487	$13,866	$13,866
	Totals	$55,464	$43,593	$42,543

14

Slide 15

"Implied savings from cost avoidances were forecasted for 36 months. A breakeven for acquisition, a Savings-to-Investment Ratio (SIR), and cost flows were calculated."

Benefits

- Benefits are derived from forecasted cost avoidance savings
- Cost avoidance saving are calculated as:
  - 75% reduction of reimbursable service call hours
  - 75% reduction of lost productive work hours
    - Productive work hours are calculated as 60% of service call hours
- Forecasts
  - Service Call Hours are forecasted for 36 months
  - 95% confidence factor is calculated for breakeven savings

Slide 16

*"Forecasts over
three years show
details of why
both discounted
values of buy and
lease-to-own are
substantially
more cost
effective than
status quo."*

Slide 17

*"Consequently,
the status quo
alternative was
eliminated.
Remaining
analysis focused
on the acquisition
of new PCs."*

Benefits (continued)

- Total ownership of *status quo* significantly higher that new workstations
  - Alternative 1 is eliminated as not cost efficient

- Analysis of two acquisition alternatives includes:
  - Breakeven period
  - Savings-to-Investment Ratio (SIR)
  - Cash flow

Slide 18

"As shown, comparison of time to breakeven for the initial acquisition of new PCs is nearly two years, with lease-to-own reached one month ahead of buy."

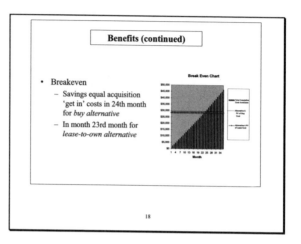

Slide 19

"A second comparison shows the 36-month payback amount also favors lease-to-own."

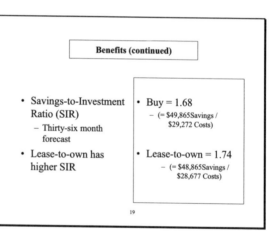

Slide 20

"A final comparison shows that cash flow out-of-pocket expenses, relative to payback due to cost avoidances, also favors lease-to-own."

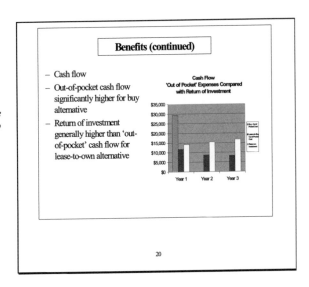

Slide 21

"Finally, sensitivity indicates that a worse case, defined as a the amount of savings required to provide a 95% chance of breakeven, is forecasted to accrue near the three-year point."

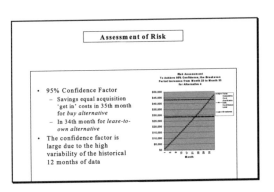

Slide 22

"While the first two indicators (i.e., breakeven and SIR) marginally favor 'lease-to-own,' it is significantly favored by the cash flow indicator.

Summary:
Comparison of Alternatives 3 & 4

- Alternative 4 is more cost efficient

  – Marginally quicker breakeven payback period

  – Marginally higher Savings-to-Investment Ratio

  – Significantly less out-of-pocket cash flow relative to Return on Investment (ROI)

Slide 23

"In summary, Alternative 4, lease-to-own, is the preferred option and is recommended."

Summary and Conclusions

- Alternative 2 was eliminated as infeasible.

- Alternative 1, maintaining the status quo, was shown to be significantly more costly that either Alternative 3 (Buy) or Alternative 4 (Lease-to-Own), and was dropped from consideration.

- Alternative 4 outperformed Alternative 3 based primarily on the time delay of payments: it was marginally more cost efficient for breakeven and SIR, and significantly more advantageous for cash flow versus ROI.

- Alternative 4, Lease-to-Own, is the overall preferred option and is recommended for implementation.
  - Note: Economic differences were close. Alternative 3 is a viable alternative, should policy prevent installment payments from being acceptable.

23

Slide 24

" The proposed implementation plan includes a 90-day monitoring period in which the vendor will replace any defective machines."

Proposed Implementation Plan

- Project Plan
  - Approval to Purchase
  - Obligate Funds by Budget Deadline
  - Install
  - Monitor (90 parts and labor warranty)
  - Close project

Project	Procure New Workstations					Nov	Dec	Jan
Starting Date	29-Sep							
Completion Date	18-Jan							
Present Date	26-Sep							
Task	Starting	Ending	%	No. of				
Description	Date	Date	Comp	Days	2	7	4	1
Project Plan								
Approval of Budget Committee	29-Sep	29-Sep	0	0				
Procure Workstations	30-Sep	13-Oct	0	14				
Receive and Install	14-Oct	18-Oct	0	5				
Monitor Service Calls	19-Oct	18-Jan	0	90				
Report Significant Problems	17-Jan	17-Jan	0	1				
Close Project	18-Jan	18-Jan	0	0				

24

Slide 25

Discussion?

25

After discussions, final notes are taken and incorporated into the *final report*, as required. The final report is then professionally bound and delivered to the client in about a week to 10 working days.

Glossary

AAM—Aircraft availability model. A METRIC (backorder) based Inventory model that calculates relative marginal benefit/costs of supply components' contributions to total aircraft availability. Developed for the USAF. *See* METRIC.

activity node tree—Schematic diagram of decomposed parent and child activities used for IDEF modeling.

alternatives—Potential 'to be' solutions to resolve the 'as is' problem.

ALERT—Air Logistics Early Requirements Technique. A stepwise linear regression model to forecast large defense budget requirements for multiple year budget horizons. Developed for the USAF.

anchoring—A decision bias to accept most recent events as beginning estimates for future events—without examining history for trends, cycles, or average levels.

'as is'—The existing (status quo) business situation.

availability heuristic—A decision bias where more frequently reported data wrongly influence judgments that could be more accurate with active research.

BCA—business case analysis.

BCR—benefit/cost ratio.

boundary location—A sociotechnical theory principle. Managers help overall processes by protecting group boundaries. That is, support is given to protect activities within functional coalitions (i.e., groups), and to facilitate coordination between them.

BPR—Business process reengineering. Often involves major streamlining of processes. *See* TQM.

breakeven analysis—Analysis of point in time where return on investment equals investment costs.

business case—A formal section of the business case analysis report that identifies the problem/study objective and qualitative pros and cons of potential alternative solutions.

business case analysis—A formal evaluation of alternatives to an existing business situation to identify the most preferred in terms of qualitative and quantitative factors.

business case analysis report—A formal written report of analysis. Includes sections on executive summary, problem statement, the business case, the economic analysis, and conclusions.

capital investment—The value of resources (for both technical and human skills) used for producing outputs.

compatibility—A sociotechnical theory principle. Flexibility of processes (i.e., rule based or employee based decisions) should match flexibility needs of the task.

compulsive organization—A dysfunctional organizational management style with emphasis on conformity and rules. Inhibits recognition and action for needed change.

conservatism bias—A decision bias of slowness or failure to change predictions in light of new disconfirming information.

consideration—A management concept of trusting, nurturing management-employee relations.

continual improvement—A sociotechnical theory principle. Design of organizations is continually changing and adapting in response to changing task complexity.

cost of acquisition—Costs for researching, ordering and shipping. One of three elements of total cost of ownership.

cost of use—Efficiency of an alternative process. One of three elements of total cost of ownership.

cost of purchase—Purchase price of resources for an alternative process. One of three elements of total cost of ownership.

CPM—Critical Path Method is a network scheduling method for determining the fastest time (the critical path) for completing complex projects.

depressive organization—A dysfunctional organizational management style where power and authority are based on bureaucratic position in the hierarchy rather than expertise. Needed change initiatives are blocked at all levels. Can only survive in protected, stable environment.

discounting—Computation of the present value of future dollars using the discount rate.

discount rate—Rate of dollar change over time. The U.S. Office of Management and budget publishes updated rates annually in OMB Circular A94 in the January–February time frame.

draft final report—A preliminary report to the study sponsor to provide background for the final briefing presentation.

dramatic organization—A dysfunctional organizational management style of egocentric, narcissistic management. Top down direction impedes upward information feedback about needed change.

DynaMETRIC—Dynamic METRIC. An inventory model that

calculates relative marginal benefit/costs of supply components' contributions, including 'parent-child' subindentures in dynamic (versus steady state) conditions. Developed for the USAF by the Rand Corporation. *See* readiness in inventory models.

EBO—Expected backorders. Used in inventory theory.

economic analysis—The quantitative section of the BCA. Can incorporate discounting, breakeven analysis, benefit/cost ratios, savings-to-investment ratios, and cash flow considerations.

entities—The fundamental objects of productive processes modeled in process models.

EOQ—Economic Order Quantity. Also known as Wilson's Q. A mathematical algorithm to calculate the minimum combined total cost of inventory due to variations of ordering and holding costs.

executive summary—A short overview of study tasking and findings. *See* business case analysis report.

exponential smoothing—A statistical forecasting technique that uses time series inference to weight the influence of historical data patterns exponentially, systematically giving less weight to older observations.

feedback—A sociotechnical theory principle. Information about performance contributions allows for individual adaptation and promotes higher motivational needs of belonging and importance.

final briefing and report—A presentation of the draft final report findings, followed by a final report that incorporates corrections/clarifications.

forecasting—Statistically mimicking past patterns as a proxy for future expected patterns.

fringe benefits—The U.S. Office of Management and budget publishes fringe benefits rates for U.S. workers in OMB Circular A76. These include additional costs for employees due to retirement set asides, health benefits, Medicare, and miscellaneous.

gambler's fallacy—A human decision bias where previous 'runs' are mistaken for future probabilities (e.g., betting unreasonably on a 'head' after three tosses of a 'head' of a fair coin—odds are still 50-50).

hindsight bias—A tendency to exaggerate how accurate one's past opinions were or would have been. Can inhibit critical self-evaluation of decisions for future events.

Hawthorne effect—An observation that individuals or groups may behave differently than normal when they perceive they are being observed. Understanding and analysis of the true dynamics and causes of behavior may be more complicated. Early studies were by Elton Mayo of Harvard University, circa 1923 at the Hawthorne electronics plant in Illinois.

ICAM—Integrated Computer Aided Manufacturing software.

ICOM—Acronym for Inputs, Constraints, Mechanisms, and Outputs used for definition of activities in IDEF models.

IDEF modeling—An Integrated DEFinition approach to process modeling using ICAM software technology.

industrial psychology—origins attributed to Hugo Munsterberg, Harvard University, circa 1912.

information flow—A sociotechnical theory principle. Information should be tailored to task roles (e.g., executive summaries for top managers, detailed operations data for foremen, etc.).

initiating structure—A management concept denoting use of prescriptive management rules. *See* University of Ohio State Studies.

IPR—In-process review.

kickoff meeting—Meeting between the sponsor and analyst to agree upon calibrations between the task order and study plan.

level of effort—Budgeted resources to pay for the study.

linear programming—A method to allocate resources using the simplex method and matrix algebra.

linear regression—A statistical method for relating strength and direction of influence of independent variables upon a dependent variable.

METRIC—Multi-Echelon Technique for Recoverable Item Control. An inventory model that calculates relative marginal benefit/costs of supply components' contributions, across multiple items, locations, and supply chain echelons, up to a finite budget constraint. Developed for the USAF by the Rand Corporation.

minimum critical specification—A sociotechnical theory principle. Degree of supervision should be balanced with degree of needed worker discretion, based on complexity of the task.

minimum spanning tree—A heuristic algorithm for determining the shortest route for entities that leave the origin, visit all points on a route, but are *not required to return home. See* network analysis and traveling salesman problem.

MOD-METRIC—Modified METRIC enhances the basic model to

also include comparisons among item indentures.

multi-function principle—A sociotechnical theory principle. Redundancy of skills is often more efficient than overspecialization, due to fractionalizing of processes.

network analysis—Evaluation of networks to determine the best methods for routing and assignment problems.

OMB—U.S. Office of Management and Budget. To find OMB circulars for discount rates and employee fringe benefits see http://www.whitehouse.gov/omb/circulars

OPM—U.S. Office of Personnel Management. To find government pay rates, see http://www.opm.gov/oca

optimism bias—A decision bias of wishful thinking, beyond supporting evidence.

paranoid organization—A dysfunctional organizational management style of institutionalized suspicion. 'Reactive' behaviors are more prevalent than 'proactive' behaviors.

participation—A management concept of leadership from the worker up, versus from management down.

PC—Personal Computer.

PERT—Program Evaluation and Review Technique. A network scheduling method for determining the fastest time for completing complex project schedules.

present value—A widely used economic concept that assumes that the value of future dollars will be different (e.g., decline) due to the time value of money (i.e., due to alternatives such as investment income or inflation).

processes—Total or partial segments of sequential and parallel steps conducted during enterprise operations.

process activities—The basic work elements of processes.

process modeling—Mathematical simulation to emulate input-throughput-output of entities through productive processes. *See* IDEF modeling.

queue—British word for a waiting line. Used in simulation.

readiness in inventory models—extends steady state METRIC models to consider shifts of requirements non–steady state (changing utilization rates) during contingencies. *See* DynaMETRIC.

schizoid organization—A dysfunctional organizational management style with internal anarchy where leadership is detached and noncommittal; worker politics set subgroup agendas; there is no consistent central policy for direction and control. Lack of strategy inhibits recognition of new information indicating need for change.

scientific method—Steps include: define the problem, derive alternative solutions, test and pick best solution, obtain feedback for verification.

shortest route problem—A heuristic algorithm for sequentially determining the shortest routes between a given location and multiple locations to prioritize first, second, third, etc. choices for lateral resupply activities. Used in network analysis.

simplex method—An iterative procedure for solving linear programming problems. The simplex method arranges linear constraint equations in a manner that allows tradeoffs (up to allowable resource or cost limits), yielding a maximum contribution to the objective function equation. *See* Exhibit 13-1.

simulation—Mathematically mimicking a process using queuing theory and statistical probability theory.

SIR—Savings-to-Investment Ratio.

social imperative—A management theory that types of organizational processes and structures are formed in response to the internal technical complexity of tasks.

sociotechnical criterion—A sociotechnical theory principle. Management should allow necessary decision discretion for workers to control problems closest to their origins.

sociotechnical imperative—A management theory that types of organizational processes and structures are formed in response to both the internal and external technical complexity of tasks.

SOW—*See* statement of work.

square root law—Theoretical equation that asserts that inventory requirements are reduced or increased at a rate of the square root of the number of locations that stock the inventory.

standard deviation—Used synonymously with standard error.

standard error—Used synonymously with standard deviation.

statement of work—Written requirements for the study. Includes background, problem statement and scope of the study. *See* task order.

statistical analysis—The use of stochastic and probability techniques to summarize data and to make inferences about data relationships.

status quo—The existing 'as is' business situation for which alternatives are being evaluated.

study approach—Identifies analytical techniques to be used.

study plan—Written reply to the task order. Restates SOW, identifies the study approach, schedule, level of effort resources, deliverables, and sponsoring activity.

support congruence—A sociotechnical theory principle. Organizational structure (formal-informal) and processes (mechanistic-organic) should match task complexity.

task complexity—A measure of organizational task difficulty, comprised of requirements for variety and stability in process performance steps.

task order—A statement of study requirements.

'to be'—The potential replacement business situation due to invoking alternative solutions to the 'as is' status quo situation.

technical imperative—A management theory that types of organizational structures and processes are formed in response to the external technical complexity of tasks.

total cost of ownership—Total acquisition cost, price, and use of the alternative product or scenario.

TQM—Total Quality Management. Involves continual monitoring of processes and minor, incremental adjustments and calibrations. *See* BPR.

traveling salesman problem—A heuristic algorithm for determining the shortest route for an entity that leaves the origin, visits all points on a route, *then returns home*. *See* network analysis and minimum spanning tree.

University of Iowa Studies—In 1937, studies under the general direction of Kurt Lewin found that leadership styles (autocratic and democratic) produce different, complex responses from otherwise similar groups. Autocratic direction tended to develop overt apathetic compliance with latent aggression; democratic direction produced a mixture of overt apathy and aggression.

University of Michigan Studies—In 1945, Rensis Likert found positive effects from participative management for both individual satisfaction of work performance, and self-initiative of workers to contribute their own initiatives when informed of importance of their roles to the overall process.

University of Ohio State Studies—In 1945, leadership studies of USAF bomber crews found a combination of 'rules' (e.g., initiating structure, autocratic leaders) and 'individual discretion' (i.e., consideration, democratic leaders) contributed to successful performance.

USAF—United States Air Force.

worker productivity rates—The U.S. Office of Management and Budget publishes rates in OMB Circular A76.

Bibliography

Ackoff, R. (1956, June). The development of operations research as a science. *Operations Research,* pp. 265–266.

Aczel, A. D. (1999). *Complete Business Statistics* (4th ed.). Boston: Irwin-McGraw-Hill.

Armstrong, J. S. (1985). *Long-Range Forecasting: from Crystal Ball to Computer.* New York: John Wiley & Sons.

Armstrong, J. (Ed.) (2001). *Principles of Forecasting: A Handbook for Researchers and Practitioners.* Norwell, MA: Kluwer Academic Publishers.

Armstrong, J.S. (2001). Judgmental bootstrapping: inferring experts' rules for forecasting. Cited from J. S. Armstrong (ed.), *Principles of Forecasting: A Handbook for Researchers and Practitioners* (pp.171–192). Norwell, MA: Kluwer Academic Publishers.

Armstrong, S., Adya, M., and Collopy, F. (2001). Rule based forecasting: using judgment in time-series extrapolation. Cited from J. S. Armstrong (ed.), *Principles of Forecasting: A Handbook for Researchers and Practitioners* (pp.257–282). Norwell, MA: Kluwer Academic Publishers.

Berenson, M., and Levine, D. (1989). *Basic Business Statistics: Concepts and Application* (4th ed.). Englewood Cliffs, NJ: Prentice Hall.

Blake, R., and Mouton, J. (1966, July). Managerial facades. *Advanced Management Journal,* p. 31.

Bouty, I. (2000). Interpersonal and interaction influence on informal resource exchanges between R&D researchers across organizational boundaries. *Academy of Management Journal,* 43 (1), 50–65.

Brannock, J. (1981). *Socio-technical Systems Theory: A Study of the Degree to Which Organizational Structure, Process and Technological Complexity Are Congruent in a United States Air Force Jet Engine Overhaul Facility.* PhD dissertation, Lincoln, NE: University of Nebraska, School of Business.

Brannock, J. W. (1987). POSSEM-ALERT: the search for a requirements forecasting system. *Air Force Journal of Logistics,* XI (2), 31–34.

Brannock, J. W. (1994). DFSC Process Reengineering. A white paper for evaluation of the IDEF Study Results.

Brannock, J. W. (2000). Challenges to process innovation at a large budget defense supply center, Paper # 2049. *Proceedings from 2000*

International Management Conference of *Society for Advancement of Management (SAM).* 6300 Ocean Drive, FC 111, Corpus Christi, TX: SAM International Office, Texas A & M University.

Brigham, E. (1975, Autumn). Hurdle rates for screening capital expenditure proposals. *Financial Management,* p. 18. Cited from R. Gupta (1996), *Managerial Excellence.* Boston: Harvard Business School Publishing, 51.

Brown, R. G. (1967). *Decision Rules for Inventory Management.* New York: Holt, Rinehart and Winston.

Burns, T., and Stalker, G. (1961). *The Management of Innovation.* London: Tavistock Publications Limited.

Cherns, A. (1976). The principles of socio-technical design. *Human Relations,* 8, 785–791.

Coyle, J., Bardi, E., and Langley, C. (2003). *The Management of Business Logistics: A Supply Chain Perspective.* Mason, Ohio: SouthWestern.

Crawford, G. (1981). Palm's theorem for nonstationary processes. *R-2750-RC.* Santa Monica CA: The Rand Corporation.

Dagli, C. H. (Ed.) (1994). *Artificial Neural Networks for Intelligent Manufacturing.* London: Chapman & Hall.

Davenport, T. (1993). *Reengineering Work through Information Technology.* Boston: Harvard Business School Press.

Defense Fuel Supply Center Fact Book, Fiscal Year 2002. Ft. Belvoir, VA, Defense Energy Support Center, Defense Logistics Agency, www.desc.dla.mil.

DLA Defense Distribution Depots: www.ddc.dla.mil.

Durant, W. (1935). *The Story of Civilization: 1.* New York: Simon and Schuster, Inc.

Durant, W. (1939). *The Story of Civilization: 2.* New York, MFJ Books, copyright renewed, 1966.

Evers, P. (1996). The impact of transshipments of safety stock requirements. *Journal of Business Logistics,* 17 (1), 107–133.

Evers, P. and Beier, F. (1998). Operational aspects of inventory consolidations decision making, *Journal of Business Logistics,* 19 (1), 173–187.

Feeney, G., Petersen, J., and Sherbrooke, C. (1963). An aggregate base stockage policy for recoverable items. *Memorandum RM-3644-PR.* Santa Monica, CA: The Rand Corporation.

Feller, W. (1968). *An Introduction to Probability Theory and Its Applications, Vol. I* (3rd ed.). New York: Wiley.

Gardner, E. (1991) *Autocast/II: Business Forecasting System.* Morristown, NJ: Levenbach Associates.

Garson, D. (1998). *Neural Networks: An Introductory Guide for Social Scientists.* London: Sage Publications.

George, C. (1968). *The History of Management Thought.* Englewood Cliffs, N.J.: Prentice-Hall, Inc.

Gillespie, D., and Mileti, D. (1977). Adapted from Technology and the study of organizations: an overview and appraisal. *Academy of Management Review,* 2 (1), 13.

Gupta, R. (1996). *Managerial Excellence.* Boston: Harvard Business School Publishing.

Hammer, M. (1996). *Beyond Reengineering: How the Process Centered Organization Is Changing Our Work and Lives.* New York: Harper Collins Publishers, Inc.

Hesse, R., and Woolsey, G. (1980). *Applied Management Science: A Quick and Dirty Approach.* Chicago: Science Research Associates, Inc.

Higgin, G., and Bridger, H. (1990). The psycho-dynamics of an intergroup experience. Cited from: E. Trist and H. Murray (eds.), *The Social Engagement of Social Science: A Tavistock Anthology, Volume I* (pp. 199–202). Philadelphia: University of Pennsylvania Press.

Hillestad, T. (1982). *R-2785-AF: Dyna-METRIC: Dynamic Multi-Echelon Technique for Recoverable Item Control.* Santa Monica, CA: The Rand Corporation.

Hillestad, R., and Carrillo, M. (1980). Models and techniques for recoverable item stockage when demand and the repair process are nonstationary—part I: performance measurement. *N-1482-AF.* Santa Monica, CA: The Rand Corporation.

Hillman, A., and Dalziel, T. (2003). Boards of directors and firm performance: integrating agency and resource dependence perspectives. *Academy of Management Review,* 28 (3), 383–396.

Hodgetts, R. (1975). *Management: Theory, Process and Practice.* Philadelphia: W.B. Saunders Company.

INFOPEDIA 2.0 (1995). Mathematics. Cambridge, MA: Softkey Multimedia Ind., a subsidiary of Funk & Wagnalls New Encyclopedia.

Isaacson, K, and P. Boren (1993). Dyna-METRIC Version 6, an Advanced Capability Assessment Model. *R-4214.* Santa Monica, CA: The Rand Corporation.

Jacobs, D. (1974). Adapted from: Dependency and vulnerability: an exchange approach to the control of organizations. *Administrative Science Quarterly,* 19 (1), 48.

Janis, I. (1972). *Victims of Group Think.* Boston: Houghton Mifflin.

Kast, F. and Rosensweig, J. (1974). *Organization and Management: A Systems Approach* (2nd ed.). New York: McGraw Hill, Inc.

Katz, D., and Kahn, R. (1966). *The Social Psychology of Organizations.* New York: John Wiley & Sons, Inc.

Kets de Vries, M. (1985). *The Neurotic Organization.* Washington: Jossey-Bass Publishers.

Kolman, B., and Denlinger, C. (1992). *Calculus for the Management, Life, and Social Sciences.* New York: Harcourt Brace Jovanovich College Publishers.

LaLonde, B. J., and Zinszer, P. H. (1980). Customer service: meaning and measurement. Cited from D. P. Herron, *International Journal of Physical Distribution and Materials Management,* 10 (8), 481–505.

Larson, K. (1990). *Fundamental Accounting Principles* (12th ed.). Boston: Irwin, p. 1136.

Levin, R. I., Rubin, D. S., Stinson, J. P., and Gardner, E. S. (1992). *Quantitative Approaches to Management* (8th ed.). New York: McGraw-Hill, Inc.

Liebowitz, J. (Ed.) (1998). *The Handbook of Applied Expert Systems.* New York: CRC Press.

Likert, R. (1967). *The Human Organization.* New York: McGraw-Hill Book Company.

Loh, M. (1995). *Reengineering of Work.* Hampshire, England: Gower Publishing Limited.

Lu, J., and Brooks, R. (1968). An aggregate stockage policy for EOQ items at base level. *RM-5678-PR.* Santa Monica, CA: The Rand Corporation.

Luthans, F. (1973). *Organizational Behavior.* New York: McGraw-Hill Book Company.

Maister, D. H. (1976). Centralisation of inventories and the square root law. *International Journal of Physical Distribution and Materials Management* 6 (3).

Makridakis. S., and Wheelwright, S. C. (1989). *Forecasting Methods for Management.* New York: John Wiley & Sons.

Makridakis, S. (1990). *Forecasting, Planning, and Strategy for the 21st Century.* New York: The Free Press.

Masters, J. (1983). Inventory management. *AFIT Course LM 6.28.* Wright-Patterson Air Force Base, OH: Air Force Institute of Technology.

Masters, J. (1993). Determination of near optimal stock levels for multi-echelon distribution inventories. *Journal of Business Logistics,* 14 (2), 165–195.

McBride, R. (1998, Mar–Apr). Advances in solving multicommodity-flow problems. *Interfaces,* 32–41.

Meehl, P. (1954). *Clinical versus Statistical Prediction: A Theoretical Analysis and a Review of the Evidence*. Minneapolis: University of Minnesota Press.

Miller, E. (1975). Socio-technical systems in weaving, 1953–1970. *Human Relations,* 28, 349–386, in W. Pasmore & J. Sherwood (1978), *Sociotechnical Systems: a Sourcebook*. La Jolla, CA: University Associates, Inc.

Muckstadt, J. (1973). A model for a multi-item, multi-echelon inventory system. *Management Science,* 20 (4), 472–481.

Muckstadt, J. (1980, November). Comparative adequacy of steady-state versus dynamic models for calculating stockage requirements. *R-2636-AF*. Santa Monica, CA: The Rand Corporation.

National Institute of Standards and Technology (1993). *Draft Federal Information Processing Standards Publication 183*. Director, Computer Systems Laboratory ATTN: FIPS IDEF0 Interpretation National Institute of Standards and Technology, Gaithersburg, MD 20899; available on the Internet at www.itl.nist.gov/fipspubs/idef02.doc.

Nightingale, D., and Toulouse, J. (1982), Toward a multi-level congruence theory of organization. *Administrative Science Quarterly,* 22 (2), 264–280.

O'Connor, J., and Robertson, E. George Dantzig. URL http://www-history.mcs.st-andrews.ac.uk/history/References/Dantzig_George.html.

O'Malley, T. (1983). *The Aircraft Availability Model: Conceptual Framework and Mathematics: AF201Report*. Bethesda, MD: Logistics Management Institute.

Palm, C. (1938). Analysis of the Erlang traffic formula for busy signal arrangements. *Ericsson Technics,* 5, 38–58. Cited from H. S. Campbell and T. L. Jones, A systems approach to base stock age: its development and test, a paper prepared for 29th National Meeting of the Operations Research Society of America, Santa Monica CA, May 19, 1966.

Perrow, C. (1967). A framework for the comparative analysis of organizations. *American Sociological Review* 32, 194–209.

Porter, M. (1980). *Competitive Strategy: Techniques for Analyzing Industries and Competitors*. New York: The Free Press.

Ptak, C. (2000). *ERP: Tools, Techniques and Applications for Integrating the Supply Chain*. New York: St. Lucie Press.

Pugh, D., Hickson, D., Hinings, C., and Turner, C. (1968). Dimensions of organizational structure. *Administrative Science Quarterly,* 13 (1), 73–76.

Rice, A. (1955). Productivity and social organization in an Indian weaving shed. *Human Relations,* 6 (4), 309–310.

Roth, J. (1999). *The Logistics of the Roman Army at War (264 B.C. – A.D. 235).* Boston: Brill.

Rousseau, D. (1977). Technological differences in job characteristics, employee satisfaction, and motivation: A synthesis of job design research and sociotechnical systems theory. *Organizational Behavior and Human Performance, 18, 18–42.*

Sanders, N., and Ritzman, L. (2001). Judgmental adjustment of statistical analysis forecasts. Cited from J. S. Armstrong (ed.) (2001). *Principles of Forecasting.* Norwell, MA: Kluwer Academic Press, 405–416.

Schein, E. (1988). *Process Consultation, Vol. 1* (2nd ed.). New York: Addison-Wesley Publishing Company.

Schein, E. (1992). *Organizational Culture and Leadership* (2nd ed.). San Francisco: Jossey-Bass.

Schein, E. (2002). *Organizational Therapy Seminar.* Eastham MA: Cape Cod Institute.

Senge, P. (1990). *The Fifth Discipline: The Art and Practice of Learning.* New York: Doubleday.

Sherbrooke, C. (1968). METRIC: A multi-echelon technique for recoverable item control. *Operations Research,* 16, 122–141.

Stewart, T. (2001). Improving reliability in judgmental forecasts. Cited from J. S. Armstrong (ed) (2001). *Principles of Forecasting.* Norwell, MA: Kluwer Academic Press, 81–106.

Sutherland, J. (1990). "Bion revisited." Cited from: E. Trist and H. Murray (Eds.), *The Social Engagement of Social Science: A Tavistock Anthology, Volume I* (p. 121). Philadelphia: University of Pennsylvania Press.

Taylor, F. (1911). *Principles of Scientific Management.* New York: Harper & Brothers Publishers. Cited from R. Hodgetts (1974), *Management: Theory, Process and Practice* (pp. 29–31). Philadelphia: W.B. Saunders Company,

Terreberry, Shirley (1968). "The evolution of organizational environments," *Administrative Science Quarterly,* 12 (4), 595–596.

Thompson, J. (1967). *Organizations in Action.* New York: McGraw Hill Book Company.

Trist, E., and Bamforth, K. (1951). Some social and psychological consequences of the longwall method of coal getting. *Human Relations,* 4 (1), 3–11.

U.S. Army Inventory Research Office (1980). Mathematics for SESAME model. Philadelphia: *Department of Army Technical Report TR 80-2.*

Wilson, R. H. (1934). A scientific routine for stock control. *Harvard Business Review,* 13 (1), 116–128.

Zinn, W., Levy, M., and Bowersox, D. (1989). Measuring the effect of inventory centralization/decentralization on aggregate safety stock: the square root law revisited. *Journal of Business Logistics,* 10 (1), 1–14.

Index

We can do anything we want to do if we stick to it long enough.
Helen Keller (circa 1958)

STS Publications

Reference/Business Case Analysis

 QUICK ORDER FORM

📠 **FAX orders: 813-707-5671. Send this form or a copy thereof.**

📠 **Telephone orders: Call 877-STSPUBZ (787-7829) toll free.
Have your credit card ready.**

📠 **e-mail orders: orders@STSpublications.com**

✉️ **Postal orders: STS Publications,
PO Box 3732-A1, Plant City, FL 33563-0013**

Please send the following books, disks, or reports. I understand that I may return any of them for a full refund—for any reason, no questions asked.

_____

_____

_____

Please send more FREE information on:

☐ Other Books ☐ Speaking/Seminars ☐ Mailing Lists ☐ Consulting

Name: _____

Address: _____

City: _____ State: _____ Zip: _____

Telephone: _____

E-mail address: _____

Sales tax: Please add 7.0% for products shipped to Florida addresses.

Shipping by air
U.S.: $4.00 for first book or disk and for $2.00 each additional product.
International: $9.00 for the first; $5.00 for each additional product (estimate).

Payment: ☐ Cheque ☐ Credit Card

☐ Other Books ☐ Speaking/Seminars ☐ Mailing Lists ☐ Consulting

Card number: _____

Name on card: _____ Exp. Date: _____